Pat Hazard

for assiduous beavering

in London & Philadelphia — et inchoante,
si ipsius verbis credendumst, Jersey!

Kenneth Lindsay.

Christmas 1974.

Everything but Alf Garnett
a personal view of BBC School Broadcasting

EVERYTHING BUT ALF GARNETT

A PERSONAL VIEW OF BBC SCHOOL BROADCASTING

Kenneth Fawdry

British Broadcasting Corporation

Published by
the British Broadcasting Corporation
35 Marylebone High Street
London W1M 4AA

ISBN 0 563 12763 5

First published 1974

© Kenneth Fawdry 1974

Acknowledgement is due to the
following for their permission to
reproduce illustrations in this book

Mauritshuis, the Hague, *23 top*;
Museum d'Unterlinden, Colmar,
© ADAGP, *39 centre*; Museum of
Modern Art, New York, *39 top*;
Prado, Madrid, *23 bottom*; Radio
Times Hulton Picture Library, 11;
Victoria and Albert Museum, *39
bottom*; all the remaining illustrations
are BBC copyright.

Figures in italics indicate colour
illustrations facing.

Printed in England
by Lowe & Brydone (Printers) Ltd,
Thetford, Norfolk

CONTENTS

Foreword
by Dame Margaret Miles DBE, BA, Hon. DCL   *vii*

Preface   *ix*

I   BBC School Broadcasting in Action Today
    1.1 In a village Primary School   *1*
    1.2 In an urban Comprehensive School   *8*

2   Landmarks of Technical Progress
    2.1 Early days   *18*
    2.2 Enter TV   *21*
    2.3 The uses of audio-tape recordings   *28*
    2.4 Radiovision   *31*
    2.5 Video-tape   *38*

3   Challenge and Response
    3.1 The fourth R   *42*
    3.2 What's in the news?   *48*
    3.3 Who'll teach us numeracy?   *53*
    3.4 What, another year of half our future   *66*
    3.5 Everyone a creator   *83*
    3.6 Hindhitches and headstarts   *93*

4   A Story of Partnership
    4.1 Council and programme committees   *106*
    4.2 In the field   *116*
    4.3 Three-letter partners   *128*

5   Problems in the Air
    5.1 'Relevance'   *138*
    5.2 'Impartiality' and 'Open-endedness'   *142*
    5.3 School Broadcasting for a multi-racial society   *146*

6   Friends and Relations
    6.1 BBC Further Education Broadcasting   *152*
    6.2 ITV School Broadcasting   *160*
    6.3 Closed-circuit television   *164*
    6.4 BBC Local Radio   *167*
    6.5 Friends abroad   *171*
    6.6 Parents generally   *180*
    6.7 The parent BBC   *182*

7   Prospects
    7.1 Recording, and its consequences   *189*
    7.2 Pressures on the BBC   *193*
    7.3 A look into the crystal ball   *196*

Appendices

A   The School Broadcasting Council for the
    United Kingdom and its Committees   *202*
B   BBC School Broadcasting series 1974-5   *204*
C   Recording of BBC programmes in schools   *209*
D   Select bibliography   *210*

Index   *212*

FOREWORD

It was a splendid idea to commission Kenneth Fawdry to write
this book for the 50th Anniversary of BBC School Broadcasting.
Mr Fawdry was Head of BBC School Television until 1972, and
had been the School Broadcasting Council's Senior Education
Officer before that, so it is not surprising that the book is informative and interesting. That it is so much more is due to the vigorous
and imaginative writing which throughout reflects brilliantly the
commitment, talent and enthusiasm of the men and women who
work for School Broadcasting.

There is a danger that the authors of anniversary works become encapsulated in the past so that the readers' appetite for
nostalgia grows as they read, and, having read, they know that
things can never be the same (i.e. as good) again. This book does
not fall into that trap; the past of course gets its due, and how I
enjoyed the recall of the old battlefields of TV versus Educational
film, and 'enrichment' versus 'direct teaching'. The tremendous
achievement of Mary Somerville and her followers, the conscientious study of the needs of the schools (often with the vision to see
a bit beyond them) are there too. But the writer also makes a
shrewd analysis of the present rapidly changing scene, both in
education and broadcasting.

The content of this fascinating history is a constant reminder
of the very high quality which has always characterised School
Broadcasting, both BBC and ITV. Its message is never sub-
ordinate; the medium is used consistently and imaginatively as
the servant of the multitudinous and varied messages of the producers and committees of the BBC and ITV School Broadcasting
Councils. There are areas in educational technology where the
hardware is terrific but where the software is poor. Not so in
school broadcasting; here the software, whether programme
content, accompanying literature, or other visual aids, has always

been first class. Now that I have allowed the jargon to creep in to my foreword, let me assure the readers that the text, as one would expect from its origins, is happily free of it.

My one sadness after reading this record of achievement is that too few people make use of the wealth of offerings which flows continuously from BBC and ITV. I certainly regret all the programmes I missed using in my teaching days. Perhaps the appearance of this book in staff rooms thoughout the country will inspire more people to seize the many opportunities presented by the makers of TV and Radio programmes for schools.

MARGARET MILES
May 1974

PREFACE

I have always found education exhilarating to be busy about, warm to talk about, chilly to read about, and torture to write about. Broadcasts are in worse case still: impossible surely to write about, unless for a reader presumed to have seen or heard them, for their essence escapes the printed page. So in accepting the BBC's invitation to write about its school broadcasting service I was chiefly motivated by the thought that if I didn't, some other fool would. But also by the enjoyment I have had from being associated with school broadcasting for quite a chunk of my life.

So this is not an objective book. I like school broadcasts – almost all of them. I have tried to write for the plain man rather than the pundit who looks for the quote from Rousseau or Spencer in support of any casual aphorism: for the plain man with an interest in schools and broadcasting – the apprentice teacher perhaps, the Local Education Authority committee man, the parent whose child is experiencing school broadcasts, the foreign student of the British scene. I assume some acquaintance with our educational structures, the character of our schools, and the ethos of the BBC; some interest in simply being informed; and some taste for historical perspective.

I am indebted to my precursors: Richard Palmer, whose 'School Broadcasting in Britain' (1947), gives a detailed picture of school radio come to maturity; and K. V. Bailey, whose study of 'The Listening Schools' (1957) explores with much insight the interaction in the educational process of programmes of quality with sensitivity of teaching. They are out-dated only in the sense that BBC School Broadcasting has vastly extended its range since then: what they say remains significant for any student of the subject. Particularly is this true of 'The Listening Schools', since the qualities which make for good handling of radio in schools apply equally to television.

Today there are over 100 school broadcast series for the United Kingdom as a whole; and 30 odd more for the special needs of Scotland, Wales and Northern Ireland. Most cannot even be mentioned in so short a compass: to the latter, in particular, I have done scant justice or none at all, though they are outstanding symbols both of the diversity of our national cultures, and of the BBC's care for the interests of minorities.

I would like to thank the BBC for putting its records at my disposal and for the valued services of Betty Smith for research and of Penny Ware to wrestle with my handwriting; the many colleagues in and outside the BBC who have generously given their time and dredged their memories on my behalf; and particularly those who, responding to my importunity, have made personal contributions to this book.

KENNETH FAWDRY

1974

1 BBC SCHOOL BROADCASTING IN ACTION TODAY

BBC School Broadcasting is almost a mini-BBC. Its output ranges from Bartók to Reggae to Music and Movement for infants; from Shakespeare to kitchen-sink drama to Morecambe and Wise; from Liverpool FC to throwing dice; from Hinduism to 'Onward Christian Soldiers'; from Czechoslovakia 1968 to what happens to your rubbish; from Broadway and the Bowery to badger tracks; from chess by computer to boiling water. Everything but Alf Garnett, in fact.

But BBC School broadcasting in action has its nodal point not in the studio, but in the classroom. That is where we begin.

1.1 In a village Primary School

The scene is a village primary school with infants, having an annual intake of about 30; thus about 200 children, one class per year plus a smaller infants' reception class. It lies in a village which has nearly doubled in size in the last 15 years. Its buildings are elderly, and supplemented by a couple of classroom huts.

The school works on orthodox 'old-fashioned' lines still: there is a timetable in the Head's study, with the days neatly divided up into 35-minute periods. But no one observes it rigidly, because each class has one general teacher for almost all the time.

The Head recognises the value of radio and television for stimulus, and for reinforcing weak spots. All classrooms are wired for radio: there is a single television set (monochrome, the Parent-Teacher Association is collecting for a colour one) which although trolley-mounted resides permanently in one classroom. This happens to be that of the second year juniors' class teacher, who was the most persuasive when the set was installed several years ago. The school makes a lot of use of its filmstrip projector; it has a sound tape recorder – a fairly recent acquisition – but only one staff member, absent today, has taken to recording radio programmes. For the most part, broadcasts are taken live.

The staff has no specialists, but a lot of stability – a very small turnover. The Head ensures during the summer term that they are aware of what BBC and ITV have to offer for the following year. He makes suggestions but doesn't impose anything: the staff tend to stick to tried favourites. He has a rule that no class should have more than one television or one radio broadcast on any one day. His limited capitation allowance sets him problems for school materials, and he has to keep a strict eye on the number of broadcast series used which require expenditure on pamphlets and other items.

Let us glimpse at television and radio in action in this school on a day in February 1974. The first programme on offer is 'Maths Workshop' on TV, but this is not a series the school takes: there's a suspicion that it would be a bit newfangled or difficult. Anyhow, it would require a very quick turn-round of classes at 9.58 in the room with the TV set, where nothing would persuade the teacher to forgo 'Merry-go-Round' at 10 o'clock.

Her classroom, at 9.58, is full of expectancy: today's programme is the first part of a play called 'The Raven and the Cross'. The classroom is also full of traces of Vikings: cardboard models of Viking longships, fearsome paintings of Viking gods, names inscribed in runic lettering, a half-finished wall map of Viking invasions. As a run up to the play there have been two programmes about the Vikings in the weeks before half-term, and the teacher has been quick to seize on the possibilities for craft activities among the children, to build up their background of experience for the play. During the two-minute signature tune heralding the start of the programme she helps the children to recall the names of some of the characters, whom they have already met briefly in the last broadcast.

Now the Vikings are on the screen, threatening to assault the Manor of Chippenham. There's a whinnying of horses as they ride off to the assault. Back at the Manor we meet Edwina, daughter of the Bailiff, complaining to her nurse Ellen that she's not allowed to go out hunting. The children's attention is glued to the screen: they seem unconscious of the noise going on in the school hall uncomfortably near, where an infants' class is assembling for a 'Movement and Music' programme. All attention is now on Edwina's father, telling her he has arranged for her to be married to the Earl of Mildenhall whose lands adjoin theirs. Disgust and truculent disappearance of Edwina, chasing inquisitive goats from the manor hall as she goes. Out in the forest riding, she catches sight of the Vikings, dashes back, screams to have the gates closed behind her, rushes in with the news. Turmoil. Her father says the gates must be opened, they can't resist. Horses careering in, swords flashing, Vikings carrying off the gold plate. Edwina's father killed. Enter Guthrum, leader of the Vikings. He stops further slaughter, tells his men that they need the conquered, to work with them, to cultivate the land. A quieter passage: the tension in the class relaxes. It grows again as the story focuses once more on the child Edwina. She's off to Mildenhall – Guthrum has been persuaded to let her go. On horseback, with Ellen following on a donkey. In the forest, suddenly she's changing into boy's clothes. Going to Mildenhall? No, she's going to the Athelney marshes – to find King Alfred.

End of Part 1. The credits. An audible sigh from the children. 'D'you think she'll find him?' asks the teacher. 'Yes, miss, she's very clever, to think of that disguise,' from a girl. A boy: 'The wolves will get her, miss' (picking up a caution from Ellen in the play). 'She's a long way to go.' A girl with an eye for melodrama speculates that Ellen will throw herself to the wolf so that Edwina can escape. 'A long way to go, yes,' says the teacher. 'Shall we try and see how far?' A modern map is brought out: Chippenham is identified and, roughly, the Athelney area. A long way indeed. Someone wonders if the story's true. Different views. Fact and fiction disentangled, the teacher guiding. Then she draws from the children some first impressions of the chief characters, and the bell goes for break. In the afternoon, the class will be taking up their group projects again. The children doing the Viking gods have finished: they're keen to try and paint the attack on Chippenham Manor. Earnest discussion with teacher as the others file out.

Meanwhile next door, in what passes for the school hall, it has been 'Movement and Music' on the radio – Stage 2, for the older infants. There's a very young girl in charge, a student teacher in

'Movement and Music'

fact: the regular teacher has gone sick, so she has found herself plunged into a new responsibility. She remembers 'Music and Movement' vaguely from her own schooldays; but it has changed its style and title since then, and she has only seen one programme used in this school, from the series for younger infants, Stage 1. She was just observing, and rather thought the teacher intervened a bit too much, wanting to lead the children. She would try and avoid this. She had palpitations now: bigger children than she was used to, would they fool about or play her up?

Well, there they were – shorts and vests and bare feet, ready to begin. She just had time for a hurried glance at the teachers' notes: oh dear! Alice in Wonderland up till this week, that must have been fun. But now some poem she didn't know, that the children would be asked to move to.

A man's voice on the air: quite a surprise – always used to be women for 'Music and Movement'. But of course no surprise to the children . . . they're scampering off happily to the quick music. Sticking feet to the floor and exploring the space around with their arms, to slow music – not badly either. Hullo, what's

4

this? Stick their *hands* to the floor and move their legs to the music? Quite a bit of overbalancing and rolling about. I'll have to call those two to order. But what are they meant to be doing? Handstands?

Never mind, we're soon on to something else. Sitting on the floor, curling into a small shape, stretching to a tall one. Into the shape of a tree with twisted branches.

Now they're farmers, dancing with heavy feet and high knees. The exhibitionists are having a field day here. Those two boys monkeying about again. Better be firm. Oh, but now they've been told to sit again. A bit of the poem. They seem to like it.

'Teachers, will you help here please? Girls, to the side where your teacher's pointing. Boys, space out.' Ah, a chance to separate those two. Good.

Now the boys are miming gates and stiles, the girls dancing in and out of them. The girls now are church spires, the boys dancing round them. Now they're windmills and watermills. It's really going with a swing: children smiling, inviting admiration as they prance past, but mostly absorbed, living in their inner world.

The broadcast's over already. Twenty minutes quickly gone. Five minutes still to break. Suppose we should practise something, really. But that might be tempting providence, or a bit of a comedown without the broadcast music. Think I'll just let them change and be off. Must get that 'sticking hands to floor' business straight before next time, though.

Eleven o'clock. Break's over. We're with the nine-year-olds. Song-books being given out – one between two. The teacher's middle-aged, genial, on excellent terms with his class. Knows his strengths and his weaknesses, too. Music's a weakness. 'Can't sing a note, old boy – but these kids will, bar a couple of growlers at the back. Taken this programme for years, I have. Eleven o'clock every Monday. A godsend.'

It's 'Singing Together' – thirty years old and still going strong in 15,000 odd schools. 'Hullo, we've got two new songs for you today and the first one is on page 4. The Cuckoo.' The broadcaster's taken the class over; within a minute they're tackling the chorus of the new song. It's brisk work, and it's enjoyed. The teacher does in fact join in – to take a back seat isn't his style; he fills in as a conductor too, to jolly his troops along, with a quip to the laggards thrown in for good measure. He loves the role, and is rather proud of the way he can draw out of them those crescendos and diminuendos.

11.20. End of broadcast. No nonsense: collect books, straight back to business end of school life . . .

School lunch is over and everyone settled at work again. The top class is in the hands of a young teacher who has inherited a fairly conventional geography syllabus, with an emphasis this term on life and work in tropical lands. He is looking for opportunities to give variety and vividness to the pupils' experience and has spotted that the radio series 'Exploration Earth' includes two programmes which might serve his purposes. The plan of the series sets these programmes in a quite different context: that of man's relationship to animals, with particular reference to the problems of conservation. There's a bit of a risk in taking them, the teacher feels: the advertised age is 10-12, and some of his 10-year-olds are a bit slow and don't find 20 minutes' listening easy; besides, they haven't got the pamphlets they're supposed to have. But today's programme at least, about Elephants in East Africa, sounds like having a ready appeal. The teacher has equipped himself with information and pictures on the National Parks, which he is sharing with his pupils. Just before the broadcast, he gets them to recall, from visits to zoos or films they have seen, just how enormous a beast an elephant is.

The announcer tells the children that the programme is, in the main, the story of Bruce Kinloch, who helped start some of the East African National Parks. Then, from among sound effects evoking the atmosphere of a tropical forest, they hear the scream of an enraged bull elephant.

KINLOCH   The scream came from the deep shadows of the forest. Wild and savage, it was so close that I was awake and on my feet in one scrambling movement. It was hot in the forest, the humid, clammy East African heat that clings like treacle and sucks steady streams of sweat from the human body. There was hardly a breath of air, and not a sound. Even the squealing baboons had been shocked into a frightened, watchful quiet. Then suddenly a whisper of wind stirred the fine dust of the forest path, and at once—

Another scream right on

hardly daring to move, I turned my head slowly towards my African companion. He pointed into the forest with a jerk of his chin.

ASHA (*Whispering*) Elephant. Big and very angry.

LOCH Scarcely had he spoken when the wall of the forest parted, and towering above us appeared a great grey head backed by mighty, spreading ears. Framed between two great tusks of gleaming ivory, vicious pig-like eyes searched short-sightedly in every direction, while a trunk like some monstrous snake curled and twisted, striving to find the faintest trace of man-scent. There before me was the first wild animal I had seen in Africa–a giant bull elephant.

A good beginning, the teacher thinks. The class's attention remains riveted while the speaker tells of the shooting of the elephant, the terrible depredations they can cause and, contrariwise, man's inhumanity towards the elephant, for gain: the poisoned arrows, the stolen ivory. Then, the story of the National Parks; the problems of population control among the elephants; the complex question of whether to cull or whether to let starve. Quite difficult stuff this: a lot of information at a stiffish pace; two or three look as if they're finding concentration difficult. The children's grasp of several points will need checking on, the teacher decides. But all in all a valuable, first-hand contribution. During the next day or two, the most graphic scenes will reverberate more than once in classroom discussion, and in playground antics too. Some of the boys, it comes out, know quite a bit from personal experience of the problems of controlling rabbits or grey squirrels in their own countryside. Good to let them air this, the teacher decides: it will help him underline the much bigger problems of pest-control in the tropics. Yes, it'll be worth taking that programme on the weaver-bird next week too. And he must work in something about locusts, of course: he could get a group of children researching on that themselves, surely.

Simultaneously, in the TV classroom, a group of 7-year-olds has been watching episode 15 of Sam on Boffs' Island. A half-class only, this: the brighter ones have been taken off by the student teacher so that the less good readers can profit from this series, 'Words and Pictures', which is especially for them. The group has seen this programme before, for 'Words and Pictures' has an unusual transmission pattern: two new broadcasts one week, each repeated at the same time in the week following. So if children are in difficulties first time, they can have a second go after the teacher has given them help and practice in between. This group has, in fact, done more: they love the puppet Boffs and their adventures, and once the teacher – months ago – had got them to act out part of an episode, they demanded to do acting every week, and often got their way.

The programme's on now: the children are reading the title on the screen (half of them only – the teacher's told the better readers to keep quiet). There'll be more reading for them here and there in the programme. But not a lot: it's a story – a story of high fantasy: Boffs' Island is a cloudcuckooland; the Boffs have been invaded by the Gurglers, but the invasion has become a peaceful fraternisation. Today there's a wedding on, Tele-boff marrying Girlgler, and a wedding breakfast: lovely grub, but Gran-boff cuts up rough – 'They'll be ill.' And all the time there's subtle teaching going on. A brush – bricks – the bride – the groom – prunes: all these words in the story, and many more, to give experience of consonant blends: gr, br and so on – spoken, heard, written, read. It goes with a swing.

Afterwards they read from their pamphlets, specially written and illustrated for the series. The girls want to do a picture of the wedding: a collage perhaps? There's discussion of materials to collect at home and bring next day. Then, a little painless revision of earlier work in the term: there's a game in the pamphlets to help with this.

1.2 In an urban Comprehensive School

Now to a different scene. The fringes of a large city: housing estate country. A big Comprehensive Secondary School: ten-form entry; about 1800 on the roll; staff of just over 100. It's a newish building, well equipped for audio-visual work: a couple of rooms fitted for sound-film projection, a language lab, TV since the school's opening ten years ago, a scatter of audio-tape recorders and filmstrip and overhead projectors; and since a year ago a couple of video-tape recorders, allowing on-the-spot play-back facilities to several classrooms conveniently accessible from the recording room.

The Head limits his involvement with TV and radio to providing the wherewithal. This covers, besides the equipment, a technical assistant whose job includes booking and making recordings on request, and looking after storage and elementary maintenance. Choice of programmes to use rests with Heads of Departments, and is discussed and agreed at departmental meetings. The Head finds he is able to meet most reasonable requests for materials associated with broadcasts: these too are channelled through the Departments.

It is the same day in February 1974. In the course of it, five TV and four radio broadcasts for secondary schools will be transmitted over the air, but no teacher is concerned with this; for no broadcasts are taken live. Only the technical assistant is checking his timetable of recordings requested for that day, his stock of available tape, the demands on his moveable VTR for classroom playback. A couple of teachers, too, have asked for previews of TV programmes he recorded last week, before they decide just how and when to use them: they'll probably have to be fitted in during the lunch break.

We are with a class of fourteen-year-olds studying British Social History as part of their Humanities course for CSE next year. They have a half-morning a week on this work, and the teacher decided to base it on a TV series of fortnightly programmes, which seemed to cover the ground pretty well. The last two, on the development of railways and motorcars, were popular. Today he's anxious, however: they're not an easy class at the best of times, and there's a Monday-morning feeling in the air: they're slouching and playing it dead pan. He'd meant, as he'd done before, to preview today's programme, 'The Palace of Glass', but hadn't managed to; and at the last moment the technical assistant had warned him that the recording was fair, but with some interference.

The teacher starts by recalling the growing prosperity of mid-19th-century Britain, referring back to the railways. He's talking too much himself, he realises, yet he can't get them to utter. He tries a suggestion in the Teacher's Notes: have they heard of the recent international exhibitions – at Montreal, at Tokyo? A blank. He tries them on Hyde Park, the Albert Hall – which someone associates with boxing – and the Albert Memorial. He recalls the programme's title, 'The Palace of Glass', and gets them to turn to the picture on page 16 of their pamphlets. The class livens up a little, and the teacher switches on the recording.

The first picture on the screen is the Albert Memorial. Glad I mentioned that, thinks the teacher, as several faces glance towards him in token of respect for the miraculous convergence of his mind with the TV's. Then the Palace of Glass itself, the camera tracking in on the huge fountain inside the exhibition hall. All quiet so far; but the voice of Queen Victoria reading from her journal, over a still of the opening ceremony, is a cue for one of the class's show-offs. 'A day to live for ever' he mimics audibly to his neighbour, his falsetto perfectly taking off the actress's rendering of young enthusiasm overlaid with primness. Titters round the class. A little later, there's the voice–and the face–of Colonel Sibthorp, a leading opponent of the exhibition: '. . . the greatest trash, the greatest fraud, and the greatest imposition ever to be placed upon the people of this country.' The mimic has another go: guffaws this time. The teacher makes to intervene, but there's irritation on some faces, and 'shush' comes from around the class–they've had enough. They're concentrating hard again at the shots of the exhibition's construction, and Albert visiting the workers on the site. 'He ordered 250 gallons of beer for the men, and was loudly cheered.' A group of difficult boys cheer too–mockingly, but they're with the broadcast all right.

Now we're being taken round the exhibition. The teacher admires the way the camera plays on the succession of stills, as he had admired the bringing to life of documentary material in the actors' voices; but are the class with him? There are some exaggerated yawns as the commentator remarks on the Victorians' lack of taste–and here, at the worst moment, there's the ropy part of the recording.

But now the focus has shifted to the people visiting the exhibition–the railway excursions, the cartoons of avid sightseers. Attention picks up again: relief of teacher. But how does he follow up this programme? As it comes to an end, he is uncertain. He plays safe–turns to pamphlets again. There are plenty of good pictures, and with their help he finds a lot is recalled including, to his surprise, quite small details.

The Palace of Glass, Hyde Park, 1851 ('British Social History'—pamphlet)

He decides the class should do some written work, and adopts the suggestion in the Teacher's Notes: 'Write an account of the exhibition from the viewpoint of a one-shilling visitor.' Groans from the class. Well, let's collect some ideas, he says. They're reasonably co-operative – it will save them trouble later, after all. Soon the blackboard is covered with jottings of ideas. They agree that men and women visitors are likely to be struck by different things: town and country ones too, perhaps. Each pupil must decide just who he is and where he comes from. Yes, include the journey too . . .

Not so bad after all, the teacher thinks, and difficult to do justice to the Great Exhibition without a broadcast. Harder to handle than the transport programmes, though, or last term's about factory and farm workers. The next one, in two weeks' time, is about the Festival of Britain in 1951. Good idea, really, to have the two exhibitions side by side like that. But that programme won't be easy to handle either. Must make sure I preview it. Wonder if I might be able to rope in one of the older staff who actually saw it?

As it happens, that is the only TV recording to be played back in a classroom that morning; but around the school there is evidence of other BBC products in use. Some years back the Biology mistress followed the series 'Science Extra: Biology' with an O-level class. She found it took too much precious class time to go on using the programmes; but she persuaded the Department Head to buy the 8mm film cassettes which reproduce some key sequences from them. The class is studying animal behaviour; the sequence she is discussing with them illustrates dominant and submissive features in the behaviour of wolves in a pack.

Meanwhile a teacher of English in the Humanities Department is talking to her second-year class about the Shakespearian theatre. She had distributed photo-copies, made in the school, of a number of line-drawings illustrating how it developed. Where did she get the drawings? She heard about them at a staff meeting of the department: they had been acquired by a colleague, a History teacher, for use with a BBC radio series called 'History in Evidence' which her class was following that term to supplement their study of Elizabethan England. A folder of documentary materials relating to the broadcasts is produced by the BBC for individual and group study: once purchased· it is part of the school's permanent resources. 'All these staff meetings have their uses after all,' thinks the English teacher (she was technically in breach of copyright in reproducing the drawings, but we all know it happens).

In the Modern Languages Department, too, there are BBC materials in use: a first-year class of children new to the language are following the radiovision series 'French for Beginners'. Radio-vision, of which more later, is a combination of tape-recorded sound and filmstrip—ideal for elementary language teaching. Originally the sound of the 'French for Beginners' programmes was broadcast, for recording at the school; but now both film-strip and tapes can be bought direct from the BBC. Another permanent 'resource', used with several classes each year; and this teacher, with years' experience of its use, is a dab at handling it. The class listened to the whole programme last week: now they're working on just a section of it. A boy is operating the film-strip projector: the teacher manipulates the tape-recorder with consummate skill, running back unerringly to the right point to give the class that bit of practice again . . .

After lunch, we have to go outside the school to follow 5X, a class that is doing its 'extra year' with no enthusiasm at all: even CSE is beyond their range. The search among staff is never-ending for something which will catch their interest for more than a moment: they are the despair of many. But this experienced science teacher is making headway; last term he got recorded and used with another class, almost as difficult, a group of three pro-grammes on practical photography from the series 'Science Session'. It went well: the class did some good work, even mounted an exhibition; so he moved heaven and earth to get the video-tapes kept for the following term (normally they'd have been wiped to make room for other recordings).

'Science Session' envisages just such an audience: to woo it, there are inviting pamphlets full of pictures – photographs, dia-grams, comic cartoons—looking anything but 'educational': something the most blasé might without loss of self-respect look at twice. The school is equipped with a dark-room. The class have followed the three programmes earlier in the term; they've made a 'camera obscura'; some had a shot at constructing an

1 Get some friends and **think up an idea**
Just in case you get stuck, and can't think of anything, try this . . .

THE DIG
A junk shop –
a musty book –
but it mentions a
mysterious burial in
a nearby garden
long ago –
Worth investigating ? –
The dig – one or two
odd surprises –
and then . . . ?

2 **Decide who'll do what**
Who'll take the photos ? Who'll act ? Who'll direct ?
By sorting it all out now, you'll avoid any arguments later !

Director

3 **Make a reconnaissance**
Go along to the places, where you hope to take your photos, with an *unloaded* camera. Look through the viewfinder to plan your shots. Decide now whether a particular shot should be a close-up or a more general view. Plan on taking no more than 20 pictures.

4 **The storyboard**
Draw 20 boxes about 10cm x 10cm on a large sheet of card (one for each photo you plan to take). Make a sketch of what each photo must show, and write CU, MS or LS beside each sketch to remind you whether it's to be a close-up, a medium shot, or a long shot. It's a good idea for everyone in the 'crew' to make a small 'miniboard' copy of the storyboard to take on location.

5 **Make a list of everything you need**
Don't forget film for the camera, clothes or props for the actors.
Do you need to ask anyone's permission ?

'Make your own Photoplay'—a section of the pamphlet pages accompanying a programme from the series 'Science Session'

actual camera, with mixed results; they've taken some snaps, working in groups with the four personally owned cameras the class could muster; some of them have tried their hand at developing and contact printing. Now, armed with viewfinders they've made for themselves, they're out reconnoitring their shots for a 'photoplay' (a 'story' told in still photographs). The teacher's glad he ventured on this: two or three girls, passengers during the technical activities, came out with some really bright ideas; and Christine, whom he'd thought only interested in her coiffure, had shown quite a talent for leading a group. She'll get her own picture into that group's story, anyway . . .

Finally, half-way through the afternoon, a dozen senior students are strolling into a bay of the Sixth Form Humanities room. A civilised place; comfortable chairs in an informal setting. One of them has the recorder and tape for a radio playback: they've opted to follow a group of five programmes from the series 'Prospect', as part of their work in General Studies. There's no teacher: a different boy or girl 'takes the chair' each week, another acts as 'rapporteur'. They're expected to turn in a coherent summary of the broadcasts and their discussion of them and during the five weeks to do some individual research with the Head of Department's guidance.

They settle down, switch on, listen. It's the first of a group of programmes about the mass communication media and their influence: an interview with William Hardcastle about News. Paul, the rapporteur, scribbles busily.

At the end of the broadcast Felicity, in the chair, asks Paul if he can remind them, from his notes, of the main points.

PAUL Well, he started with the election broadcasts, how you had to have a balance–not like the USA where you can buy time on the air. But he thought personalities in the TV broadcasts were boring–same ones all the time (murmurs of agreement). Then I've got down: newspapers better than radio and TV, more information and you can read it quicker. Then he said objectivity is impossible. You have to select the news. . . .

LICITY Oh yes, he meant that was a kind of comment, didn't he, when you choose one story rather than another for the headlines.

PAUL That's it. Then, I've got readers' complaints–Solzhen . . .

LAIRE Solzhenitsyn. He had to leave Russia.

LICITY Why were readers complaining?

PAUL Because the papers went on so about him. Then I've got; news is gloomy. M1 pile-ups. But in Russia all that is suppressed in the papers . . .

CHAEL He would say that, wouldn't he? Not true of course. There's a lot of criticism in the Soviet press (some groans as this well-known leftie gets under way). What about the capitalist press anyway? He never talked about . . .

LICITY Michael, can we stick to what he did talk about, please? Perhaps we've enough points to be going on with. Thanks, Paul. Now what about the election news–d'you agree with what he said? Any comments?

And so they go on. They collect most of the important points, note the one about fact and comment not really being separable as a job for research on some actual newspapers. Not an earthshaking broadcast, Felicity reflects, but plenty to chew on.

The broadcasts featured in those two accounts were actual ones: the schools and their activities fictional but, I hope, recognisable. A little better than average reality, no doubt: in the hurly-burly of school life there are more stresses and strains, more slips between cup and lip than we saw there. Some broadcasts simply flop; some teachers are less conscientious or less imaginative in handling them than any whose activities we observed or whose thoughts we shared. Most schools would probably not draw quite so much on BBC products in any one day: other possible sources of comparable material—ITV, local radio, closed-circuit television—I have, to avoid cluttering the picture, ignored. My intention has been to sketch the variety of forms which BBC school broadcasting and its associated products take today, and the variety of opportunities and problems inherent in their use. The following chapters, using a 'lines of development' pattern familiar to teachers of history, will trace the vicissitudes through which over its fifty years the service has come to be what it is today.

2 LANDMARKS OF TECHNICAL PROGRESS

School broadcasting's development has depended, at both producing and receiving ends, on a lot of educational thinking and a lot of creative imagination. Yet, as with so much of human activity, it can be seen also as the resultant of intelligent application of the clever inventions of engineers. In the comparatively young field of broadcasting, hardly a year passes without some innovation which extends its scope or lightens its burdens—a more sophisticated microphone, a more discriminating receiver, a lighter camera, a cheaper or more flexible method of recording: the list is unending. But this chapter is not about technicalities: it aims, much more simply, to chart the main landmarks which have enlarged, over the last quarter of a century, the range of school broadcasting for producers and for users. For users particularly, since technical developments applied to the production of school broadcasts are, in the main, part of the story of broadcasting generally, whereas the problems of using them are unique.

Seen in this context, our landmarks are easily identifiable: the coming of television; the advent of magnetic tape and the tape recorder; the new field of radiovision which tape recording opened up; and finally the development of video-tape. Colour television, for all its attraction, is not a landmark of this order. It does not, until virtually universal, extend the range of what school broadcasting can attempt, nor change in any fundamental way the situation of the user. It simply enhances enjoyment, and often understanding as well, by being 'natural' television (just how 'natural' can be argued about) instead of television with the artificial limitation of colour-blindness.

2.1 Early days

The start of school broadcasting came hard on the heels of the beginning of the British Broadcasting Company: its pioneers shared in the hazards of all those early in the field. Some of them were masters of the art of the extempore: Walford Davies, the doyen of them all, never used a script, but spoke from scribbled notes. It was as well, for in the earliest days rehearsal and production as later developed were scarcely known, and facilities minimal. George Dixon, who joined the BBC in 1925 and was its first—for many years its only—specialist school broadcast producer, relates how he once found himself allotted a studio without a gramophone deck for a programme in which Walford Davies wanted to include short excerpts from two recordings of classical pieces. 'Clutching the two discs, I dashed down a couple of staircases to another studio, got disc 1 on in the nick of time, and sat down with relief—on disc 2. Just time to hare upstairs again and warn Walford. He didn't bat an eyelid. "Well children, I did promise you an attractive piece by Brahms, but Mr Dixon has just sat on it."' Live broadcasting: intimate atmosphere.

Virtually all school broadcasts were transmitted live, right up to and during the war. Some were recorded on transmission, but for the purpose of demonstrating them to teachers and others: a script might be used again, but the programme would be remade. There was a mystique about it: the essence of broadcasting was felt to be 'this man in person, talking directly to you, now'. A unique thing, made for a unique occasion. Professional actors, mostly more used to stage than film, played up well of course: old hands swear that live broadcasting brought out heightened performance, and far fewer fluffs.

By the thirties engineering skills and programme production were already highly professionalised: far otherwise at the listening end of school broadcasting, where the struggle for standards was long and arduous. The BBC was well aware that schools would need help to achieve good reception: its first 'Education Engineer' was appointed in 1925—in the days when most domestic listening was still on earphones. Their number rapidly multiplied. The report on the first thorough study of the listening end of school broadcasting (the 'Kent Inquiry' in 1927, of which more later) had much to say about choice and maintenance of

The first school broadcast—Walford Davies in the studio with the Temple Church choirboys.

receivers: in 1930 the newly created Central Council for School Broadcasting set up a Technical Sub-Committee, with a BBC Engineer as secretary, to take the matter in hand; and the Council's Chairman referred in 1934 to 'a group of teachers and technical experts sitting on panels for a total of 514 hours last year, in connection with the completion of the Council's list of broadcast receiving apparatus suitable for use in schools'. He went on, 'If the experiment of school broadcasting is to proceed, the duty of securing good reception in schools must fall on the Local Education Authorities and not on individual teachers.'

The LCC took this so much to heart that for some years it forbad its schools to listen unless their installations had been vetted by BBC Education Engineers: this did not endear the BBC to all the Heads concerned. But few other Authorities were as rigorous, or as concerned. A lot of school sets were gifts, mainly unsuitable, from well-wishers – if they were not School Managers' cast-offs. And the only real expertise on reception in acoustically difficult classrooms and school halls was in the BBC itself. Its

Education Engineers conducted technical surveys in hundreds of individual schools. 'Baffleboards' were recommended for loud-speakers to project the sound forward and give adequate bass response: aerials had to be made more efficient (the transmissions were on long-wave). Reception was often improved by touching the aerial terminal: some teachers detailed a boy to keep his finger on it throughout the programme.

Aerials, indeed, were often a bone of contention. Before TV hardened our senses to universal rooftop outrages, battles over their unsightliness were frequent – particularly where schools, still symbols of parish dignity, were concerned. The role of arbitrator might well fall to the lot of the village constable.

Some teachers adopted bizarre solutions to their problems. John Wiseman, who was to serve the longest of all the BBC's Education Engineers, recalls hearing a school broadcast loud, if not entirely clear, as he entered the high street of a small village. The school teacher, who lived next to her single-class school, had a personal wireless set in her sitting room. The school had none, but she would not deprive her pupils of this new joy. She turned her volume to maximum and distributed her largesse to the whole village.

School often neglected proper earthing, too; so they were advised to embed the earth wire in damp ground as near to the set as possible. One Head interpreted this very keenly: the classroom floorboard next to the set was taken up, the earth wire implanted, and a pupil instructed to water the ground at regular intervals.

Thus was progress made, but haltingly. BBC engineers continued – up to the war, through it, and beyond – to do a job which really belonged to the Education Authorities. Despite their efforts, the Beveridge Report (1951) expressed concern about the quality of reception in schools. Much has improved since then, but much remains to be done; and recording in schools has brought fresh problems.

In some ways the wheel has come full circle. The portable battery sets of the 30s were quite inadequate for school use in most circumstances: the ideal aimed at, and normally fulfilled in the crop of new post-war schools, was a cabinetted central set with extensions to fixed speakers in as many classrooms as possible. Today, transistorised portables are infinitely more sturdy and sensitive than the battery sets of thirty years back: handy tape recorders give satisfactory reproduction; and work in small groups is the norm in many schools. The costly and elaborate installations of twenty years ago are becoming white elephants.

2.2 Enter TV

The BBC started TV in 1936 and resumed it after the war in 1946. Its attraction for children was quickly in evidence: its educative potential equally so. By the end of the 40s there were plenty of people working in TV who were anxious to exploit this potential for schools, and groups of school radio producers were going into huddles about it. In 1951 agreement was reached for a pilot experiment in School TV the following year.

The Pilot Experiment

This was to be a 'house' experiment, not involving profound mulling over by educational committees beforehand; for the Television Service itself was still living a somewhat hand-to-mouth existence, and as it expanded its facilities were continually stretched to their limits. For a few weeks' programmes, to go 'on the air' was pointless, for there would be no incentive to invest in receivers: better, anyhow, to cut milk teeth in relative privacy. An arrangement was therefore made with the Middlesex Education Authority to equip six conveniently situated secondary schools and to link them with the studio at Alexandra Palace by micro-wave for vision and P.O. line for sound. For observing response to the programmes, six schools could be well covered by the School Broadcasting Council's team of Education Officers, while their engineer colleagues kept an eye on the technical side; how were the twenty programmes themselves, due to be broadcast one a day during May, to be created?

They were made, to put it mildly, under difficulties. Only three of School Radio's producers had had any training in TV production: they had to team up with others, ill-spared from other TV departments, who lacked experience of the educational situation. The many essential back-up services, too, had to be squeezed out of an already overstrained general service. It was remarkable that the results were as good as they were.

Viewing circumstances were bound, of course, to be quite artificial. The twenty programmes—four in each of five different fields—were all discrete entities, unrelated either to each other or, except by chance, to other work the viewing classes were doing at the time. The experiment was conceived, therefore, as a try-out of a wide variety of television production techniques in the context of a number of programmes addressed to children in schools, and not in any sense as a foretaste of what an educational service might eventually offer (the original intention was to follow this 'pilot experiment' by a longer 'main experiment', planned to take account of school realities and seeking to offer just such a foretaste). But it is difficult, perhaps impossible, to assess the effectiveness of production techniques and styles of presentation without passing judgement on the programmes as a whole, and this was in effect what the teachers and other observers mainly did.

Still, it was an exhilarating experience for all involved; and the programmes were certainly varied. One of them, in a group on the visual arts, showed how to make tiles out of plaster (and assumed immediate practical follow-up); another, from a science group, explained just how an aeroplane stays up; a third took us on a leisurely tour round a modern dairy farm; a fourth explained volcanic action, demonstrating with a studio model spouting porridge for lava.

What was learnt from these pilots? From the responses of children and teachers it was possible to draw up a number of elements of promise in the various programmes. The report on the experiment listed them as follows:

The clash of personalities in unscripted discussion on a topic of moment; studio discussion on matters of personal interest to children; the personal story, e.g. of a traveller, supplementing his own film; young people at their jobs; the poetic quality of artistic skill allied to the personality of the artist; the stimulating illusion of being 'on the spot', created through 'faked' studio resources (the volcano); the straightforward informative outside broadcast (the dairy farm); clear exposition reinforced by visuals

E is for Edwina and Ellen

F is for fraya. hoo is a god. and Fite. when pepol Die.

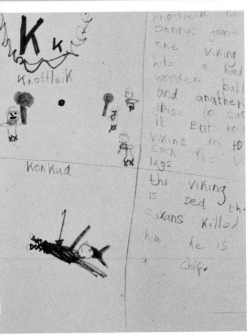

Knottleik

Konkud

Knottleik is Danmes game one Viking hits a hard wooden ball and another trise to cac it But for vikins tri to cach the legs thi viking is Ded the Saxans killed him he is a chif.

Q is for Queen

'Courtship and
Marriage in Painting'
– *Head of a girl*
(detail) by Vermeer
(right) and *The
Sunshade* by Goya
(below)

outside the range of the average teacher's equipment (the aeroplane).

A useful anthology: most of these elements were to find a place
in the permanent service later. But not all: outside broadcasts
proved inadequately amenable to the selection and control
needed for educational purposes; while talking faces, even in
discussion, were to get fairly short shrift.

Personality

The stress on personality was important, and for two reasons.
First, participants in School TV were likely, as in the pilots, to
be mainly amateurs at the forbidding business of communication
in front of the camera; yet assurance and ease of manner—particularly in the 'anchorman'—the person who held the programme
together and was usually the main speaker also—were of cardinal
importance: children are merciless towards failings here. Yet
where to find such people, and how to train them except on the
job? The problem dogged the early years of regular School TV
also: was one to choose the man who really knew what he was
talking about, and risk the consequences of inexperience in the
studio—or to go for a hardened professional (probably an actor)
without any deep knowledge of the subject in question, and trust
him to learn his lines and cope?

Producers usually plumped for the first—the bolder—course.
Particularly in science programmes; for supposing, for instance,
a studio experiment failed: how was a non-scientist to know why,
or what the chances were of a second shot's coming off? A speaker
who was doing things as he spoke would tend, too, to be less
self-conscious than one with nothing between himself and the
camera: the artistic skill of a potter in one of the 'pilots' had won
sympathy for her not immediately engaging personality. But
often a scientist doing an experiment in the studio would, to
allow the camera to present a clear picture, have to act un-
naturally—manipulate apparatus with his left hand, for instance.
There were no easy solutions.

Today, these problems are much less intractable. There are
many more professionals and experienced amateurs to select
from; the arts of communication are diffused much more widely;

'idiot boards' set in strategic positions for the anchorman's guidance can be replaced by a script unfurling on the 'autocue' screen; and pre-recording, followed by video-tape editing, makes instant retakes possible. Yet the choice of presenter remains, for many programmes, a crucial decision.

TV and educational film

Screen personality in School TV was important for another reason: it distinguished television's contribution from that of educational film. Most films made for schools were instructionally conceived: the emphasis was on carefully shot and edited pictures, combined in a logical sequence, and accompanied by an out-of-vision commentary, precise, economical – and aloof. Some were brilliantly done, and most of course were in colour. By comparison, many TV programmes of an informative nature – and most of those in the pilot experiment – looked amateurish; yet often they had a warmth, an intimate sense of personal communication, that the more professional film lacked. It is not to be inferred, of course, that a film designed primarily to inform necessarily lacks personality: common experience, for instance of 'Alistair Cooke's America', disproves this. I am only saying that the films made for school use twenty years ago failed to exploit personality; and that the TV studio was the crucible in which the expression of personality and the transmission of information were first fused into a new, and more powerful, visual message. The sound studio had done the same for oral communication: School TV then had, indeed, much more affinity with School radio than with educational film, both in its nature and in the circumstances of its use. It was noticeable already in the pilot experiment that those experienced in handling school radio also used TV to best advantage.

It was not surprising, however, that makers and users of educational film were quicker to see the weaknesses of the new medium than to appreciate its strengths. They also pointed out that whereas educational films for classroom projection were under the teacher's control and could be previewed, shown and repeated at his convenience, TV programmes had to be taken as they came, planned to someone else's timetable.

Indeed, in the aftermath of the experiment, a kind of 'battle of the books' raged between the users and would-be users of educational film and the advocates of classroom television. The experiment might have been meant as a 'house' affair; but of course it was widely reported. The programmes had been re-corded (involving some loss of quality with the technical means then available); and there was a passionate interest among educationists in seeing what the BBC was up to. When they did, the best of the experimental programmes often got a chilly reception; and even when people liked what they saw, the cry was 'Why can't we have this on film?' The rather arid debate was prolonged by delay in moving on to the next experimental stage: the economic climate was frigid, the Ministry of Education (whose agreement to allowing TV receivers to rank for grant-in-aid to Local Authorities was crucial) sat tight. In the event, the idea of the 'Main Experiment' was abandoned, and five years elapsed before School TV came again – this time to stay.

The partisans of educational film had a point of course: they were genuinely alarmed at the possibility of the BBC's showering on the schools second-rate material, likely to be poorly used. But there were powerful counter-arguments. Several teachers participating in the experiment had compared children's response to the TV programmes favourably with their reactions to educational film. There were large areas of school curricula for which educational film had little or nothing to offer – and the hunger for more visual material in the schools was intense. The conditions postulated for the proper use of educational film were rarely apparent in practice. And when School TV really started, it would be buttressed by the guidance of educationalists, and executed by a specially chosen professional staff, fully trained in the medium, and backed by adequate finance and support services.

The School Broadcasting Council, reinforced now by a Television Sub-Committee, took great pains to examine the extent to which educational film was actually used, and the circumstances of its use: their findings, save here and there, were disquieting. Not all educational film was of high quality; much was out-of-date; and anyhow few teachers were trained to handle 16mm projectors: convenience of operation was to prove a prime advantage of TV in this respect (not that reception conditions in class-rooms were by any means uniformly good, nor yet are). The Council went even further in its determination to substantiate the overwhelming need for school TV: I remember preparing a paper which hypothesised plans for a number of school TV series, and noted beside them the topics on which educational film had something reasonably up-to-date to offer. They were few.

The dust has long since settled on this controversy: educational film continues to do a useful job for schools, though a limited one by comparison with TV; and many of the films shown in schools are not the less valuable (sometimes the reverse) for not having been made specially for that market. The BBC itself has for many years now, through its Television Enterprises Department, been one of the agencies supplying 16mm films to schools, both for sale and on hire. All these films were originally broadcast as tele-vision programmes; so to those who exclaimed 'Why can't we have this on film?' justice has, in a measure, been done; while the earlier notion that an educational film and an educational TV programme were and would remain two fundamentally different things has been exposed for the nonsense it really always was.

The educational TV producer

The pilot experiment also illuminated the problems of producing school TV programmes. In school radio creative responsibility is usually shared between a producer, who plans a series, com-missions and edits scripts, and looks after associated publications; and a director who takes over in the studio. The two jobs are quite often combined, but are separable whenever a fully fashioned script is prepared which the one can hand over to the other. In much of television production a similar division of labour, though with many differences of detail, is possible. It is possible in educational television too, but the hazards are greater; for writing the script in its final form is usually the last thing to be done: it is conditioned by what is to be seen on the screen. More-over, many of the decisions made in studio rehearsal—decisions about timing, about what to cut, about balance—require an educational mind behind them no less than an understanding of the medium. The same is equally true of work in the cutting-room, if the programme is mainly or entirely on film. If two share the tasks of production and direction, their minds must work as one: both must know television inside out, both must be instinct with educational purpose. Communication can falter; even if it does not, there can be an extravagant overlapping of two people's time on the job. For the producer, as he assembles his material, must carry in his mind a picture, constantly readjusted, of the programme as a whole. There are clear advantages in his being the final executant also.

So in BBC School TV that is how we mainly work: all responsible staff are educators, all are fully trained in the arts of television. Within this framework, there is of course specialisation in terms of subject, and of the age-range being catered for. But not invariably: many of our producers move willingly, indeed with relish, from a secondary school series to a primary; from, say, a geography series to a series on careers. Some producers will show a special flair for film, others for studio work: the talents of each are of course given the maximum scope.

The qualities expected of such all-rounders are formidable. First, they must have a knowledge of their subject and how it is handled in schools; they must know how to deepen this knowledge by extracting relevant advice from busy experts; they must have an instinct for shaping it so that it is attractive to children and pertinent to teachers. Then, they must be able to 'think pictorially'; they must know the likely sources for the visual material they need; they must understand how designers and graphic artists work and be able to give them clear briefs; they must be sensitive to the contribution music and sound effects can make to their programme. Again, they must be able to work with skilled technical staff, professionals at their job, and judge when to stick out for the effect they want, when to accept contrary advice; they must be discriminating in selecting their 'cast' and able to handle both professional actors and nervous amateurs; they must write with precision and economy, whether scripting programmes or composing 'Notes for the Teacher'. Finally, they must manage a budget (nearly always reasonable, never fat); live with decisions they regret; work at need a seventy-hour week; and be eternally buoyant.

These are not paragons, just ordinary men and women, but

they earn their keep. In September 1957 we had half-a-dozen of them, all trained, none with any depth of experience in TV production. A few hundred schools, this time following carefully the technical advice offered on reception, had sets and were waiting: it was time for the first programme. The series was 'Living in the Commonwealth', the producer, Peggie Broadhead; the subject, 'British Columbia'; the presenter, Bernard Braden, star comedian: he was born and bred there. BBC School TV was launched.

2.3 The uses of audio-tape recording

Tape recorders are household articles today: some people, whether from passion or sloth, conduct much of their private correspondence through them. It is difficult to imagine the world of broadcasting without them. Yet the handy, portable tape-recorder is a development of the last twenty years only.

The BBC did in fact have tape-recorders as early as 1932: big machines, anything but portable, using steel tape–a spool running twenty minutes weighed twenty-one pounds. Three years later it introduced its own direct recording to disc – previously, disc copies of programmes for preservation had been commissioned from the Gramophone Company, as they involved elaborate manufacturing processes.

Direct disc recording gave mobility, and made recording in the field a possibility, but first only in large, cumbersome vans. The recording car, much more manoeuvrable, came in just before the war; midget disc-recorders (not all that midget, but portable) during it. Meanwhile technical staff were developing extraordinary skill in editing disc recordings for transmission, jump-cutting with infallible dexterity from one part of the disc to another.

School radio made some use of the pre-war vans for outside recording, and very effectively. 'I am standing in a pothole,' a Yorkshire voice is saying, 'called Weathercote Cave. On either side of me tower the sides of the pot, high limestone walls covered with mosses and lichens. Above, I can see the overhanging trees and the blue sky . . .' It was an insert for a programme on the rural West Riding. A new dimension had been added to School Radio.

According to plan, the voice should have come from a more famous pothole, Gaping Ghyll. But the recording van could not get near enough; and apart from their limited mobility, field recording facilities were not easily come by (during the war they were pre-empted for more vital tasks). Moreover, an outside recording was rarely in those days as crystal clear as a transmission from the studio, and account had still to be taken of adverse reception conditions in many schools.

Suppose, then, that a school radio producer was making a programme on The Thatcher, in a series 'Living in the Country'. Today, no doubt, armed with his tape recorder he would climb up on the roof where the thatcher was working and get the man himself to talk into the microphone about what he was doing. But at the end of the 40s (when that programme was actually made) he would have climbed up—or sent his scriptwriter up—armed only with a notebook, conversed with him, made jottings, returned to base, and composed a piece for an actor representing the thatcher to speak in the studio. It would probably sound phoney today: at the time, at its best, it did not.

Even discussion programmes involving youngsters would be produced, well into the 50s, on similar lines. The boys and girls—and perhaps some experts too—would be interviewed; then a script written, incorporating what they had said. Then they all came together in the studio and an effort was made to produce them into sounding as spontaneous as when first interviewed.

The BBC started developing the use of the now familiar magnetic tape-recorder in 1950 only: gradually, through the next decade, it was to supersede most disc recording—at least in the field. Soon it was reproducing sound of a quality indistinguishable from that of the studio. A programme made by Denis Mitchell in 1955, now a classic, gave a foretaste of a new dimension in radio production: it included the midnight confessions of a cosh-boy, recorded on a patch of waste ground in an industrial city. Today the handy tape-recorder is an indispensable instrument for much of School Radio's programme making: many are built substantially out of field recordings, edited like film and given coherence through studio links.

Tape-recording in these days is of no less importance for users of school broadcasts in the classroom. Its application to this purpose was longer in coming, because although tape recorders were finding their way into schools in the latter 50s, to record broadcasts was in fact illegal: when BBC staff visiting schools saw or heard of its happening, they had to look the other way. In 1961, however, the BBC was able to secure an agreement with the interested parties that recordings of school broadcasts could, subject to certain restrictions, be made in schools for their own use: details of this agreement, which has now been extended, are given in Appendix C. Soon afterwards the School Broadcasting Council published a pamphlet of guidance for schools, later revised and amplified.[1]

Many schools first learnt to exploit the tape-recorder for purposes unconnected with broadcasting – the Modern Language Departments of Secondary Schools in particular. But the right to record school broadcasts gave a strong impetus to this development. It freed teachers from the tyranny of the broadcasting time-table. It made a broadcast available to several classes where before, probably, only one could use it effectively. By enabling teachers to listen to a programme before using it, it made for better preparation and a more discriminating choice of what to use. It permitted repetition of what had been inadequately grasped first time, or clamoured to be heard again simply for pleasure – sometimes the whole broadcast, often just part of it. In short, it gave scope for both more use of broadcasts, and better. And in secondary schools, it came just in time to save radio from a slow decline. Larger schools, with more complex administrative problems; more pupils with attention focused on examination courses; television supplanting radio in popular estimation – all these were militating against radio in secondary schools; and for some years listening figures had been static, then declining.

Today, tape recorders are standard equipment in all types of school. Young children handle them as adeptly as teachers. Their effective use requires a modest financial outlay; some organisational effort; a care for technical quality; and thought. Because they demand something more from teachers than off-air listening

[1] 'School Radio and the Tape Recorder', BBC, 1972 (latest revised edition).

does, they usually get much more. That is their strength – as a recently published survey[1] on the use of broadcasts in schools amply testifies. They have also made possible a totally new development in school radio, important enough to have a section of its own: Radiovision.

2.4 Radiovision

A radiovision programme consists of two elements: a sound element which is broadcast for schools to record, and a colour filmstrip (or set of slides) which schools buy in advance and which is easily synchronised in the classroom with the tape carrying the recorded programme. Beginning in 1964 BBC School Radio now produces each year about 40 radiovision programmes, spread over a dozen or more different series.

Pictorial accompaniments to sound broadcasts were not, of course, new: since quite early days, many series had illustrated pamphlets which children were asked to refer to during the broadcast, but for the most part intermittently only. Radiovision normally has pictures throughout the programme.

Even the use of filmstrips in association with sound broadcasts was not entirely novel. As far back as 1936 a note in the annual 'Programme of Broadcasts to Scottish Schools' ran as follows:

An extension of the combined aural and visual appeal has been developed in an experiment whereby broadcast talks are illustrated by specially prepared film strips. On its formation last year the Scottish Educational Film Association undertook to continue the practice of preparing film strips to illustrate talks in the Junior Geography series from lists of topics supplied by the Scottish School Broadcasting Council's staff. A number of teachers have made trial of this combination of sight and sound and have found it satisfactory.

Since its use presupposes a darkened room where pamphlets cannot play a part in the broadcast, a general use of this particular method of illustration would involve the reconsideration of broadcast technique.

[1] 'Using Broadcasts in Schools: a Study and Evaluation', by C. G. Hayter, published jointly by BBC and ITV, 1974.

While it is clear that the value of these films in preparation or in follow-up work could be considerable, how far a class may both listen and look is a matter for further question and experiment.

Not many schools participated in this experiment, however, and no broadcasts were adapted for use in this way. Two years later the idea was abandoned—as it transpired, for a quarter of a century. In the 50s there was much discussion about the place of filmstrips in association with broadcasts—but only as a supplement, in follow-up work. Their effective use simultaneously with broadcast sound was dependent on schools' ability to pre-record the latter.

The Head of BBC School Radio saw radiovision programmes from two or three European countries and one African successfully illustrated at a World Conference on Educational Broadcasting held in Rome in 1961: this was one incentive for the BBC to enter the field. A second was, of course, the now rapid spread of tape recording equipment in British schools. A third was the emergence of School TV, which School Radio naturally, and quite properly, saw as a rival as well as a partner. If radiovision involved schools in substantial expenditure, it also offered freedom from transmission timetables and scope for all the variety in use that tape recording had opened up: if its pictures lacked movement they had, in compensation, colour; and if the context called for pictures requiring a long and detailed look, the very absence of movement could be turned to advantage. Stillness of picture could be an asset, for instance, not only in obvious fields like the study of art and architecture, but in the rigorous observation underlying exploratory work in science. How, other than in a still picture, could a joint on the famous Iron Bridge in Shropshire be examined as an instance of traditional methods being applied to the use of a new material? How else could the fascinating shapes within the transparent wings of a dragonfly be properly studied, or the outline of a moth camouflaged against the lichen-covered bark of a tree? The recorded sound to match such visual experiences might be no more than straight talk (perhaps punctuated with music)—but talk economically and precisely composed to guide children's observation; and talk, often, imbued with the particular qualities a gifted radio personality could give it. Johnny Morris explaining a weather map in the programme 'A Depression South of Iceland will move . . .' might be doing direct teaching, but it was direct teaching with a difference.

The producers who pioneered the new medium in 1964 were experienced hands in all the arts of radio; and from the first they wanted to make of radiovision not simply a succession of pictures with commentary, but a medium which exploited, in association with pictures, the full range of radio's resources. Some of the most interesting of the earlier programmes, if not necessarily the most successful, were those which used pictures and sound in a kind of counterpoint to create an emotional experience. One of these was called 'Courtship and Marriage in Painting'.

'This,' said the announcer, 'is a sort of dream. You'll hear voices, but they're not talking about the pictures. They're telling the story of their own courtship—Leila and Johnnie falling in love now, and Old Bet remembering how she got married long ago . . . It begins with Leila . . .'

The voice of Leila: 'Mum says, back in Wicklow—she never left Ireland until she was married—they were always looking out of the window. Watchin' the street. Watchin' the boys without being seen.'

We hear the voice of a singer: 'As I went out one May morning . . .', then Johnnie's voice: 'I was at this dance see. Not wiv' any-one, not really. Just gone for a bit of a lark that's all. Well, we're dancing anyhow, and then the music stops. Sudden like. And I see this girl. Across the floor . . .' As he speaks, we are looking at the first picture: it is a detail from Vermeer's 'Head of a girl'.

A little later, we hear again a man's voice singing, 'O lady I will give to you a fine silky dress . . .' and the 'lady' replying 'Indeed I won't accept of you your fine silky dress . . .'; this leads into

'Johnnie: What's your name?

Leila: Leila.

Johnnie: Leila. That's nice. Unusual like (*pause*). 'Ere, coming for a ride? . . .' The picture on the screen now is Goya's 'The Sun-shade' (facing page 23). It depicts an elegant young lady of the Spanish court sitting in the sparkling Spanish sun from which a young servant (one supposes) is shading her with a parasol.

For some adults this is hard to take. A moving dialogue with a still picture is not unacceptable, any more than the illustration which 'freezes' the narrative of a book; but what are Vermeer and Goya doing in this *galère*? Do they illuminate the radio story? Hardly: children's imaginations can create their own satisfying Johnnies and Leilas. Does the story illuminate the pictures, then (as was the writer's intention)? Not of course in any sophisticated sense of 'illuminate': it is scarcely possible to imagine that either artist had anything like the situations in the broadcast in mind. But adults bring to the sight of an Old Master a historical per-spective which a child does not: to fuse picture with story, the child has nothing first to clear away. Or has he? Vermeer's girl has a very old-fashioned head-dress. But then it is her eyes that steal the picture. Her eyes as they become aware of Johnnie's, across the floor?

Matter for endless debate. But the child who said 'It was telling you about the feeling' had sensed the producer's intention. And the end of the broadcast would not be, for the children, the end of their experience of these pictures. The filmstrip was a school investment, theirs for keeps and for teachers to handle at will: for discussion of the pictures – the Vermeer and the Goya among them – without the soundtrack, for instance. Any art teacher who found the programme a kind of sacrilege could, if he thought fit, apply a corrective. And he could use the children's involvement with the pictures as his launching-pad.

There were weightier and less controversial tasks for radio-vision than 'Courtship and Marriage in Pictures', however; and most notably in the field of Modern Languages. School radio had for thirty years been offering splendid programmes here; but it could not reach down to the level of a beginner in French or German. Increasingly, therefore, for elementary work in so-called 'direct method' teaching schools were investing in one of the audio-visual courses available from the commercial market. Some of these were in effect 'radiovision' courses except that the sound element had never been transmitted over the air: similar indeed to the BBC course we met briefly in the first chapter, and which one might describe as a 'retired' radiovision course, its tapes now put on sale to schools along with its pictures.

To launch a beginners' course in French which would rival,

and improve on, these was a big undertaking. A programme a week meant thirty-one in all, each with its filmstrip of twenty or more frames. There were difficult questions to resolve, such as whether to have photographs for pictures, or artist's drawings: the latter were chosen because they can better exclude distracting elements. To embark on the course entailed a big investment for the schools, too; so it had to be right. A whole term of pilot programmes was prepared – to sample response to one or two only was not enough, since the rate of progression envisaged had also to be tested. An officer of the School Broadcasting Council, himself a specialist in Modern Languages, made consultation with the producer, field study of response to the pilots, and promotion of the forthcoming series his main business for a year. By 1964-5 'French for Beginners' was on the air, and it has been in use ever since. Soon afterwards came a similar German series, 'Frisch begonnen'.

Radiovision offered wide opportunities for experiment. 'Joan of Arc', in the series 'World History' for age 8-10, had a fully dramatised sound track, resonant with music and effects, to accompany a filmstrip of forty-six frames. A generous allowance of pictures for a radiovision programme: 'a low-budget colour film' was the producer's description. By this definition it lagged a little of a movie's 1440 frames a minute; but it was very popular. So was 'Pompeii and Vesuvius' – from the same series, but with quite different problems, and therefore a different approach. Pictures of ruins on their own are dry stuff for young children; and the normal sound broadcasts in this series attuned them anyhow to expecting a story approach. So the editor, Duncan Taylor, wanted to bring to life the Pompeii of AD 79, just before the famous eruption: to show the people who lived, worked, shopped, bathed and amused themselves there. He engaged an artist and together they discussed, by reference to the visible remains of Pompeii today, what the characters in the story should be shown doing, and in what setting; while the sound track he built up largely out of a series of imaginary interviews with them. Later in the film we saw the evidence, among the actual ruins of Pompeii, for the scenes the artist had depicted (facing page 38).

The field of art appreciation also gave radiovision scope for variety of approach. For 'Vincent van Gogh', in the series 'Art and Design', the sound-track was composed from documentary sources: the words of Van Gogh's brother Theo, of Gauguin, of other friends and acquaintances, and of Vincent himself. A programme on Stanley Spencer in the same series chose to concentrate on his paintings in the Burghclere Memorial Chapel, which reflect his experiences in the First World War as a medical orderly, particularly in Macedonia. Again, the sound track does not talk directly about the pictures, but presents a radio drama which attempts to catch the spirit of Spencer's whole work in the chapel. We follow Arthur, a fictitious, diffident young soldier, in his daily routine experience of a military hospital; we hear of camping, cooking, route marching and preparations for kit inspections in Macedonia. As the story unfolds in the broadcast, the scenes depicted in Spencer's paintings are shown on the filmstrip. There is time to savour them as the dialogue proceeds, the speakers' words helping the viewing pupil to slip into the mood of the pictures, and the pictures heightening the effect of the words. The broadcast conveys Spencer's own feelings and thoughts, especially in the words of the main character, Arthur.

Recording a radiovision programme in the 'World History' series

Dozens of radio series have, over the years, generated their radiovision element – related to, but not of course an essential component of, the succession of normal programmes in sound. In Chapter IV we shall meet another, and very significant, pair of them, made for the series 'Nature' several years ago. But I must end this section with a reference to a recent one, 'Everything New', from the series 'Stories and Rhymes' for children of age seven to nine. I say a reference only, because no description in words alone can conceivably do justice to it. It is rich in sources of stimulus to young children's sensory experience of nature and to creative work of every kind: in speech, writing, movement, music, art. But above all the programme is a joyous experience in itself, for people of all ages. It is the story of the Creation, told in picture, poetry and music drawn from the widest variety of sources. It describes, first, day breaking over the darkness; then the sun, moon and stars moving across the sky; rain falling; trees, vegetables and flowers growing, birds flying and singing, fish darting through the water. Then man is formed out of the dust of the earth; and men, women and children name all the creatures and see how different and special each one is. Finally, accompanying the last picture we hear the voices of children over the music:

ᴅʀᴇɴ Hullaballoo!
  The sun is high.
  The clouds are whooshing across the sky,
  Birds are soaring and winds are free,
  Trees are tossing and we are WE!
  (Nobody else we would rather be)
  Hullabalay baloo!
ᴄʜɪʟᴅ I eat from the dish of the world
  Trees, fields, flowers.
ᴡᴏᴍᴀɴ I drink from the glass of space
  Blue sea, sky.
ᴄʜɪʟᴅ I pour the sky over me
  In blue showers.
ᴍᴀɴ Look, I light up the day
  With my eye.

Readers may be able to gauge something of the total effect, even if they must imagine the music, from the short excerpt from the programme (facing page 39).

I hope I have given enough clues to radiovision's nature to justify its claim to be an art-form in its own right. A hybrid art-form, perhaps – there are moments when one longs for the picture to spring to life with the living word – but one that has added lustre to the annals of BBC School Radio. Radiovision programmes are not as widely used in schools as ordinary radio, or television programmes: one could hardly expect this, because half of each programme has to be paid for by the receiving school. But a diminished quantity of use is compensated by a higher quality. We have seen this effect already when considering the responsibilities laid on teachers by tape-recording. For effective radiovision the responsibilities are greater, though mastered easily enough in return for a little time and trouble. It is heartening to see how well the challenge is answered.

2.5 Video-tape

Video-tape needs no long treatment here: the pattern of its development largely matches that of audio-tape, and so does its importance for school broadcasting. First introduced into BBC Television in 1958, it has transformed the planning of programme production and transmission: today virtually no programmes except news, current affairs, and public events go out live. The viewer is hardly conscious of this, if at all: the mystic virtues of 'instant communication', cherished in the early days of TV as of radio, have largely evaporated.

There was recording of television before video-tape of course, but on to film, with loss of quality, and a substantial time-lapse for processing before replay was possible. In the early days of video-tape, editing was a time-consuming process too; and even when programmes were being recorded a single 'take', as if for live transmission, was aimed at whenever possible. Now with sophisticated electronic editing available, studio programmes of any complexity are mostly planned with recording breaks; and professionals in the studio are well used to having plays, in parti-

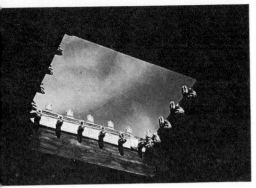

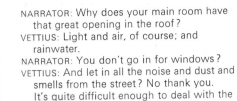

NARRATOR: Why does your main room have that great opening in the roof?
VETTIUS: Light and air, of course; and rainwater.
NARRATOR: You don't go in for windows?
VETTIUS: And let in all the noise and dust and smells from the street? No thank you. It's quite difficult enough to deal with the smells from our own kitchen. Keep that door shut, confound you.
SLAVE: Very good, sir.
NARRATOR: Can I see the kitchen?
VETTIUS: Well, as you please. You'll excuse me if I don't go with you? The smell's appalling.

*mpluvium' in roof of 'atrium', House of the
ii.

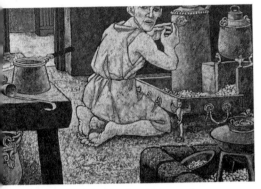

SLAVE: How can I help the smell? These are sauces I'm cooking for tonight's dinner. We serve dinner at about four or five in the afternoon and it may be over in an hour or so, or it may go on till pretty late — like last night's.
NARRATOR: What's it like being a slave?
SLAVE: Well, being a gladiator's a lot worse and being free's a lot better, as my master may have mentioned to you.
NARRATOR: You mean he used to be a slave?
SLAVE: Of course. And you mistook him for a gentleman? Ho! That's good. Still, we've got a real high-class family just across the way. Them that's got the mosaic pictures on the floor. May I have the pleasure of introducing you?

*chen in House of the Vettii, with stove from
ples Museum (reconstruction).*

LADY *(fade up)*: And there was this rumbling, and everything shook and cracked and when it was over, half Pompeii was in ruins.
LADY: Stop it, Marcellus. Look at this. We had his portrait done, in mosaic. And look at our little *faun* there, in the rain-water tank. What'll happen to him if there's another earthquake?

from 'Pompeii and Vesuvius' (Radiovision)

*use of the Faun (reconstruction, the dog mosaic
s actually in a neighbouring house).*

The Starry Night *by Vincent Van Gogh*

LEFT: *Taureau detail of tapestry* La Flamme et L'Océan *by Jean Lurçat*

BELOW: *Detail of* Rainstorm at Night on the Mountain of Oyama *by Toyokuni II*

Music, Moon, begins

WOMAN The white mares of the moon rus
    along the sky
    Beating their golden hoofs upon
    the glass Heavens:
    The white mares of the moon are
    all standing on their hind legs
    Pawing at the green porcelain
    doors of the remote Heavens.
    Fly mares!
    Strain your utmost,
    Scatter the milky dust of stars,
    Or the tiger sun will leap upon yo
    and destroy you
    With one lick of his vermilion
    tongue.

Music, Moon, ends

Music, Sun, begins

MAN The red bull-sun is blazing on the
    mountains;
    He stretches his burning bulk upo
    the rock-horned mountains;
    He stamps and snorts, and from h
    flaming nostrils
    Red-bellied mists escape and
    rise . . .
    Music, Sun, ends

NARRATOR The sun set, and the moon rose.

    Music, First Rain, begins under
    narration
    The first rain began to fall, and the
    raindrops brought life to the
    earth.
CHILDREN Noise of the rain falling.
    Where are the black clouds rising?
    Where is the rain falling?
    In the east the clouds are massing.
    Noise of the rain falling.
    In the west the rain is falling.
    Noise of the rain falling . . .

from 'Everything New' (Radiovisio

cular, chopped into small sections and recorded out of order, to accommodate the demands of design, wardrobe and make-up, and thereby save time.

Some educational programmes in dramatised form require, to do their job properly, not only high-quality performance but the precision of camera work one associates with a scientific demonstration. Consider an elementary language programme, for instance: the close-up on the plate of apples must exactly coincide with the actor's 'des pommes'; the camera must pan immediately and precisely on to 'des poires' next to them. These, and other dishes, must have been so set on the table that the shots will exclude any possible source of misunderstanding – for instance, the cherries: yet the laden table must look perfectly natural when seen in mid-shot. A simple example, but such problems arise several times a minute in a programme of this sort. To sustain a flawless performance through twenty minutes and up to 300 shots is hazardous, to say the least: video-tape recording with post-production editing is an indisputable asset to both director and cast.

Video-tape recorders are now coming into the schools: by 1973 already nearly a quarter of Secondary and a scatter of Primary Schools had one or more. These are of course simpler, less sophisticated and much cheaper machines than the BBC uses for transmission; nevertheless, when one adds in an adequate supply of tapes they represent a substantial investment, and it is difficult to see them becoming universal in Primary Schools, though no doubt they could be one day. They are not, in their handiest form, substantially more difficult to use than audio-tape recorders, and they offer the same advantages. This is not the place to go into details: again, there is a pamphlet of guidance available.[1]

Given this facility many television programmes, just as with radio, will serve teachers' purposes better if they can be easily replayed in sections after an initial complete viewing; and some are already being structured with this in mind. 'Tout Compris', for instance, is a short series shot in colour on location in France and designed to support the study of French in about the third

[1] 'VTR and School Television', BBC, 1971 (under revision).

year of secondary school: it was first transmitted in Summer 1973. To quote from the Teacher's Notes,

The programmes do not follow a linguistic or thematic progression: each rather presents a variety of 'slices of life' in which young French people are seen in real situations stemming from their own interests and experience, expressing themselves naturally within them and presenting them in their own unscripted words . . . The programmes contain three or more quite self-contained sequences, each covering a particular situation or episode: this 'modular' format makes the series particularly well suited to video-tape recording.

The programmes, in short, are designed to be worked on in class, sequence by sequence; and to supplement them (particularly for those who have no recording facilities) an audio-tape of the sound track is available separately, and also a filmstrip (ninety frames for the five programmes) which may be synchronised with it. Together these elements make up, to use the current jargon, a complete 'resource package'.

'Tout Compris' represents, therefore, a new development in broadcasting: it is a part of that revolution in educational technology which has brought to the schools a whole range of new equipment and 'software' to further the objective of efficient learning. This variegated 'software' of audio- and video-tape cassettes, films, discs, and still pictures comes from a multiplicity of sources: commercial publishers, Local Education Authority Resource Centres, Teachers' Centres, and indeed from within the schools themselves. Its very richness creates formidable problems of communicating information about it to its intended beneficiaries. The BBC is only one of the providing agencies; but its basic job as a broadcaster of the living and the actual make it peculiarly fitted to march with the vanguard of development and to be sensitive to the need for constant renewal of its products. At the same time, this development is tending to enlarge the gap between the classic broadcast and the 'resource' which best serves the needs of schools: a gap reflected not only in the time lapse between the original creation of the 'resource-type' broadcast, through transmission and recording in school, to the moment when it has finally served its purpose there and is 'wiped'; but even, as we have seen with 'Tout Compris', in the nature of the products themselves.

It is hardly too soon, therefore, to pose the question: If programmes for schools are no longer to be intended for use 'off air',
and if in consequence their nature is so changing that they are
scarcely recognisable as complete and unitary programmes, then
has broadcasting to schools any long-term future? We shall take
this up in the final chapter: meanwhile, it is time to revert to
square one and trace some of the ways in which school broadcasting has interacted with changing educational needs.

3 CHALLENGE AND RESPONSE

The story of school broadcasting is also a story of challenge and response. The challenge of altered circumstances, of a change in the climate of the times, of new aspirations and new needs in education; the response of the BBC to the opportunities thus opened up.

In the 1920s H. A. L. Fisher's Education Act of 1918 had enlarged the national vision of what education for the ordinary child might be: for the upper reaches of the elementary school, the reforms proposed by the Hadow Committee in 1926 came as a powerful reinforcement. But change was not rapid. In the 20s our elementary schools were still dominated by the three Rs: Reading, 'Riting, 'Rithmetic. Now there was a fourth: Radio. How was it to be used?

3.1 The fourth R

The prime inspiration of BBC School Broadcasting was unquestionably Scottish. Reith, a son of the manse, was imbued from the outset with a sense of the BBC's educational mission. He brought in Mary Somerville, a Scot, to partner J. C. Stobart[1] in giving creative impulse to the enterprise. Mary Somerville, in 1927, brought in Rhoda Power, Scots Irish, to fuse historical scholarship and a flair for communication with children into a new concept of scriptwriting. Other pioneers of the 30s—Edith McQueen for environmental studies, Jean Sutcliffe with stories

[1] Stobart, acquired from the Board of Education, was the author of those classics of Classical popularisation *The Glory that was Greece* and *The Grandeur that was Rome*. A pillar of wisdom and experience in the early days, he had flashes of insight too. In 1926 he handed Reith a draft scheme for a Wireless University, anticipating Harold Wilson by 37 years.

for young children – came from Scotland; Duncan Adam stayed there to blaze the trail in Scotland itself; and the greatest all-rounder in school radio's history – as scholar, writer, producer and performer – was a Scot, Douglas Allan, later to become Head of Scottish School Broadcasting and Secretary to its School Broadcasting Council.

Scotland, indeed, claims to have originated the very first, experimental, school 'broadcast' (to a single school apparently), early in 1924 – before any regular service began, even (it seems) before Mary Somerville's celebrated vision on the road to Damascus. By all accounts, that vision was worth waiting for: a participant describes the first experiment thus:

Mr Herbert Carruthers, Mr Swinton Paterson, Professor Charles Martin of the French Department, Glasgow University, a young lady whose name I cannot recollect, a male violinist and myself assembled for the great occasion. Carruthers announced me, and I spoke for fifteen minutes on The Ballad. Then Professor Martin read from a French classic: then the violinist (very nervous I remember) played his 'piece' . . . When the show was over we repaired to the school to receive the plaudits of the children.

What I have called Mary Somerville's 'vision' was really a very homely affair: she would no doubt be horrified at so much being made of it. But much-quoted as it is, it bears repetition:

The first time that I ever heard a broadcast was by accident in a country schoolhouse where the sailor brother of the schoolmistress had installed a wireless set. There in her little parlour she and I and the three most musical of her pupils listened turn and turn about – for there were only two pairs of earphones – to a talk on music by Sir Walford Davies. It was not a broadcast to schools. He was speaking, I fancy, in the early evening some time in the spring of 1924. No matter, he was teaching, and he was making music, and the impact of his personality, and of his music, was tremendous. Things happened in all of us, in the children, in their music-loving teacher, and in me. The children's eyes were round with wonder. We grown-ups were exalted. Science, as Bridges later wrote, has 'outrun all magic, spiriting the dumb inane with the quick matter of life'. Beauty now could enter every home, and every classroom!

After the broadcast we made our own music; the children sang and their teacher played to us some of the themes we had heard on the air; and then, far into the night, she and I talked of what this brave new medium of communication might mean for schools.[1]

As Dickon Steele,[2] a close associate of Mary Somerville's from 1936, has observed, this story enshrines in itself the essence of school broadcasting. There is the vivid, personal communication in the act of telling. There is the sense of a unique occasion. There is the concern with what is happening to the listening children. There is the evidence of the broadcast experience as springboard – to action, to participation, to creative enjoyment.

None of these qualities were quickly manifest in school radio. There was a nationwide flurry of enthusiasm to have a go: BBC programmes in the mid-twenties were originated from a wide scatter of studios the length and breadth of the country, and school broadcasts with them. The schedule for Spring Term 1927 (the first under the newly formed British Broadcasting Corporation) lists over forty series for schools in all, some from cities which had to await the coming of local radio in 1967 before joining the ranks of programme originators again.

Most of these broadcasts were simply lectures by experts probably knowing little of schools or of children, and certainly unaware that speaking on the radio was an art with its own disciplines. They were not much different – except, mercifully, in length – from the original Scottish programme. Mary Somerville herself at this stage thought of school broadcasting simply as providing a substitute for things a privileged school could have in the flesh – a distinguished speaker from outside, a taste of a professional string quartet. But in 1927 the BBC, in association with the Kent Education Authority and with the help of a grant from the Carnegie Trust, organised an inquiry into the response to school broadcasts in seventy-two Kent schools. Early reports were disquieting, so Mary Somerville did a lot of school visiting herself. She learnt how wide of the mark most broadcasts were, and how detached from the ordinary business of teaching. She at

[1] From *School Broadcasting in Britain*, by Richard Palmer, BBC, 1947.
[2] Later he was for 17 years Secretary to the School Broadcasting Council for the United Kingdom.

once brought into her team Rhoda Power, with a series of talks on 'Boys and Girls of the Middle Ages'.

The Annual Programme of School Broadcasts for 1927-8 introduced her thus:

Miss Rhoda Power has already given a very successful course of afternoon talks on Village Life in Olden Times. She is a proved broadcaster, and has experience of teaching. She will collaborate very fully with class teachers during this course, giving suggestions for the conduct of the lessons, and for relating them to the ordinary school work in history, in an illustrated pamphlet to be issued in September.

This was a landmark. Innovations in broadcast presentation were yet to come – these were straight talks. But with a difference: the difference of a broadcaster able to talk to children, and determined to enlist the classroom teacher to work with her. The pressing necessity for this was one of the cardinal conclusions of the report on the Kent inquiry.

Mary Somerville saw as her other main task the exploration, with her BBC collaborators, of the special properties of radio. One day Rhoda Power was giving a talk about medieval London. She was describing the crowds crossing London Bridge – the hubbub, the jostling, the singing. George Dixon was producing. 'Those songs are extant, you know, why don't we have them sung? A voice approaching the microphone from a distance, then receding.' The illustrated talk was born. Then the traveller's tale with sound effects, the 'nature walk' with inserted sound and song from moor or woodland; the inquiring adult – or indeed the inquisitive child – as observer ('What the Potboy Saw' was another landmark), or as explorer of his own locality; the dramatised insert; the full dramatisation; the imaginary interview; and the 'actuality' outside recording we met in the last chapter.

Whatever form was chosen – and my list is far from exhaustive – the basic aim was the same: to offer imaginative experience, to involve children's feelings as well as their minds. It brought school radio, within twelve years, from the dry, detached lectures criticised in the Kent Inquiry report to programmes like, for instance, 'The Five Members', about Charles I's ill-fated attempt to arrest Hampden and his associates for high treason.

Towards the end of the programme we hear the King enter a tense House of Commons and take the Speaker's chair. We feel the silence, then the stir as he protests that he is careful of members' privileges, but that these men have to answer a charge of high treason.

THE KING   ... Therefore I am come to tell you that I must have them wheresoever I shall find them.

Is Mr Pym here? Mr Hampden? Mr Holles? Mr Haselrigge? Mr Strode?

Mr Speaker, are any of these persons in the House? Do *you* see any of them? Where are they?

SPEAKER   May it please your Majesty: I have neither eyes to see, nor tongue to tell in this place, but as this House is pleased to direct me, whose servant I am here, and I humbly beg your Majesty's pardon that I cannot give any other answer than this to what your Majesty is pleased to demand of me.

THE KING   Well, I think my eyes are as good as another's. I see all the birds are flown. I do expect of you that you shall send them unto me as soon as they return hither. If not, I will seek them myself, for their treason is foul, and such a one as you will thank me to discover. But I do assure you on the word of a King, I never did intend any force, but shall proceed against them in a legal and fair way, for I never meant any other.

I see I cannot do what I came for. I think this is no unfit occasion to repeat what I have said formerly, that whatsoever I have done in favour, and to the good of my subjects, I do mean to maintain it. Good afternoon, gentlemen!

There is a movement as the tension relaxes, and then softly at first, but swelling and swelling to a great cry, the word

VOICES   PRIVILEGE ... PRIVILEGE ... PRIVILEGE ...

Children cannot respond to the predicament of Charles as an adult can. But they can sense his bewildered recognition that even his, God-given, authority could be defied. They can share in the drama of one of the crises of our history. And they can absorb, however unconsciously, an English the more beautiful for being hardly less plain than their own.

The traveller's tale was always popular ('Travel Talks' as a series lasted for thirty years). An early one, 'The Mangrove Swamps of the Rufiji Delta', by Granville Squiers, remained in demand for years as a demonstration piece to teachers. I have not unearthed a script, but the outline in the Programme for Schools is inviting enough:

The river Delta—the sailing ships of Arabia and India—Mud, Mangroves, Mosquitos and Monkeys—Walking fish, Crocodiles and Hippo—What the work was like—The Arabs arrive—Coasting on a Dhow—A Burst Sail—Walking Back—A Dog at the Delta—Three Days Lost in the Swamps.

Shades of Rider Haggard and G. H. Henty! But this time for real.

Mary Somerville stood by her early determination to bring also the best of existing literature and music to the schools. And people of the highest distinction too: broadcasters in 'Talks for Sixth Forms' between 1935 and 1937 included Sir William Beveridge, G. K. Chesterton, T. S. Eliot, Edith Evans, E. M. Forster, J. B. S. Haldane, A. P. Herbert, the Hon. Harold Nicolson, Sir John Boyd Orr, Bernard Shaw, and Sir Henry Tizard. Sixth Forms in those days were expected to digest tough meat also: in 1938, talks on Plato, Aristotle, Epicurus, the Stoics, Roger Bacon, Machiavelli. Their attention was called, too, to a twenty-programme series in the BBC's general service on Mondays at 12 noon, and suitable also for pupils of sixteen-eighteen. Its title: 'An Outline of Church History.' Compare four recent consecutive programmes for the same age in School TV's 'New Horizons': Kenneth Galbraith in conversation with Sixth Formers; The Calley Case; The Immigration Bill; The Alternative Society.

Of the other end of the spectrum of school life, the Kent inquiry report had concluded that school broadcasting had doubtfully anything to offer to children under nine. Mary Somerville brought in Ann Driver, with Music and Movement, to disprove it. Someone coined the phrase 'memorable interruptions' (of school routine) to describe what broadcasts meant for schools; but Rhoda Power had already shown how they could be woven into the texture of school work, and Ann Driver used them to introduce, for most, a wholly new activity on which she could build from week to week.

Virtually all that school broadcasting has since achieved has been raised on the foundations Mary Somerville laid. Not all the programme forms she and her team devised were of course innovatory in the sense of being peculiar to school broadcasting: they shared in broadcasting's general development, drawing ideas from and adopting the techniques of other departments too. Looking back with hindsight, one is tempted to believe it was bound to happen. But this is to forget how narrow and formalised most teachers' concept of their business was in the elementary schools of forty years ago (for all the promise held out by the Hadow Report), and how wide must have seemed the gap dividing their world from the strange new world of broadcasting. To respond to the challenge of bridging this gap, to cause these two worlds to interact, required a personality that serenely ignored obstacles. To invent the means to do it required an original genius with a flair for attracting producers, writers and artists of the highest quality. Mary Somerville was both of these, and more; Dickon Steele puts it thus:

She was also very humble. Like Socrates, she really believed herself ignorant; hence her insistence that the quality she demanded must be based on audience study. One was often amazed – sometimes irritated – by the attention she paid to the opinions of quite ordinary people.

Too fulsome? She could be interfering also – and apologise handsomely afterwards. I record what her collaborators have said of her: I only spoke with her two or three times, after she had left school broadcasting. She was of the stuff of which legends are made.

3.2 What's in the news?

The war set school broadcasting its own particular challenges. Production had to move from London – first to Evesham (where for lack of available actors a small 'Schools Rep' company, still extant, was formed), then to Bristol. The pamphlets which had become an integral element in many series were discontinued. Expert professional advice was harder to tap. Producers were more on their own.

But there were great opportunities too. Hundreds of thousands of children were evacuated, with their teachers, to unfamiliar places. Worse off scholastically were others due for evacuation, their schools being in danger areas, but whose parents preferred to keep them. For the teachers of both, but the latter especially, school broadcasts were a special boon. In Sheffield, for instance, a system of home instruction was rapidly improvised for 50,000 children whose schools were unsafe. Householders were invited to reserve a room where up to a dozen children could forgather; peripatetic teachers called daily on each group for an hour or so to guide and direct their work; and school broadcasts added an extra dimension to what they could learn for themselves between their teacher's visits. They were also a means of the central authority's keeping touch, and a symbol of 'carrying on as usual' – the conventional British rallying cry in times of crisis. An official directive drew attention to their value in keeping young minds active in air-raid shelters.

Wartime broadcasts

Broadcasts which contributed to a sense of national cohesion by inviting nationwide participation were especially appropriate to the times. Two such series were born during the war – to survive it triumphantly and continue to this day. One, of Scottish origin, was 'Singing Together' (which we met in the first chapter); the other, the weekly Religious Service for Schools – an act of worship for a whole school assembled in the Hall. Throughout this time there was a dearth of experienced teachers, of course; so broadcasts which simply took direct command of listening classes, as 'Singing Together' did, were much valued by hard-pressed Heads.

Another long-runner of wartime origin was 'How Things Began' – the story of life on earth from earliest beginnings to the flowering of the first settled civilisations. Again there was the child as enquirer, now a familiar technique of presentation; in fact two children, almost excruciatingly avid for information and for 'evidence' of what they were told by a knowledgeable uncle-figure. The high-spot of each programme came when the uncle-figure (originally christened 'Bernard Bumblebee', later a more demotic 'Jim Smith') turned into an 'observer' of prehistoric events, suitably announced: 'This is the BBC Service from the past. Here is our Observer, Jim Smith, speaking from a coal-age forest.' The pedigree is clear: this is the commentator on Wimbledon, or more contemporarily on the war front, describing events as they happen – brilliantly adapted to feed the imaginations of learning children. Each observer episode was a cliff-hanger, too – Jim Smith desperately scuttling from a brontosaurus or whatever.

Reports from the front – the voice of Churchill – the impassive newsreader's 'seven of our aircraft failed to return': these were experiences older children were sharing with adults. They were involved with the instant present of the big world as never before. Here was a new incentive for school broadcasts too – to explain to them what was happening there simply, straightforwardly, and authoritatively.

This was not a new job for school broadcasting: there had been Current Affairs talks as early as 1932, and on knotty, controversial topics too – the Means Test, the Irish question. There had been a series of Friday afternoon 'Unfinished Debates' on current issues. But these were mainly suitable for older, abler pupils. The war gave a great fillip to broadcasts about the news and its background for ordinary children of about thirteen. The legacy survived and flourished in the post-war decades – into the late 60s, when the impulse petered. It is worth following the story through.

Current Affairs for schools

In the summer of 1940 a daily News Commentary for schools was started, 'to elaborate educationally items in the news; to give children any special instruction or exhortation which may be necessary under abnormal conditions; to reassure them on points that may be worrying them, and to serve in an emergency as a link between central authorities and schools.' Almost an imperative to listen; but after the war, when the brief was of course modified, the habit continued. A team of distinguished journalists was drawn in to contribute regularly. There was a longer, weekly Current Affairs programme too, often tackling difficult topics like 'The Marshall Plan', explaining its significance for the day-to-day needs of a single firm, or a single family. The concrete realities behind the generalisations of statesmen: good popular journalism, in fact.

For the school TV experiment in 1952, one programme anyhow on an issue currently in the news was a 'must': the topic chosen was the Canal Zone. The background to the Suez Canal was built up with the help of library film; the issues explained; and an Englishman and an Egyptian each argued his case. Not an impressive programme by today's standards; but children recalled the indifferent film shots with exactness; and the Egyptian, so passionate the words tumbled over each other, created a profound impression. Politics was not dull stuff if people could feel like that about it.

So for regular School TV in 1957, Current Affairs became a 'must' too – a first priority, along with Science; and 'Spotlight', with such spokesmen as Richard Dimbleby and Christopher Chataway in the early years and Dick Taverne, Erskine Childers and David Holden later on, became a firmly established series, running for many years. Yet in 1968 it was wound up, and 'Current Affairs' had also vanished from the radio output: why?

Back in 1947 the age of compulsory schooling had been raised to fifteen, giving teachers much to think about. The extra crop of school-bound adolescents, for the most part in the Secondary Modern schools deriving from the Butler Act, were almost all there reluctantly: their focus was on the working world they had been expecting to join, and there was no shortage of jobs. The more imaginative teachers concluded that these youngsters' last year in school should be no mere prolongation of the conventional syllabus studies. It was to be an outward-looking year.

Schools were short of resources for making it so; but one at least they had, almost all of them by now: their radio receiver. Within a few years, several new radio series were devised to meet the new situation: Current Affairs, an established one, again received a new impulse. Many teachers took great pains to make this weekly occasion a worthwhile one, associating with it the study of newspapers and world maps, local inquiries where appropriate, class discussion and debate. Even curriculum-bound schools usually made their weekly bow to this non-curricular item: it was 'important', and it was something few felt competent to tackle on their own. 'Spotlight' suited the early, honeymoon years of School TV particularly well: vision brought, or appeared to bring, the affairs of the world within the range of a wider spectrum of children, and twenty minutes viewing followed by twenty minutes discussion could stand as valuable on its own, without disturbing the pattern of schools' main activities – which there was an unwillingness at that time to allow TV to do.

The School Broadcasting Council's report on the first eighteen months of school TV conceded as a basic problem of 'Spotlight' that it was offering children material beyond their capacity to grasp fully. It continued, a shade sententiously:

It is no use worrying unduly about this. Understanding the world's problems is the business of adults, and requires a long pilgrimage through the mists of partial comprehension during adolescence: whatever means are used, there is a limit to the extent to which the presentation of these problems can, by simplification, be nicely adjusted to each phase of the child's development.

True enough: but the problem was perhaps not so much the inherent difficulty of some of the material, as the fact that it was offered almost *in vacuo*. A Current Affairs series which 'follows the news' is necessarily a patchwork of weekly, unrelated topics. To be up-to-date, each programme has to be selected as late, and prepared as rapidly, as possible: two or three days for a radio programme, usually two or three weeks for TV (though much less, with all hands to the plough, for major unforeseeable events – the launching of Sputnik, the assassination of Kennedy). Minimal forewarning to the teacher, therefore: a bare title, no notes. Nothing much to build on, really. Such a programme belongs to the category of the 'memorable interruption' – but a weekly event is not all that memorable, nor is a programme on, say, the housing situation.

This weakness became increasingly apparent during the 60s. There was a new professionalism abroad in the planning of secondary school courses, given fresh impulse from 1965 by the work of the Schools' Council; and a much more intensive examination of what adolescents were really interested in. 'It's important: you like it' was out. There was much more concern, too, to dovetail broadcasts in with other work: the tenuous links offered by current affairs programmes were no longer, for the conscientious teacher, enough.

So 'Spotlight' was wound up. There are plenty of broadcasts on current topics in the school schedules today, with a strong emphasis on social problems; but they are part of the total patterning, and chosen for their closeness to adolescents' own situation. In the field of world politics there are no programmes which chase the news, but in both media there are substantial series on twentieth-century history, providing a firm background against which current events can be intelligently discussed.

There is loss as well as gain, however. As I write, we are in the throes of a national crisis, with a general election pending. Not a word about it has been prepared and transmitted specially for schools. Unimaginable ten years ago; and not all the evening snatches of news, politicians' and pundits' faces, and party politicals glanced at or half-heard by the impatient young can compensate.

3.3 Who'll teach us numeracy?

Through the 50s and early 60s we were all being told till we were blue that a technological revolution was upon us. Automation, computerisation, atomic energy, space technology; cybernetics, systems analysis, DNA, $e = mc^2$ – we had to come to grips with these or we were sunk. So more science and maths graduates were required, and more skilled technicians as back-up; while the population at large needed to be better taught and better informed – more 'numerate', to use the jargon of the times.

The schools were patchily staffed and equipped to meet these demands. Their specialist forces were dwindling rather than growing: there were other, better paid jobs to attract young people equipped with degrees or A levels. How might conventional teaching be reinforced and updated? That was the challenge to broadcasting: what was the response?

Science broadcasting in the 50s

School radio in the 50s was doing its useful modest bit: there was the 'General Science' series dealing with some of the basics, and 'Science and the Community' helping to broaden the outlook of pupils in their 'extra year'. But the potential of a blind medium was very limited, and maths virtually outside its range. TV by contrast held high hopes. A programme in the 1952 'pilots' had shown us how an aeroplane stays up. We saw clear visuals, logically arranged; we followed a simple, orderly exposition. That teacher doing it was very competent too (no teacher, in fact, but an actor who knew his lines and could look a camera lens in the eye). But a good teacher on the screen was just the rub. Too good a teacher, perhaps—a rival, if not a supplanter? So the watchword for school broadcasting was 'enrichment': no usurping of the classroom teacher's role; and school TV started in 1957 with science sights firmly set on 'enrichment'.

After two years, there was a review of what had been achieved and where the signposts to the future seemed to point. The review questioned the dichotomy of function implied in the contrast of 'enrichment' with 'direct teaching'. 'But there is', it went on,

a broad distinction to be made between a series whose function is to extend the range of children's experience of the world of science, deliberately avoiding what the specialist teacher can do himself, and often exploring aspects of the subject which the conventional four-year syllabus might barely touch on; and a series designed to be the nucleus of a class's work in science and to set some pattern of activity for the teacher not naturally very much at home in this field. Both jobs, surely, are within television's capacity, and there is a need for both.

If the shortage of qualified science teachers is as serious as it is said to be, this second type of series might be expected to make a strong appeal to a wide variety of schools: for some classes, it might make the difference between doing some science and doing none. Television would not be a substitute for the class teacher, but it would be giving him a very strong lead. The series need not avoid the more conventional 'syllabus' topics and the simpler scientific principles they illustrate—indeed, it should embrace them; for there are surely few areas of elementary Science teaching to which it is unlikely that television could make a useful contribution, and schools will want evidence that it is prepared to take on a really solid job. A series for first-year classes would probably be easiest both for the BBC to plan and for the schools to use. The essential point, however, is that it must be able to carry the non-specialist teacher along with it: it must not therefore require in him a wide background of scientific knowledge, even of an elementary kind; and it must be accompanied by very full notes which will give him both a precise forecast of the programmes' content and firm direction on preparatory and follow-up work.

'Discovering Science'

This was the point of departure for a new, additional series, 'Discovering Science', launched in 1960, with Notes for the Teacher (assumed to be a non-specialist) and Pupils' Pamphelts in support – or rather, built into the concept of the course as an integral part of it. Its aims subsumed a full year's series, with a single presenter. He had to be an experienced teacher, of course, and with a flair for communicating the excitement of science. Making the programmes involved the closest collaboration of Gerd Sommerhoff, the teacher we engaged, with two BBC staff, both equipped to direct as well as produce, who transferred from School Radio where they had had long experience of working together on science programmes. The basic plan for the twenty-eight programmes was recognisable by any teacher of science to eleven-year-olds as central to his purposes: one term on air and heat; one on water; and one on simple physiology and life histories. There was, indeed, 'direct teaching' too, but teaching enriched by a wealth of film illustration, animations and practical experiments – nothing like the pedestrian programming current in the USA, where teachers were simply being transplanted to the studio to give arid lessons with exiguous resources. To 'carry the non-specialist along' with the series, the Notes on each programme gave background information, an analysis of programme content, and instructions (with illustration) on what to do before and after the broadcast; to give scope to the child with initiative, the Pupils' Pamphlets contained plenty of experiments he could do on his own, at home as well as at school.

In 1963 reports from the School Broadcasting Council's Education Officers who had observed the programmes in use, and the comments from teachers on them, were summarised as part of a major review of Broadcasting and the Teaching of Science in Secondary Modern Schools. It was found that only a quarter of the teachers using 'Discovering Science' were without qualifications in Science: nevertheless these amounted to some hundreds, quite apart from others in Primary Schools who were following the series. From such teachers, the usual comment was simply that they would be hard put to manage without it.

But what of the specialist teachers who used the series, though presumably competent to teach on their own? To some, it was the wealth of illustration that appealed:

Far from resenting 'direct teaching' on the screen, he was at pains to point out how much there was in this programme that he could not do, such as the Italian balloon.

To others, the clarity of the exposition:

Not only are experienced science teachers using it as revision, not only are they finding in it techniques such as animated diagrams which they cannot use themselves, but they are also attracted to an efficient piece of exposition.

In other Education Officers' reports, there are reservations:

In schools where the amount of time is limited, a large part of the science allocation is taken up by broadcast and note-taking, talk and redundant demonstration around the broadcast, to the detriment of active experimentation. The Teachers' Notes are recognised as excellent, but even they may (unintentionally) encourage this.

It must be recognised that some of Her Majesty's Inspectors in science and many Local Authority Advisers do little to encourage the use of broadcasts, believing that they are conducive to a 'taking facts on trust' attitude.

And what of the missing customers—the teachers who could surely have profited from the series, but did not use it? This report, too, is significant:

Inexperienced teachers tend to fight shy of broadcasts, not because they have all the answers, but because they haven't. They know that ques-

...rd Sommerhoff, with the aid of models, explains the dependence of life on the sun ('Discovering Science')

tions, and maybe desire for experiment, will come from the class and they prefer to have things entirely under their control. This may apply to some specialists also. A Headmistress observed: 'My Head of Department (a biologist) is terrified of physics and chemistry and would be incapable of using units such as you outline'.

The way of the world: to him that hath shall be given. Yet much help was being given to many also who had not; and teaching apart, there was time and again the evidence of children's involvement with the programmes:

During the yacht club episode—the actuality sequence to establish the speed of sound—they were totally absorbed as if by a moment of high drama at the cinema. They worked out the answer to the little sum as soon as it was set, and before the broadcast was formally over some were scribbling down figures in their jotters to get the speed of sound in m.p.h.

Involvement first, and through involvement, learning. The place of 'Discovering Science' in the BBC's annual provision of broadcasts was secure. But its form did not long remain static: in 1966, under the guidance of Geoffrey Hall, one of its original producers, it was completely revised. Geoffrey Hall focuses on one feature of the series as a pointer to the need for change:

57

The new series aims to interest children in science, to stimulate them to find out, to get them thinking scientifically, to provide them with a basis of facts on which to work, and to relate science to life. It aims, too, to avoid conveying the idea that science always has a clear-cut answer to offer. The old 'Discovering Science' ended every broadcast with a concise three-line summary of 'what we've learned today'. Many teachers liked this summary and so did most children. It buttoned-up the topic neatly and assisted memorising. But we (and many with us) now feel that this buttoning-up conveyed a wrong impression of what learning science is all about, and its air of finality might well have inhibited any desire to find out more. The summary helped in the aim of providing *facts* – but at the expense of all the other aims of the series. Its omission from the new 'Discovering Science' is almost symbolic of the change of attitude in science teaching that made the new programmes necessary.

From science as certainty to science as provisional: a big step, and one which has informed the thinking behind all the many studies in curriculum building and teaching methods which have come, in recent years, from the Nuffield Foundation and Schools Council projects. The revised 'Discovering Science' has gone into limbo now, to be replaced by 'Exploring Science', which more closely reflects this thinking. It gives more scope to television, too, and balances better the roles of class teacher and broadcast, by concentrating on showing how science in the classroom relates to real situations and problems in the outside world. It is designed, therefore, for selective use by teachers assumed to be fully competent at their job. More no doubt are than was the case ten years ago; and if television does not march with the vanguard, it risks losing the respect both of the pioneers and of those who would follow them. Yet a teaching deficiency does not disappear overnight, nor even over a decade; and there are still schools in which the 'Discovering Science' of 1960 would be an asset, rather than mark a regression.

Other science series

We have dwelt on 'Discovering Science' at some length, because its beginnings – and its end – so well reflect the educational climate of the times. But it has been a small part only of BBC School TV's contribution in science: to the rest I can only refer much more summarily. There are the many short units in the Sixth Form series addressed not to science specialists only but to Sixth Formers as a whole: from the early days when the emphasis was on bringing scientists of high distinction to the studio (not always with happy results, for not all were amenable to the disciplines of TV presentation) to, in more recent years, 'People and Computers', 'Monkeys, Apes and Men', 'Research in Progress', and 'The Mind of the Scientist'[1] – a particularly stimulating quintet of imaginary conversations between Dr Michael Hoskin of Cambridge University and actors impersonating Galileo, Newton, Herschel, Darwin and Pasteur. There are the 'Science Extra' series in Physics and Biology with their illuminating resources of specialised film and animation for teachers of GCE classes to quarry; there is 'Science Session' for the less able (which we met briefly in Chapter 1), anchored not to Science as such, but to those actual interests of all adolescents from which simple scientific principles can be drawn. And there is the whole field of Primary Science.

Here radio, despite its limitations, was first in the field. Primary School Science was only beginning, in the late 50s, to move beyond the range of Nature Study: radio's 'Junior Science' was soon helping teachers to extend its scope. Its producer, Eurfron Gwynne Jones, engaged as scriptwriter and presenter a brilliant teacher of young children, Harry Armstrong, who exploited to splendid effect the freedom that radio leaves them (since it requires the attention of the ear alone) to do small experiments even during the broadcast itself. Later, both he and his producer moved to television, with equally happy results in 'Exploring your World'.

Not totally happy, however; for while 'Exploring your World' was watched and enjoyed by children in thousands of schools, and though it included incentives to personal exploration afterwards, the weekly succession of programmes seemed to many teachers almost self-sufficient, and associated work was rarely ambitious, often perfunctory. So 'Science all Around', its successor series, adopts a different approach. It asks, firstly: what kinds of work, giving what kinds of experience, do we aim to involve

[1] Published by the BBC in book form in 1971.

59

children in as a result of this broadcast? And only secondly: what should the broadcast include, and how present it, so as to give them this stimulus? Thus, in one year the early autumn broadcasts aim at getting the children (aged nine and ten) to make careful observations and recordings, and in so doing to come to an appreciation of the capabilities and limitations of their own senses. Later ones lead to the idea of classification; then to the designing of simple measuring instruments and their calibration; then (through a broadcast on Clothing) to devising tests on fabrics for strength, wear, and stretch. By the second term, the children are ready for topics giving them opportunity to plan and carry out experiments on their own. Throughout, they are necessarily absorbing the principles of scientific method. The programmes themselves (once a fortnight only) are relaxed in style, their elements often loosely linked by association rather than patterned within a rigid framework, and more questions are posed than answers given.

Here is a BBC Education Officer's description of the responses of a class of ten-year-olds to a programme from this series on 'Streamlining'. He explains that normally the children would set to work on group projects after the programme, but on this occasion the whole class joined in discussion with him.

The pupils were enthralled from beginning to end. All the subjects dealt with seemed to arise naturally one from another and provided a tremendously rich and varied diet of interesting material. At the outset of the programme, when the possibilities of dropping a feather through a vacuum were mentioned and the vacuum pump was shown, a boy remarked 'Oh, good, I have always wanted to see this', and the rest of the material seemed to evoke comparable anticipation.

Afterwards they commented on things that had interested them: a girl singled out the wind tunnel experiment and was able to describe, very loosely, the way the experiment had been made to work using smoke trails. A boy picked on the streamlining of the Bullet Express: he could remember the speed at which it travelled, where it travelled to and from, and many other details relating to it. When the teacher drew on the board a diagram of a speed engine acting as wind-break to a speed trial cyclist, several children were keen to explain to me the effect of the partial vacuum behind the locomotive and the additional propulsion given to the cyclist by the turbulent eddies of air behind him.

Not one of them spoke of vacuum sucking, but all based their discussion on the air pushing in to the empty space.

We went on to consider the pros and cons of streamlining bicycles, ships' funnels and chimney pots: this drew in a lot of discussion on the nature of air pressure, slipstream effects, and so on. I have no doubt at all that some of the experiments given in the pamphlet will be carried out as the children start putting into practice ideas they suggested to me for examining streamlining effects without using wind tunnels.

A bright class, of course; and with bright ten-year-olds what is not possible? Anything is, if their diet has the piquant to match their mettle. Too often in school it does not: here it did.

Maths on the air

The air did not, at first sight, suit maths: at least no one put it on their list of priorities for trial. But among the first BBC TV producers was a former Maths teacher, Donald Grattan—so it did not have to wait long. The approach was suitably experimental, and the initial response fairly tentative: secondary school maths teachers were not natural television users. Yet 'Mathematics and Life' succeeded in making topics like averages and probability interesting to ordinary children; while a more substantial series, 'Middle School Mathematics', explored areas of the subject, such as binary numbers and vectors, almost untouched in many schools. Meanwhile we put on the air for Sixth Forms, besides some more adventurous series, two years of conventional maths, offering quite openly a substitute for the specialist class teacher, who was by now in desperately short supply.

By contrast, our first contribution in maths for Primary Schools was imbued with a new, exploratory approach to mathematical ideas. For thousands of teachers it was an illumination: in terms of viewing figures, it was outstanding for a new series. For the breeze of the 'new maths' was blowing, and the Primary Schools, as usual, were quickest in the uptake. Not that the series went whole-hogging for 'new maths' concepts: it was a judicious blend of new and established ideas (and so-called 'new maths' anyhow could trace its ancestry back over more than a century).

But the resources of TV transformed the presentation even of familiar ideas; and the whole was informed by the conviction, now a truism, that children learn best by discovering for themselves.

Two years later, in came 'Maths Today', a two-year course for secondary schools which really did take the bull of 'new maths' by the horns. The timing was just right: perhaps ten per cent of schools had followed the lead of the pioneers and revolutionised their approach: many more were shuddering on the brink, for it demanded an enormous effort and much courage to plunge into these, for them, uncharted waters. It was School TV's first essay in drawing teachers and pupils together along a totally innovating course.

As with 'Science all Around', the Teachers' Notes were far from being a mere appendage to the broadcasts: they had to lay the foundations of the course and provide most of the superstructure as well (there were eighty closely printed pages for each term). The fortnightly broadcasts were 'to provide starting points for the work in the Notes, from which teachers can select and develop according to the interests of their pupils.' It was suggested that teachers should copy questions in the Notes on to work cards, on which pupils would work in small groups.

Everything possible was done to achieve a successful launch: the producer, John Cain, held explanatory meetings with potential users up and down the country, at which pilot programmes were shown; and there was a special short series of broadcasts, 'Teaching Maths Today', for those who had committed themselves to the enterprise. 8 mm loop films were made and put on sale, too, to help teachers consolidate key concepts in the programmes.

The production method, as well as the content of the course, was new. Hitherto BBC producers had themselves been, after appropriate consultation, the prime initiators of series content: in this case the main responsibility for both structure and details of the course lay with two expert mathematical teachers engaged from outside. The producer (also a mathematician) worked in close co-operation with them, particularly in determining what elements were appropriate to television presentation: the team's style of collaboration, therefore, has parallels with what later became established practice in the broadcast productions of the Open University.

Was it all a success? Partially. It certainly put new approaches to maths study 'on the map' in many hundreds of schools. It provided a spur to many teachers to discard practices ingrained through familiarity but known to be rejected by a high proportion of pupils as tedious. Many of the programmes were found stimulating; some of the concepts, as abstract as they were polysyllabic, were apparently more easily grasped by the uncluttered minds of the young than by middle-aged teachers. But the series also proved too ambitious: too ambitious, perhaps, in its double target—in hoping, by addressing itself to pupils, to draw struggling teachers along with it; too ambitious, surely, in aiming to cater successfully for all but ten per cent of the whole spectrum of pupil intelligence. For the rigidity of the pattern imposed on class progress by the fortnightly arrival of a new programme with new material proved its undoing: however skilful the plan, once behindhand a class and its teacher began to feel lost. Admirably timed to capture interest, the series was premature in being offered with the ineluctable time-table attached to it that off-air reception imposes. It cried out for the flexibility that video-tape recording in school would one day give.

Let us end, therefore, this rapid mathematical survey with some recent comments on another maths series ('Maths Workshop', for age nine-eleven) where the teacher—unusually, in a Primary School—does have access to VTR:

I find the series very worth while. Not only from the children's point of view, but also because it has given me more time for preparation, and also more detail to base follow-up suggestions on . . . A TV programme can soon be forgotten by children, but with a VTR it can (by repetition) constantly be made 'fresh' . . . I showed each programme in its entirety to the whole set. I then used the programme material selectively, replaying that part which was applicable to the area of study we were involved in; for instance, when the children were considering tessellations, the relevant part of the Maths Workshop programme 'Pattern and Shape' was viewed again from the tape.

Round-up Two 4

Guess what? 5

These are some of the numerals the Romans used.

1, 2, 3, 4, 5, 6, 7, 8, 9, 10,-- 50,--100,--500,--1000,
I, II, III, IV, V, VI, VII, VIII, IX, X,   L.   C.   D.   M.

How far is it from the milestone on the left to York?

How long did John Smith live?

Try doing these two sums in Roman numerals.

Why do you find them difficult?

DCCII + LVII =

LXXVI − XXXI =

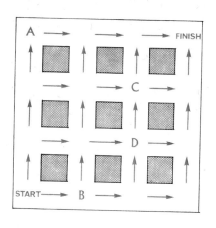

Here is a maze of one-way streets.
In a journey from START to FINISH, how many different possible routes go through corner A?
How many routes go through B, C, D?
How many routes use **both** corners B and D?
How many routes use **three** corners B, D and C?

'Maths Workshop'—pupils' work cards

The broadcast had become a resource completely under the teacher's control; and let us note in passing how easily TV bridges, and encourages teachers to bridge, 'subjects' once as disparate as maths and art. There is no dividing line, in 'Maths Workshop', between mathematics and the rest of life; and still less is this so in 'Countdown', a series specifically devised (like 'Science Session') for the young school leaver whose academic potential stops short even of CSE aspirations. 'Countdown' is rooted in real-life situations, often presented dramatically, and the mathematical ideas which are subtly and painlessly drawn out of them are all ideas which have a manifest practical application. Admirers of the film adaptation of 'The Railway Children' may not readily associate Sally Thomsett with maths; but there she is, in 'Countdown', involved in a succession of real-life problems, and a powerful incentive to solving them. The broadcasts themselves do not, of course, solve pupils' problems for them, either in 'Countdown' or in 'Maths Workshop': they are starting points for the pupils' own mathematical explorations, and here again the associated publications–work cards or work book–are a cardinal element in the total resource offered to teachers and children.

Should TV teach?

In this section I have wrapped up in a single package a consideration of two questions: what has been TV's contribution, up till now, to the study of science and maths in schools? and, Is TV a good teacher? I have done so because the interest in TV's role as a teacher (whether mainly through broadcasts directly, as in 'Discovering Science', or through literature closely associated with broadcasts and other aids, as in 'Maths Today') happened to coincide with the development of our maths and science programmes, and seemed particularly pertinent to this field. That TV has contributed substantially to school work in maths and science by offering teachers visual resources incomparably rich, varied and up-to-date is not, I think, in question. As a teacher, in the sense of an agency which can take over for a time the planning and selection of most or much of a child's experience in a particular discipline, TV certainly cannot be dismissed: we have all, I think, seen worse alternatives in action. But it is, of course, out of tune with today's concept of children at work: as a regular weekly ritual it throws the accent too much on teaching, too little on learning. Yet there is no reason, it seems to me, why TV should not from time to time teach how an aeroplane stays up, or its equivalent: it can do it so efficiently. Not all learning, all the time, can be discovery; authority is not yet that suspect; and a teacher, as we have seen, can appreciate TV's capacity to save him time. Nor should there be any objection to a TV series setting a pattern of activity which the teacher is invited to follow with his class, provided its plan allows him and his children the flexibility to develop it in their own ways. VTR adds greatly, of course, to this flexibility; but it is far from being a *sine qua non* of the good use of science and maths broadcasts in any circumstances.

Meantime, let us exorcise 'direct teaching', which has always had a bludgeoning ring, to describe TV's role in the classroom;

A tennis service photographed at 50 frames/sec. (Middle School Physics)

and 'enrichment' had better go too: TV is so much more than the icing on the cake. 'Resource' is a pallid word when it stands for the excitements of strobe photography or the macabre fascination of a bluebottle's life-cycle; but it must serve.

3.4 What, another year of half our future?

We have noted the impulse given to the study of Current Affairs in schools by the extension of compulsory schooling to age fifteen in 1947, and the crop of new radio series designed to encourage an outward-looking final year: 'Science and the Community', 'Looking at Things', 'The World of Work', 'For the Fourteens', 'Citizenship'. This last was short-lived: the title evoked too strongly the yawns that opened on schools' well-meaning efforts to explain the workings of Parliament and Town Hall to roaring boys and pudding girls. Nevertheless, even conventional subjects could fit the new bill, given the appropriate face-lift and make-up: add 'life' to them and they too could be enlisted in the new progressive army. So over the years BBC School Broadcasting came up with 'Science and Life', 'Mathematics and Life', 'The Bible and Life', and 'Religion and Life' (for which you qualified in the Sixth Form). This is not mockery–just pity for the hours in the bath spent title-searching, only to find the cherished one already commandeered.

By the time of the next raising of the school leaving age (henceforward ROSLA for short), there were series in plenty, on both radio and television, with the young school leaver as their primary target. For to the inheritance of the past had been added the new spur of 'Half our Future', the Newsom Committee's Report, published in 1963, on the education of average and below average boys and girls aged thirteen-sixteen. John Scupham, Controller of BBC Educational Broadcasting, who was a member of the Committee, wrote afterwards of it: 'This is the first major report on education in this country to treat the revolution in communications–and broadcasting is no less–as a new educational force, and not simply as a new educational tool.' He was thinking, of course, of the impact of broadcasting gener-ally, and not only in school: the report called it 'the most signific-ant environmental factor that teachers have to take into account'. One conclusion of the report, therefore, was that school leavers should be given courses in critical appreciation of the media, especially TV and film. As it happened, in BBC School TV we had recently broadcast such a series, 'Looking at TV', for ages thirteen-fifteen; in subsequent years we gracefully left this terrain clear for Granada TV's series 'The Messengers', while continuing to make our own occasional contributions at a rather more sophisticated level.

As for the classroom uses of broadcasting, the Report dwelt on the special value of 'its powers of presentation in terms of the actual, the concrete and the sharply individual for children who will perhaps never move easily in abstractions'. We were already applying these characteristic powers of television to maths and science; of radio, to English literature; of both, to history and geography. But beyond these there were the series which took as their starting point the young school leaver's personal situation; and first among these, TV's 'Going to Work' and radio's 'The World of Work'.

'The World of Work' and 'Learning about Life'

TV had of course great strengths in the field of careers guidance which radio lacked: it could actually show the man on the job and the routines he went through; it could convey directly the feel of the factory floor. 'Going to Work' was one of the 'founder' series of School TV; it was soon drawing in the largest Secondary School audience of any series; and it has stayed for a decade at the top of the league. But radio has, within its obvious limitations, its own strengths too. Here Rita Udall, producer of 'The World of Work', describes how she sees her job:

What subjects do we choose? Self-assessment, of course. How can a young person possibly explore the field of education, training and employment if he hasn't reached a point of beginning to think of himself as an individual with his own needs, strengths and weaknesses? Similar, perhaps, to other people he knows, but with important differences which he must be encouraged to discover. Then, we take a broad look at what job opportunities mean. Third, and most importantly, our programmes are about relationships. What does it mean to the young person when he ceases to be a pupil and become a young worker? How does he learn to get on with older workers and those of his own age? What are his attitudes to authority, to trade unions, to money, to leisure, to his changing relationship with his parents? Does he need to be involved in the community or did he leave community caring behind when he stopped doing the half-day of social service organised by the school?

The majority of my audience, girls as well as boys, will have to settle for jobs which, in themselves, may give little or no job satisfaction. The broadcasts try to help them begin to think in some depth about what they are expecting to get from their job and what they are expecting to give. By going out with a tape recorder and listening to young people in schools, colleges of further education, youth clubs and places of work, I am able to encourage them to examine their attitudes in some depth, and I can then translate some of their feelings into programme terms;

sometimes by including extracts from the tape, sometimes by using the ideas as the basis for a dramatised scene or a full-length play. This is the kind of material I get from these young people:

from Lancashire:

GIRL We wouldn't suit in an office 'cos we're only working class, aren't we?

GIRL Yeah, we don't come from where they do.

GIRL We're not snobs like they are in offices.

GIRL They'd be able to talk better than us. I mean, I couldn't talk to a person if they could, you know, talk proper.

GIRL They could use their words well.

GIRL They use great big long words.

from Bristol:

GIRL I'd like to get a job where I got promotion and could be in charge of everybody else, because I think I'd feel superior over everybody. There would be responsibility but I wouldn't mind that as long as I was in charge.

BOY I wouldn't like to be a boss because it's too much responsibility. If you do things wrong then you have to take the blame. I'd like to be an ordinary worker earning enough money to put some away.

Rita Udall also produces 'Learning about Life', it too concerned with relationships: with home, family, friends; relationship of boy to girl and girl to boy, maturing to love, marriage, parenthood; to child care and community involvement. Here too she builds many of her programmes from what youngsters give her in discussion:

Discussion sessions are exciting, exhausting and rewarding. Exciting because there are always surprises–some pleasant, some upsetting. Exhausting because so many young people have a great need to be listened to. Rewarding because, as the discussion progresses, you can see new ideas being formulated, old prejudices being re-examined, hopes for the future being formed. There is rarely, for instance, a group meeting that does not want to talk with feeling about their relationships with parents–some with love, some with resentment, some with despair:

BOY It took an accident for me to get to know my Dad. It was exactly a year and two months ago that my brother was killed. It shook my Dad because my brother was in the services and our Dad was the proudest man that could live because of my brother. I used to think that our Dad was real hard. You know how hard a man can be. But there's many a time I've seen our Dad upset now. So I communicate with him more now, just to keep his mind off it. I don't know how I do it but I just start talking and our Dad tries to forget about it. The main thing I want at the moment is to reach 18 for my father's sake because he was waiting for my brother to reach 18. To stand at a bar with my Dad at 18 and drink with him, that's what my Dad's ambition is and I'm going to make it mine now.

GIRL   Parents these days don't bother teaching their children. You have to go out into the world and learn for yourself and from friends whose parents have been bothered to teach their children so if it wasn't for schools and teachers we'd have a problem of being taught. At one time I think you could sit and talk to your father and have a quiet conversation with him. Today, you can't. They just don't want to know. I can't speak to my Dad at all. You just sit down talking to him . . . he just says 'Shut up!' You just sit there talking to yourself.

The young people I listen to for hours on end provide the material which encourages small group discussions in schools after the broadcasts. The boys and girls, making an attempt to sort out and assess their attitudes, will be truly adult in a few years' time. Most of them will follow the current trend of marrying young and becoming parents at a relatively early age.

Radio also devised, as a contribution for the beneficiaries – and the victims – of ROSLA, a new series, 'Inquiry': outward-looking, focusing on topics which might be expected to rouse youngsters' concern, and asking questions rather than supplying answers. Typical units from recent years: Waste and Want, Sporting Life, The Family, A Place Fit to Live In. The primary objective: discussion after listening; an important secondary one: to encourage further exploration or research of the topic in the class's own locality.

'Scene'

School TV, meanwhile, introduced 'Scene', with similar objectives but ranging rather more widely – partly because in its origins it inherited a little from the Current Affairs series 'Spotlight', which it replaced. The other, and more significant, strand in its pedigree was a sense of a missing element in the programmes we were offering young people in dramatised form. We had achieved some distinction with our 'Drama' series of carefully selected plays mainly from the classical repertoire; and we were using a dramatised format where appropriate in a wide range of other contexts too, and for children of varying age and abilities. The former however made heavy, sometimes excessive, demands on the least able section of our audience, where these were viewing; the latter were thoroughly competent pieces of craftsmanship, but hardly aspired to be more. Why could we not engage some of the ablest of contemporary playwrights to create half-hour plays specially designed for our audience? They must be writers whose existing work revealed, or suggested, an interest in young people and a feeling for what is of concern to them – but we could think of several with this quality. Thus over the years the series has included plays from such writers as Keith Dewhurst, Alan Plater, Peter Terson, and Colin Welland – to name only a few: it has also brought in younger writers, some with their first play for TV. Ronald Smedley, the producer of 'Scene', has written an account of the making of one such programme, '£60 single, £100 return', which will interest any aspiring School TV playwright or producer.[1]

When planning the first year of 'Scene', Ronald Smedley had the idea of combining with each of the four plays he had commissioned a documentary on a related theme, so that viewers' experience of the play could reverberate through their subsequent discussion of some of the realities underlying it. We will look now in some detail at two examples of these 'paired' programmes, and the responses to them. One is from the early days of 'Scene', the other from 1973.

'Last Bus'

The very first play for 'Scene' was 'Last Bus'. The scriptwriter, Keith Dewhurst, had chosen from a number of possibilities suggested to him the theme of violence in young people and

[1] In *Scene Scripts*, editor Michael Marland, published by Longman Group Ltd, 1972.

society's attitudes to it. His play told the story of a group of boys, in high spirits, getting on the last bus home; trying to dodge paying their fare; picking a quarrel with the Irish conductor; and finally getting off but returning immediately to punch him up quite brutally, and steal his purse. There were several other people on the bus – a middle-class woman, an elderly man, and a young engaged couple – but none of them intervened; nor did the bus driver, a West Indian.

This short scene was written with an edgy terseness and an eye for visual effect; it achieved a mounting dramatic tension as boisterousness soured to malice. It was near-documentary, too: one could read of similar incidents almost any week in the papers. It provokes the question, Why did these people act, or fail to act, as they did? So in the second half of the programme, the author decided, the 'cast' would be brought into the studio and questioned in turn about their reactions to the incident, and their reasons for behaving as they had. There was no script for this; and while there was rehearsal, Ronald Eyre, the 'inquisitor', warned the actors that he would vary his questions a little on the final 'take', to preserve an element of the impromptu. Finally, he would turn to the viewers and put three questions to them: Who was to blame for what happened? Can anything be done to stop it happening again? and, Was the BBC right to show it?

The last question was a mistake. Put to the viewing youngsters, it was highly disingenuous: clearly, if the programme had held and stimulated them, they would answer 'yes'; if it had not, it was best buried anyhow. To expect of this audience a sophisticated discussion of the rights and wrongs of portraying violence on the screen was quite unrealistic. The question was, I think, addressed more to teachers and casual adult viewers, and it was defensive, as if to say 'We do realise we are treading risky ground with this'. It revealed, in fact, our own anxieties about the programme.

What were these anxieties? Not about the principle of showing an act of violence on School TV: violence, particularly among teenagers, is a perfectly proper subject for discussion by fourteen- and fifteen-year-olds, and a strength of TV is that it can demonstrate forcefully just what one is talking about: not playground scuffles, but humanity temporarily brutalised. But the programme was not simply about teen-age violence: it posed also the question, Am I my brother's keeper? The other characters in the play were faced with this question, and at the crisis their actions answered No. They shared in the responsibility for what happened: with mitigating circumstances in each case, they too were guilty. Would this guilt somehow appear to diminish that of the boys (or the yobs, if you prefer)? The interviews had brought out what might be adjudged mitigating circumstances in their case too—poor family backgrounds, lack of places to let off steam harmlessly, and so on.

The ringleader of the boys, Robbo, was personable too—sexually attractive. (It was not he who stole the purse, either, but one of the others, as an unpremeditated afterthought). To some of the viewers Robbo would appear, initially at least, a heroic figure. A few would probably, on their record so far, seem to their teachers budding Robbos themselves; more would qualify as potential Robbo-followers. They would have been up before the Law already, and have acquired kudos among their mates for it. What would be their responses to the programme? Robbo had shown a strong revulsion when the conductor, cool and sweetly reasonable in the face of provocation, put his hand on Robbo's shoulder. Young people are very sensitive about being touched: would they find this too a 'mitigating circumstance'? All in all, a heavy burden could lie on some of the teachers coping both with the programme and with the old lags in their midst. Had we, by explaining or half-explaining so much, blurred the issue of personal responsibility?

To launch a programme with all such questions resolved is to take no risks; and without risk-taking there is no progress. We were confident that we had a programme which would engage youngsters' interest and be found by the great majority of their teachers challenging and fruitful of discussion. The School Broadcasting Council's Education Officers reported their experiences in schools in some detail, and their reports justified our confidence. Here are extracts from two of them:

The children reacted sympathetically to the boys in the café, enjoying their cheerfulness and the pop music, but the atmosphere tensed as the boys got into the bus. They were rather amused by the boys' cheek to the conductor and his replies, particularly his pride at being Irish, but there was no reaction to their abuse of the woman passenger, whom they seemed to accept as the typical adult 'pain in the neck' (the teacher said that the language used would be quite normal for this class, even mild). They were very attentive as the boys discussed whether to get off the bus or not, and very serious and absolutely silent while the conductor was beaten up. I thought it possible that some members of the class might even enjoy this episode, but they took it very seriously indeed – possibly because it was all too familiar. One of the more talkative, blasé boys asked rather anxiously whether it was only a story. There was an outburst of talking and general relief at the end of this sequence, and although they were never completely inattentive, they did not follow the rest of the programme with anything like the same concentration.

However, I think they grasped the significance of the second part and in the discussion which followed they mentioned each character's excuse. It was interesting that when the youth was interviewed and pleaded that he dared not go against the gang leader, one boy whispered the name of the school bully (who, according to the teacher, terrorises them in the school and out).

This kind of programme with an arresting, provocative but simple story line is a certain way of getting through to this kind of child, who has little reading ability, is bored with traditional teaching and anxious to leave school. In fact it may be the nearest they will get to any depth of thought on current social issues.

The next example shows how tiny, unforeseeable factors can affect the mood in which a class of adolescents approaches a broadcast. The title sequence for 'Last Bus' described it as 'A Scene with Interviews, concerning A Conductor, A Driver, A Lady . . . ' and so on. As each character was named, we saw him momentarily in action, then his picture 'frozen' on the frame. A useful and unremarkable convention, one would have thought – but not for this class:

They roared with laughter as each character was 'frozen', and loudly chanted out the accompanying word. This was clearly a jolly old giggle. The real scene began therefore on a slightly hysterical note, and the girls hooted with admiration at the close-up of Robbo in particular. Attention became riveted and the level of sheer hilarity reached its peak when the dustbin was kicked over. At this stage one vaguely got the impression that we were about to experience something akin to

Golding's *Lord of the Flies*! The impression was further heightened by the class's reaction to the cheeky retorts to the Irish bus-conductor.

A note of genuine malice could be detected in their reaction to Robbo's disgust at being 'handled' by the bus-conductor. The class seemed to be carried away by a sort of mass hysteria: the violence that *The Observer* tells us is in us all was certainly not far from the surface on this occasion.

The class was suitably hushed by the furtive references to the 'spade', and the mood unmistakably changed at the beating-up. Several girls winced very noticeably at every blow. If the class had previously identified with the young lads, they certainly rejected their behaviour now, together with the behaviour of the other protagonists who looked idly on.

I am convinced that they had really lived through this whole incident: they had been caught up in those feelings of devilment, arrogance and hatred that presumably account for many acts of teenage aggression; they had, in a very real sense, experienced violence – first as aggressors, but then as the aggressed. I think this was a sobering experience for all of them.

Afterwards this large group of forty-five children jostled and shouted to be heard. They all had something to say and more than half of them probably said it. The teacher controlled this torrent of keenly-felt views and allowed as many as possible to have their say.

The basic technique adopted was to talk about each character in turn. The teacher nevertheless had to cut short the discussion rather abruptly in order to be able to move on to another character; but even then, he had no time to go through more than the characters of the woman, the bus conductor and Robbo. At the end of the lesson it seemed that the class had an enormous amount still to say and that the impression made on them would last long enough for them to be able to talk meaningfully for quite a long time yet.

Other reports reflected some of the hazards, and the weaknesses, of the programme. This one, for instance:

We discussed the protagonists in the drama. Predictably, 'society' or 'the system' was the chief offender, and this was extended into 'the pressures of town life . . . lack of opportunity . . . boredom' etc . . . Gradually the boys, chiefly the ringleader, came in for a share of blame. I tried not to induce this change of view but at the same time to draw attention to the question of the responsibility of the individual. On the passengers and crew, and their action or inaction, these boys were not, I think, inclined to ponder so much as on the problem of urban disorder and the circumstances that make our neighbours, if not ourselves, into Robbos.

Or this:

It was not a particularly bright class – very much like, I should imagine, the bulk of the audience for the series; yet the programme had, I think, almost every sociological problem in the book: Irish immigrant conductor, West Indian driver, middle-class mother with children at public schools, old age pensioner, housing estates and their attendant lack of amenities, gang leadership problem and so on. Consequently these very unsophisticated pupils, quite unaccustomed to discussing this kind of material, really needed a lot of help to understand what motivated or failed to motivate the various characters. I think, too, that the Investigator's questioning of the passengers was altogether too high-powered for this audience. If one of the objects of the programme was to get the pupils to recognise the problems of the society in which they live, it was a bit much to throw the lot at them all at once.

Very fair comment. The complexity and variety of the issues raised by the interviews was, in part, the price paid for unscripted spontaneity – though we never expected any one class to pursue them all! Today, many teachers with access to video-tape recorders would, I believe, opt to use the first part of the programme only – though they might well get useful ideas about the handling of it from their 'private view' of Part 2.

'Last Bus', however near the bone of real life, had been fictitious and about crime: 'The Sentence of the Court', the following week, was to be documentary and about punishment – the sort of punishment that is adjudged to fit that sort of crime. It could take us, for instance, inside a probation office, a detention centre, or a Borstal prison – perhaps all three. The producer decided the programme would be stronger if it carried on the story of two of the 'Last Bus' boys – Robbo, the ringleader, and Arthur, the youngest of the four – after their arrest. And so it proved. The work of a real probation officer and a real Borstal governor could be related to the specific cases of 'Robbo' and 'Arthur', whom the audience knew, and for whom they were just as 'real' as two genuine delinquents would have been, and unlike these could be shown face to camera.

'The Sentence of the Court' worked very well. It was ingeniously done (the actor impersonating Robbo was not allowed to set foot in a Borstal, but the viewers were convinced they saw him there, in his cell); it was well constructed, informative, and thought-provoking: more stylish a programme, I thought, than 'Last Bus'. But it was 'Last Bus' with all its faults that set the pace for 'Scene', breaking new ground and opening up new prospects for School TV.

'The Ballad of Ben Bagot'

Five years later, and with much else that was experimental and mainly—not always—on the mark in between, came 'The Ballad of Ben Bagot', by Peter Terson. It opens with a Rank cinema-style gong, then a naked torso appears on the screen, as of one striding forward, and the words:

They call me Bagot, the stalwart one,
I am an awesome sight,
Such road I travel I travel alone,
No one is equal in my might.

Then the titles: The Ballad of Ben Bagot, A Fantastic Tale; and we are in a shoe-shop.

NAGER Bagot, are you going to lunch, or are you going to sit in the customer's chair all day?

BAGOT I have an appointment for lunch, Mr Hillmorton.

NAGER Are they interviewing for a new James Bond?

BAGOT Actually, it's a private lunch, Mr Hillmorton . . .
He seizes one of the shop's long shoe-horns, and as he makes ready to go, the sound track echoes his thoughts:
With brow uncreased, with mind unworn,
The youth on yon Promethean point
Straps on his trusty weapon which in blood he did anoint,
His own, his trusty, brave shoe-horn.
And out into the street:

Bagot 2 . . .

Out he shone from the seething mass,
A man alone, a paragon,
Stand aside, proles, trade unionists, office boys, let me pass,
For to my love I must be gone . . .

Now he's with Laura in her sordid little room. She's getting his
dinner. She is pregnant. The smell of dinner takes him back to
thoughts of school: we see him with his teacher, who is trying to
cajole him into appreciating Kubla Khan. There's some sparring
between them; they like each other, we feel, but Bagot floors him
hands down. Caption on the screen:

Bagot 2, Williams 0.

Back with Laura:
  'What did you think when you first saw me at school, Baggsy?'
  'A right scrubber.'
  'But what did you think when you saw me at the dance?'
  'I thought you were the slinkiest, sexiest thing' – and we see her
there, looking like a TV commercial . . . 'And what do you

think now, Baggsy?'

'I think I was right first time.'

He's trying to chat up his father. 'You're on your own now, son': no Laura in his house, thank you. He muses gloomily on the prospect of life with Laura: 'I'm eating for two now, Baggsy' . . . the midwife . . . the rent collector.

In the shop again: enter Splendid Bruce – his schoolmate, in the Sixth Form now, with a fistful of O levels. No getting girls pregnant for him.

'Get out of it, Bagot.'

'I have responsibilities.'

'Only to yourself. Get out of it, boy. Never look back. It might hurt her now, if you go; but if you stay it'll cripple you for ever . . . In ten years' time, when you're a man of the world, with an interesting, sun-tanned, weatherbeaten face lined with experience, you'll relate the tale with mild amusement. Stay now, and you'll never get beyond a day-trip to Blackpool. Think big, Bagot.'

Bagot chucks his job. We see him in imaginary situations of great success. Back with Laura, more fantasies as he lies in bed –

'Get out of it, Bagot!'

the big money jobs, pipe laying, North Sea gas, motorway building—while she tries to bring him down to earth. Then he sees:

'An angel, writing in a book of gold.

"What are you writing?"

"It's the book of fate."

"Am I in there?" he asked.

"You, you stupid git, you're just too late."'

The angel turns as he answers. It is the face of Ben himself.

To encapsulate a high fantasy of vision and sound within a patchy fabric of words alone is to reduce it almost to ashes; but perhaps enough survives to suggest a programme which is at the same time a salute to life and a wry comment on the pathos of the human condition. What did schools make of it?

A mixed group of below-average pupils, just fifteen years old:

Ben was described in turn as 'imaginative', 'a dreamer', 'daft' and 'stupid'. Laura was condemned as being 'silly and immature' to get herself into that situation. Most felt that Ben and Laura would marry,

'I have responsibilities!'

partly because they thought they should and partly because they obviously felt a great deal for each other. Everyone was convinced that
Laura was in love with Ben. Ben's position was a bit more difficult to
analyse. Some felt that he was happy because he could day-dream but
others were convinced it was his day-dreaming that made him dis-
contented. One girl maintained throughout this discussion that the
happy part of Ben's personality came from his being a prospective
father.

There was some consensus that Ben felt that everything would go
right for him. He was the eternal optimist. Things turned out badly for
him because he could not think beyond tomorrow and he had no staying
power. Ben should not marry Laura in his present state of mind. Nor
should Laura allow Ben to marry her. There were plenty of people who
could look after the baby: parents, grandparents, social workers, etc.
Some people wanted to get married and others did not. Ben and Laura
were in the Don't Know category.

A class of fourteen-year-old girls, above average:

The class warmed very quickly to Bagot's sense of humour, though they
were to reject him as a person later. They had grasped the essentials of

the Bagot philosophy and predicament very well, even if they saw the situation in rather simple terms. It took a certain amount of questioning to bring out the complexity of the decisions facing Bagot and his peers and the far-reaching interpersonal effects of those decisions. In the end they did see that it was Ben's eight O-level friend, who knew how to play the system, who was the real winner.

Bagot was rejected as an irresponsible layabout who should have felt more and done more for Laura. Confronted with an actual case, albeit fictional, they changed their minds about paternal responsibilities. Suddenly, conventional family ideals began to surface and trendy liberalism evaporated.

A double class of average boys, aged fourteen:

The interest of these boys had been high. They had found Ben a likeable lad, but thought that he had not grown up – 'We used to have fantasies like that when we were about 12'. Ben was unreliable and was not efficient at running his life – though he kept trying. He wanted more from life than he could really have. Ben should not have married his girl even though she was to have a baby. He did not love her enough to be able to go home to her every night for the rest of his life. In five years' time he would be bored by her. He should have paid for the baby but not married the girl. He would be a bad husband and the girl would become unhappy. But if Ben had not married her she might have found it difficult to get someone else to marry her.

A mixed class of sixteen-year-olds, above average:

These intelligent pupils simply lapped up this broadcast. As far as I could see, they appreciated all the allusions, literary, visual and musical. Unfortunately, at the end, there was not sufficient time to develop a real discussion, but some of the questions did provoke argument. For example, 'Was Ben's imagination a help or a hindrance?' Some said that it was a hindrance because it prevented him from coming to grips with reality, while others said it was a help because it enabled him to escape from the humdrum surroundings of Bradford where 'the turgid river ran'. They were largely in agreement that Ben and Laura should not get married just because she was pregnant. In their opinion, she seemed to be the sort of girl who would turn into a stodgy conventional 'mother of ten' and with nappies and feeding bottles put an end to Ben's aspirations and flights of fancy.

Two documentaries followed 'Ben Bagot'. The first dealt sensitively with a number of case-studies of young unmarried mothers. The second was called 'How Good a Parent?' Some quotes from this latter:

'A child's education starts long before he gets to Infants' School.'

'For a child, play is really working.'

'Talking, just talking with the children is probably one of the best things we can do in the playgroup.'

An educational pundit speaking? Not quite. It's Mark, a shock-headed, freckled fourteen-year-old reflecting as we see him at work in a play-group – admiring this child's brick-building control, encouraging that one down the chute, sorting out an incipient quarrel between two more over who's to have the trike. An Education Officer noted:

To hear these ideas and comments coming from youngsters so close in age and background to those in the viewing group was more than remarkable: it was quite breath-taking, and made a deep impact on this audience. The teachers agreed it was a first-rate programme – nothing false or authoritarian about it. 'Could we please have more of this teenage-centred, teenage-presented kind of programme?'

If 'Scene' has had more than its share of attention in this chapter, it is because, as here, it seems so often to point towards new possibilities in school broadcasting. Such a series owes everything to the quality of its production team. I am proud to have had the opportunity of giving it benevolent encouragement. I believe I even thought of its title, and without soaking in the bath.

3.5 Everyone a creator

Until recently, school broadcasting was thought of, above all, as a magic carpet on which schools could escape from the classroom's confines. Escape in the imagination, by radio, to a crofter's cottage, to Achilles' tent, to the coal-age forests; by television, in reality almost, for there it was on the screen, to the research chemist's lab, the markets of Singapore, the surface of the moon. Escape anywhere, provided it was away from the classroom, the one place children saw enough of anyhow. But in school TV today, cameras are continually taking children back *into* classrooms: to see other children making shadow puppets, setting up experiments, preparing local surveys. No need any more to tag 'and Life' on to curricular subjects to give broadcast series the tang of relevance: call it a 'workshop' and you're home. So we have 'Maths Workshop', 'Music Workshop', 'Drama Workshop'. For that is what classrooms at their lively best now are: from being boring places to escape from, interesting places to look in on. And not to educational pundits only: to other children in other classes also.

It has not happened (when it has) all that suddenly, of course. Learning by doing is hardly the most novel of educational ideas; and lively broadcasts, imaginatively handled, have always tended to issue in lively activities, to set children creating as well as just talking and doing the more obvious things. The history broadcasts of Rhoda Power and her inheritors have often stimulated children to recreate the past in their own fashion, sometimes pictorially, sometimes dramatically; so too with 'How Things Began' and its successor 'Man'. The gothic fantasies of Tolkien's 'Lord of the Rings', adapted as a serial broadcast in the mid-fifties, evoked from children a range of pictures lurid and macabre, portentous and comic, which often brilliantly reflected the fertility of the author's imagination. The series 'Poets and Poetry', devised about the same time by the poet Robert Gittings, then a producer in School Radio, also drew original poems from many children. K. V. Bailey's 'The Listening Schools' is a rich source of documentation on these and other instances of creative work derived from the experience of broadcasts.

If new crops have sprung from more recent broadcasts it would be wrong, therefore, to suggest that a new inspiration is at work. Nevertheless there has been manifest in the last decade, within the schools themselves, a growing enlargement of teachers' view of the educational process – rooted in the concept of the child as creator, and reflected in a new adventurousness about what ordinary children can be encouraged to undertake; and in this development could be discerned, if not a wholly fresh challenge to school programmes, at least a new soil in which they could cast their seed. It has been especially in evidence in the fields of English and of music.

In school radio's English series of twenty years back, the legacy of Mary Somerville's ideal of bringing children the best in literature was still potent, and 'the best' still meant, for the most part, 'the classics'. The range was far from narrow: Victorian classics loomed large, but the Bible, Homer, the Arabian Nights, and such traditional material as ballads, folk tales and miracle plays all had their due. Fewer than half the programmes were based on twentieth-century writers. What was expected of the listening children, and most often but not of course always got, was a lively appreciation: a capacity to sense the atmosphere the author had created and to involve themselves with the characters of the story. Until Robert Gittings invited original contributions from children for 'Poets and Poetry', no one had thought of using English broadcasts to foster children's own creative impulses. And even 'Poets and Poetry' drew its response mainly from the more gifted teachers and children; while the very concept of the series – a whole series devoted to poetry – was in a sense an act of reverence towards traditional values.

'Listening and Writing'

In the 60s, on the inspiration of Moira Doolan, radio series in the field of English for children aged between nine and fifteen took on a different emphasis. The new titles suggest its direction: 'Listening and Writing', 'Speak', 'Living Language'. 'Listening and Writing', one of the first of the 'new wave', has a target age of eleven-fourteen: its aim is for the listening child to share in the writer's experience, but also to go on from there to explore his own experience, to value it and try to put it into words. As Moira Doolan explained it:

Children start level with the adult writer, in that their raw material is within and around them; their fresh impressions of the world and their experience of it exist and are of value in their own right. Apart from this they can help themselves towards maturity by digesting their experiences into words. Children start behind the adult writer in imperfect mastery of the tools of the art: vocabulary, grammar, spelling. But if children have something they want to say they will learn to use these tools because they need them for a definite purpose, and then they can find pleasure in using them. Radio can supply the immediate impact of a story and clear impression of the writer's thought and feeling. The material broadcast is chosen not for its perfection of 'literary' quality, but primarily for truth and tension of expression and closeness to the listener's experience, for that shock of recognition that may disturb the listener, and make him search within, and draw out.

The material of 'Listening and Writing' and its fellow series is offered to children straight, virtually without comment: the skill of the programmes lies in the selection and arrangement. The bias is towards contemporary writers, and not necessarily big names either: it is to the accents of today that older children most readily respond. Not that response is necessarily immediate, nor easily won: to share in a writer's experience, even to grasp at all what he is at, can need practice by the child, and a change of stance on the teacher's part.

The very first broadcast in the series was a short story by Ted Hughes, 'The Rain Horse'. One child's comment: 'It made no sense. Sounds raving mad.' Another's, in the same class, 'I felt as though it was me. I was living it too, it was exciting and unusual. The ending made me think.' A teacher remarked after the broadcast, 'I think this class is not yet capable of appreciating anything which contains so much description of mood and feeling.' Another: 'Interest is amazing. I'm quite sure they don't understand it all, but they do get very vivid images, which they reproduce.'

Each term's 'Listening and Writing' concludes with a programme of children's own work. It comes in abundance for the producer to choose from, and by no means from the older and abler children only. The personal vision, distilled in vivid and often homely language, is what he looks for: not the finished, precociously literary, product of language manipulated into verse, but this, for instance:

A SHARK OF THE RIVER

A shark of the river was on my hook,
Waiting for me to write in a poem.

ildren's paintings inspired by 'The Horses of the Sun' ('Living Language')

The day I caught a shark
A shark of the river, a pike.

The struggle was long,
The fish was strong,
Like a war submarine,
With motor and fin, on my hook.

I fought like a tiger,
'Twas four feet long,
'Twas terribly strong,
'Twas on my hook.

It's tiring now,
I can see its size,
It's four feet long,
With glowering eyes.

It's now in the landing net
All four feet,
Twenty-five pounds of long, strong pike,
Except one fin, dashed against a rock.

It's in a glass case now, all four foot
Of fighting fish,
Four feet long, fat and strong,
Except one fin, dashed against a rock,
Of a tiger, of a shark of the river.

Or this:

THE FOG

When you walk in the fog
All the houses are like
Big, black blind eyes
Staring at you.
The fog is like a misty
Blanket, covered around
The house and we are
Inside this blanket.
You see no one.
What they wear
Or who they are.
It is as if

We are blind ourselves.
It is dark!
Everything is silent!
In my mind I expect
to see no one.
But there
At the top of the road
A panther shape creeps up
With gleaming yellow eyes
and passes slowly.
When it gets near
I see it is a car.
Then comes a bus,
I laughed. For to me
It looks like a monster beetle
Wriggling across the road.

'They are looking at and talking about the world around them with new voices and new eyes', said an enthusiastic teacher about her class, 'and their writing is of an entirely different quality.' She added that the series was also extending her own range and stimulating her reading and appreciation of literature, as well as encouraging her to put pen to paper on occasion. Small wonder that school broadcasts are often referred to as 'the teacher's permanent refresher course'.

'Living Language'

A few years after 'Listening and Writing' came 'Living Language', for slightly younger children. The producer again:

Language lives in our own mouths if we use it well. We speak and write with freedom, power and insight if we can draw on the full range of our personality and being – the strength of intellect, the depth of feeling, the fire of imagination. Language is the one art we all practise all our lives, well or badly. The artist's use of language, in myths, stories, plays and poems, contains the wisdom and the imaginative life of the past and of the present. It can help us to develop and to unlock our own powers of creative speaking and writing.

A more catholic range of material here, with the traditional far from neglected. The series explores three main areas of the imagination: morality, truth and feeling; broadly represented by the myth, the novel or true story, and poetry. The work inspired by the broadcasts is varied too: besides writing, there is painting, drawing, modelling, mime and drama. Discussion, of course, is important still: the prelude, very often, to creative work – and may not discussion itself be creative? Here are some children talking with their teacher about Phaethon, after listening to 'The Horses of the Sun':

TEACHER What did you think of Phaethon? What sort of picture of him have you in your mind?

CHILD I think that he had black curly hair with long sideboards and a scarlet cloak on with a sort of tunic thing underneath and he went around all proud and haughty and I wouldn't like him at all and he used to go and boast to all his friends because his father was the sun god.

CHILD Yes, but that was only in self-defence because his friends were teasing him saying that he wasn't the son of the sun god, their teasing made him only more haughty.

CHILD I imagined him as a person easily led by other people.

CHILD I would like Phaethon as a friend but he never stops saying about his father being Apollo.

TEACHER But you can understand him can you? You can understand why he boasted about his father?

CHILD I think that he thought if he never told anybody he would forget about his father you know, he wanted to know about him, you know, tell everybody else.

TEACHER You think that he didn't have his father with him all the time like you do and therefore he's got to talk about him more so?

CHILD I think he was driven to haughtiness and boastfulness because many people have a father but he didn't because he was away up in the sky.

And for children's writing, I like this: perhaps you do?

THAT PESTY BABY

A new baby always causes an eruption. I've never seen the like of it. My baby sister who was born on Saturday, has caused the biggest eruption. I can't watch television but someone is knocking on the door wanting to see the baby. I have to sleep on the couch because my room is FULL of presents. Worst luck for me that it's half-term and I have the Monday off. Get the baby's nappies, get her bottle, get the powder, find her mits, do this, do that, do the next thing. All attention is put on that pesty baby. They call her beautiful, they would be shocked if they heard my description of her. I had to make my own tea last night because Mum had to put her to sleep. If it weren't I was so kind-hearted, I wouldn't do a thing for her. Well, it's the last time I'll ever want a baby sister again. I wouldn't have minded a brother so much although I suppose he would have been just as bad. And just to think seven years later no one could ask for a kinder sweeter nicer sister, than my sister Sharon.

'Making Music'

Music had established itself, by the end of the war, as a main element in radio's contribution to schools: indeed, many children's experience of music in the Primary School was based on BBC programmes throughout. Yet here too, among the more enterprising schools, new trends were in evidence in the 50s. Some of the new approaches were inspired by continental teachers, particularly Carl Orff, the essence of whose approach is the development of sensitivity to sound not only in musical instruments but also in nature and in language. The basic principles of Orff's 'Schulwerk' include giving children opportunities to express themselves in music by using instruments that are easy for them to use, and teaching rhythm as a fundamental part of musical education by its natural connection with speech rhythm and children's own rhythmic activities.

These ideas were first exploited in a quite novel series produced by John Hosier for School TV, to which he had recently transferred after several years' successful leadership of the group of school radio music producers. For him therefore the challenge lay in the medium itself as much as in the opportunity to explore new ideas in musical education. He decided to build the whole term's programmes on a mini-cantata, 'The Midnight Thief', for which Ian Serraillier wrote the words, based on a Mexican folktale, and Richard Rodney Bennett composed the music. It was made up of simple unison songs and speech accompanied by percussion; and it was specially written for performance as a class activity, away from a piano, using instruments (both pitch and non-pitch) that could be found in every school. There was scope

SAY

They munched their lunch together
Then merrily played leap-frog round the field.
They sat on the ground side by side
And waited, waited, waited . . .

PERCUSSION

Till lo! across the face of the moon there flew
With radiant sweeping wings
A Bird of Paradise,
And lighted on the corn
And pecked and pecked and pecked . . .

Fernando cocked his gun,
Then lowered it – how his heart did ache!
'Bird of Paradise,
Bird of beauty brighter than the sun,
Must I kill you for my father's sake?'

He raised his gun and tearfully took aim . . .

'The Midnight Thief'—a page from the children's pamphlet

for creative percussion work wherever words were to be spoken to percussion accompaniment: here children were left to improvise in any way appropriate to the mood and atmosphere of the words. Musical sensibility was of course expected of class teachers in guiding this, but no special musical expertise was necessary.

Each week a class from a local Primary School, who had already rehearsed with their teacher the material for that week's programme, came to the studio to serve as a model for the unseen, distant viewers who were to participate too. Jack Langstaff, a professional singer who was also a music teacher, took over in the studio as conductor and trainer of the children there, working closely with John Hosier as director, and gradually building up to the complete performance of the work in the last programme. Then, the broadcast series completed, the viewing classes would stage their own performances of 'The Midnight Thief' in their own schools.

Story, music and setting were all lively and colourful; children were active throughout; there were pamphlets of course to help with practice in between programmes; it was a glorious experience for all. And not only a musical one: the Mexican scene was a source of inspiration to many schools, and painting, modelling, even geography were incidental outcomes of the new stimulus.

'The Midnight Thief' had several successors, each with a composer of high reputation. 'Making Music' has gone now; but school radio followed closely in its wake with 'Music Workshop', adapting to radio many of its predecessor's ideas, and bringing in new ones of its own; and it too characterised by the belief that children can not only appreciate and interpret other people's music, but by skilful guidance and encouragement can be led to express the music that is within themselves.

A few years later John Hosier came up with something even more adventurous. He had found a Comprehensive School where, under the leadership of teachers not only musically gifted but with a deep understanding of and sympathy for adolescents, an 'Opera Band' had been formed of youngsters, mainly aged about fifteen, who co-operatively devised, practised and performed their own musicals. A group of eleven boys and girls from this band were invited to present, for their peers in the viewing schools, a series of programmes about music-making in the 'pop' idiom: 'Making a Musical'. Very few of the group had any academic pretensions, or any musical training: several played an instrument—guitar, drums, piano—but mainly or entirely self-taught. The most surprising thing about them, however, was their readiness to sing on any occasion—sing solo or in parts, improvise vocally without self-consciousness.

There was discussion—and illustration by the group and others they brought in—of how music creates atmosphere and mood, of musical ensemble, of the relationship of words to music, of how to compose chords, how to arrange simple orchestral backing, how to devise and use electronic music; and finally a performance of the Opera Band's own musical, 'Cave'. A real attempt to talk to average fourteen- and fifteen-year-olds about *their* music and to point to what lay within *their* capacities to create with it.

'Making a Musical' did not, of course—could not—achieve the success of 'The Midnight Thief' in terms of what was inspired by it in the schools which viewed it. To the majority of specialist music teachers in Secondary Schools it would be far too revolutionary, or perhaps make demands on them they were simply not equipped to respond to. Both in what it presented and in the manner of its presentation it was something of a 'tour de force'. But it was a pioneering effort to bridge the gulf which separates 'establishment music' and its frequently high-quality performance in secondary schools from the music which is the staple of most teen-agers' genuine, but often so passive, experience outside school. It showed popular music in action – and with the action supplied by the very youngsters so repeatedly assumed to be nothing but the willing dupes of commercialism. It pointed forward, and its day will surely come.

Meanwhile we have, on radio, 'Music Club', for this same audience. Some of the fare is intriguingly exotic: 'The next broadcast, "Cement Music", returns briefly to jug-playing and then introduces the major triad in a variety of guises. The producer demonstrates some more ways of using a tape recorder to produce "musique concrète".' But its affinity with 'Making a Musical' is clear. To quote from the Annual Programme of broadcasts for Schools:

One of its purposes is to encourage all sorts of private, group or class activities. Projects on song-writing, 'wallpaper' music, making a blues, playing with tape-recorders, singing folksongs, improvised vocal harmony . . . and making a reggae have all brought first-class response from schools in the past.

Once more, then, the accent is on creation; and once more, the audience is being met on its own ground.

3.6 Hindhitches and headstarts

How can educational effort be deployed to compensate children handicapped and left behind through adverse environmental factors? The question has increasingly, over the last quarter of a century, engaged the attention of researchers, of practising teachers, and of political decision-makers. In the 50s, remedial education for the least able was becoming a significant feature of the work of most Secondary Modern Schools: these children, usually at best semi-literate only yet with an intelligence quotient which qualified them for an ordinary rather than a 'special' school, were normally handled separately from the main body of their peers, by teachers who had had special training in the needs of the backward. Where the personality, skill and devotion of such teachers matched their responsibilities, a visitor to their classrooms would often find a particularly warm atmosphere there, and even evidence of an unusual sense of achievement. Had broadcasting a contribution to make to their special needs?

Broadcasts for backward secondary children

Teachers of backward children were free from the claims of the formal curriculum, but their material resources tended to be meagre and the search for new kinds of stimulus was continual. What books the children were capable of reading would be much too babyish for them; the school radio programmes available were almost all too demanding for their limited vocabularies and defective powers of concentration. Scotland, however (pioneering once more), tried out an experimental term of radio programmes specially designed for such audiences; and it was sufficiently successful for London to take up the idea and launch a whole year's series, with the format of a family serial, for what our publicity described as 'less able children'.

'The Jacksons', as this series was called, went pretty well; but when School TV came in it was in this direction that teachers mainly looked for help and encouragement with their backward children; and after an earlier experiment of promise we started 'Television Club' in 1962. Again, a family provided the framework: the format had proved its value in offering that background of security which many of the audience missed in their own lives; but television could also range much more widely over the practical activities and problems which form the surest centres of interest for children of this kind.

The producer added to his broadcast plan one other idea which was quite new. To extend the value of the series, he suggested a pupils' booklet in the form of a reader. Each chapter would be based on one of the broadcasts: there would be illustrations showing the activities of members of the family; and the vocabulary and syntax of the stories would be carefully checked by experts to conform with the average reading abilities of a child of about eight (the target for the series was age eleven-thirteen). The idea was that having enjoyed the broadcast and become familiar with its content, pupils would find the task of assimilating it in print both rewarding and relatively easy. Thus confidence in their capacity to read – the heart of the struggle at this age – would grow and with it, we hoped, a recognition that the effort of acquiring the key to what is to be found in books was worth while.

The producer's ideas were readily accepted and the series ran with success for a decade in this form. Teachers did find the booklets contributed to reading progress; they were equally enthusiastic about the encouragement given by the programmes to children's individual work, and it was moving to see the effort put into this by pupils for whom conventional schooling had achieved little. If the future of 'Television Club' is now more uncertain, it is not because of doubts about TV's uses in this quarter, but because the trend now is against hiving off the least able in the school community, and towards allowing them to work alongside their peers in more loosely organised classes, with scope to operate at their own pace.

'Look and Read'

Meanwhile, however, the concept of TV as a provider of the 'hitch up from behind' was being applied at an earlier age also, and with reading progress as a main and no longer a secondary objective. We had recently appointed a producer, Claire Chovil, with experience of secondary teaching and also of producing for children's out-of-school radio. I wanted her to work in the primary field, so she went at her own request to teach in a junior school for a spell. Here she was struck by the preoccupation of the staff with children's progress in reading, and felt that if only TV could be harnessed to help directly in this it would be doing something quite central to teachers' purposes. None of us had thought of trying to use TV to assist in the actual acquisition of reading skills, but she convinced us all, and went on to devise two experimental groups of programmes within the established series

'Merry-go-Round'. Having proved her case, she launched a complete new series 'Look and Read' for age seven-nine, which still flourishes today and has acquired a younger partner, 'Words and Pictures', seen in action in the first chapter; while radio has now no less than three series of 'Listening and Reading' contributing at different ages to this same field of experience.

The essence of learning to read (as I have suggested in discussin 'Television Club') is confidence, and the spur of adequate motivation. Television can provide the motivation by basing the experience of reading on an exciting story, specially written and specially shot, with child hero and heroine of course. In 'Look and Read' the story unfolds in short episodes; between them, words which are of key importance in the reading scheme are examined, pulled to bits and reconstructed through animations.

For the encouragement of reading television has further outstanding assets. It is associated with home and entertainment; it therefore suggests enjoyment and not the drudgery that slow learners have often associated with reading. It is, moreover, the medium of learning most common among ordinary people at home – children and adults alike; so children are used to it and feel it more 'natural' than books. Then, some children are backward readers partly because their experience is too limited to give meaning to what they read: the filmed TV story helps to make up this deficiency. Again, television itself holds attention because of the luminous screen and movement. In particular, the various techniques used in the teaching sections of 'Look and Read' focus attention to a degree impossible with blackboard or books; animation especially, as used in the programmes, is often both surprising and amusing. Finally television, given the essential co-operation of the teacher, can work with groups of ten to twenty children, whereas the teacher doing similar work on her own would have to concentrate on one or two only at a time; while the backward children themselves, far from being the butts of their peers, gain prestige by being a group selected for special television lessons.

The planning of the teaching element requires of course the co-operation of an expert: we have been lucky to have the outstanding services of Dr Joyce Morris for this. Its execution calls for much ingenuity and for adroit timing. As for the story, it

needs to be not only exciting but as carefully researched and prepared as any documentary. Here is Andrée Molyneux, producer
of 'Joe and the Sheep Rustlers', one of the more recent stories in
the series, describing how she went about this:

I wanted a new background, which would provide more than a back
drop, for an exciting tale to keep them reading from beginning to end;
a background which would be full of valuable leads to further classroom
work. Not just reading work, but all kinds of project work across subject
divisions. A farming story, perhaps? All kids love animals, and now
there are many kids in the cities who have never seen a cow, never
touched a sheep or seen piglets. We would remedy this and make them
curious about life in the country. But we wouldn't do it in a middle-
class 'the wonderful country life' style. We would do it in an area where
town and country are permanently cheek by jowl. In the north west,
where the factory chimneys grow up taller than the tallest trees and out
on the moors, 15 miles from the nearest town, you touch the grass and
your hand is striped with soot. Halifax, Hebden Bridge, the outskirts of
Rochdale, Todmorden – yes, above all, Todmorden, where the factory
smoke rises from the valley to beautiful hillsides and farms that are
isolated by snow in even the mildest winter.

So on a cold January week-end we took a writer who had worked
before for 'Look and Read' and other school series round the farms up
there, and with him we talked to the farmers, talked even to the rustlers;
and the true tales we were told and the humorous incidents we heard
were woven into the plot by Leonard Kingston. The farming had to be
right. A local farmer was wonderfully co-operative and for a very
modest fee appeared almost every day to help, advise, assist. So we were
able to include a sheep shearing sequence in which the farmer played
the part of a travelling sheep shearer, and Leonard wrote the script so
that he hardly spoke at all, and made it dramatic to boot. The shire
horses were our farmer's own. The horse which our heroine rode was
provided by a local man who had done television and film work before,
and was wonderful. A champion shepherd provided Sweep the sheep
dog, taught the hero the whistles and gave him useful tips about the
way to behave. We knew we were all right because as we filmed our
actors doing jobs around the farm there was frequently the most expert
of audiences looking on – the farmer's friends and relations. An admiring
audience: 'Oh, he does take the part good, that Joe'; 'He looks a real
farm lad'. The actors were all either Northerners or at least committed
to the idea of the story and the principles behind it. Joe used to help the

farmer on his days off from filming and Jill used to go riding for pleasure. It's important to make everything you print in a reading series *worth* reading.

A bolt from the American blue

While 'Look and Read' was cutting its teeth the Plowden Report,[1] surveying the field of Primary education, was published. Its findings did not seem to call for immediate new initiatives on school broadcasting's part; but one of its main recommendations, a substantial increase in nursery school provision, was within a few years to be reverberating with some force in our counsels. If the Plowden Report furnished the powder for this, the spark was applied by a meteor from the USA, 'Sesame Street'.

'Sesame Street' was produced by 'Children's Workshop' in the USA as a contribution to a nationally sponsored project known as 'Headstart', which was designed to give pre-school children in disadvantaged circumstances the opportunity to start school more on a level with their more privileged peers. In particular, it aimed to compensate for the often deplorable living conditions and very limited backgrounds of young children growing up in the central areas of large cities. Statutory schooling begins in the US at age six, a year later than here; so 'Sesame Street' had no compunctions about including quite a strong (and rather old-fashioned) teaching element aimed at interesting, even drilling, children in letters, word-building and number. Equally strong, however, was its emphasis on social education: its setting achieved an atmosphere which reflected American folksiness at its more engaging, while steering well clear of cosiness or condescension.

Most remarkable, however, were its pace, its humour, its verve, and the great variety of brilliant techniques it used to sustain interest and carry young viewers along with it (it was a daily programme, and each transmission lasted a full hour, not to mention Saturday's jumbo repeat: five hours off the reel). It was highly professional; confident in the virtue of its products, it cheerfully espoused the 'hard sell', but being produced for 'public service'

[1] 'Children and their Primary Schools': a report of the Central Advisory Council for Education (England), HMSO, 1967.

television it was also quite free from shoddy commercialism. Among the contemptible products which pass for children's entertainment on the big US networks, it stood like a beacon light.

When shown to interested people abroad, 'Sesame Street' was accompanied by a blaze of publicity and a keen anticipation of added prestige from exposure on foreign networks. German television bought it and re-vamped it to make its own version, 'Sesame Strasse'. Some who saw it in England said 'Why don't you put it on here?'; many more, 'Why don't you put on something like that?'

We all enjoyed and admired 'Sesame Street'; but direct transfer to BBC, as part of either School Television's output or that of the department responsible for children's out-of-school programmes, was never on the map. First, the programme's background and idiom were of course American; and one might surely question without being accused of chauvinism whether this alone did not rule it out as an educational contribution to British children of so tender an age. There were doubts, too, about its educational approach. As one of our consultants said,

'Sesame Street', and possible imitators in this country, would present a serious challenge to the professional judgement of our teachers, basically because it raises the issue of the permissible or desirable degree of structured conditioning as an educational method, contrasted with methods more concerned with provoking thought and appreciation.

As for doing likewise, our first thought on the production side was that 'Sesame Street' was very expensive and anything similar would leave an unacceptably yawning hole in our anticipated departmental budgets. An equally powerful brake was the belief that once you started feeding very young children a diet of high-key, hard-sell programmes they would end up by being unable to respond to quieter, simpler ones. America loves to dramatise its educational crises and acclaim the brilliant novelties which might seem, in part, to resolve them: we tread more warily, with eyes on the long haul. 'Blue Peter', first launched in 1958, is alive still, and kicking, and perpetually renewable – and renewed. So is 'Play School', born in 1964; so, in School TV, is 'Watch!' (for six-year-olds), started in 1967.

Moreover, at that time the Plowden Report's recommendation of more nursery schools had not yet, except to some extent in the designated 'Educational Priority Areas', been translated into action: this had to await Mrs Thatcher's White Paper on 'Education: a Framework for Expansion' in 1972. My own belief was that School TV should not embark on educational programmes for children under five until there was evidence of substantial new man-power being directed to the task of nursery school expansion; for at this level of education, above all, there is no substitute for trained staff in generous numbers: nothing less could begin to compensate for early deprivation. Given such action, television could well come in as a useful additional resource; but to imagine that television on its own can make inroads into the problem is in my view chimerical. 'Children's Workshop' had high hopes that 'Sesame Street' would do this; indeed they made plausible claims that it was doing so: dispassionate observers greeted the claims with scepticism. So far from narrowing the gap between privileged and underprivileged, I fear television can only increase it: good programmes, whatever their primary target, will always offer the lucky with the built-in headstart more which they can turn to their advantage than the less fortunate will find in them. This is not to argue against television, of course; sources of experience that can help all, no matter if in varying degrees, are to be fostered and cherished, not rejected. It is simply to reiterate what everyone who has worked in educational broadcasting knows: that the context in which the experience is received is as important as the experience itself.

'Playtime' and 'You and Me'

Once there was the assurance that the basic needs of increasing numbers of children would be met through the provision of more nursery school places, it was time to start planning a contribution from broadcasting. Of course, we hoped that this would reach young viewers and listeners not only in nursery classes, but in playgroups also, and indeed in any situation where an adult was present with a child or children, including the family group in the home: these would be, therefore, the first 'school broadcasts' where we were consciously seeking to involve parents as well as teachers. But it is in the nature of things that adequately disciplined viewing or listening is most likely to take place, and creative work to ensue, where there are trained staff to guide it—however informal the circumstances; so nursery classes would be the primary target.

Thus School Radio's 'Playtime' came on the air in September 1973, closely followed by TV's 'You and Me', which has three programmes a week (of twelve minutes each, not an hour!). 'Playtime' has a group of children from a local nursery class in the studio who can respond freely to a rich variety of songs and games for movement; of stories, sounds, rhythms and poems, offered to them (and simultaneously of course to the unseen listeners) by a regular presenter, Judy Bennett. Even within the studio class, there is a lot of individuality in response: I watched a West Indian toughie majestically striding out his own movement game, superbly oblivious of his English classmates. Perhaps he knew the score in the Kingston test match.

'You and Me', as always with television, calls for more elaborate preparation and involves greater hazards, if the real potential of the medium is to be exploited. I asked Claire Chovil, who took charge of it when it was no more than a glint in anyone's eye, and saw it through its early productions, to recall some of her thoughts about its opportunities and problems during the year of its gestation: a kind of diary, perhaps. Here is what she wrote:

You begin with a very clear idea of what you want—but it's like a view from the top of a hill a few hours before it's going to rain. It's a fantastically clear landscape, full of colour and detail. Everything appears solid—you know it so well you think you could touch the hedges and pick up the houses and replant them. The light is very even—in fact it's being sucked away into the clouds, but you don't know that. And when they've really got into position, the view from the top of the hill is blurred by rain, the mist hangs in patches among the trees and the hedge corners, and everything that seemed clear and near becomes distant and obscure. So with your new series: you have that clear view, but as soon as you start to research and do the ground-work, you realise it was foolish to be so certain, because there are things to consider which are not really at all clear, but you hadn't noticed. You progress from a false clarity into a confusion of ideas and impressions, and try to fight back to simplicity.

So I would never keep a diary about work. It would be a record of hesitations, doubts, contradictions, circular arguments, and occasionally a hop forward – confused like tracks in the snow round a bird-table. Looking back over the year, it's impossible to remember how one's thought went. So this is nothing more than the recollection of a few land-marks. For example:

Middle-class obsession Everyone said that of course the programmes must not be middle-class. As easy as that. No posh voices, no smart surroundings, no experiences that might be beyond the understanding of a deprived city child. It still sounds easy. Actors with good diction and southern voices are out, kitchens with modern equipment and chrome fittings will be suspect, children should only be called Billy, Tom and Anne, not Jason, Julian and Nicola.

Woods are outside the experience of some children, so woods are middle-class. It's such a mixture of truth and nonsense; if you carry it to its extreme you end up twitching because even birthdays seem middle-class; if you ignore it you end up with pretty ladies in long skirts and everything is cosy. But one thing we have learned is that many enlightened radicals have an astonishingly Dickensian stereotype of so-called working-class people, which ignores the fact that nearly all of us aspire in some way in our clothes, furniture, cars, hairstyles, to look as if we could fit in to the consumer society.

For the record, Jason is a popular name because television made it so. There was a hero-figure on ITV about 6 years ago, called Jason King.

Asking Questions Right from the beginning it seemed clear that programmes should include repeated sequences, with a chance for children to answer questions, and thereby start putting thoughts and ideas into words. It's much more difficult to devise questions than one ever suspected. Questions that have the answer 'yes' or 'no' stop any attempt at self-expression. Questions that ask for factual information or recall are not much better. We're told by the consultant that children won't respond to that kind of bombardment.

So how can you ask the questions in terms of real curiosity, giving the impression you're not too sure of the answer? 'I wonder' . . . 'do you think' . . . 'can you tell me'. Certain phrases become over-worked quickly. In the end, it's what you choose to ask as much as how you ask it that matters. There's a temptation to ask too obvious questions.

Puppets Pre-school programmes are groaning with puppets – as if the young cannot take any kind of information unless it is squeaked at them by something with a funny face. I like puppets – in their place – but it

'You and Me'

was hard to think of any which wouldn't seem borrowed from another show, or have the same sort of intensive jollity as a garden gnome. We argued about this constantly. Someone said there should be two puppets—a crocodile and a rat, I think. Someone else said 'Domestic animals. What animals do children have?' We went from a hamster to a dog to a cat, to a mouse, to a canary, a tortoise, and back again to a hamster. 'Fur is difficult', said the puppet-maker, so we went round and round again, and almost decided on the tortoise. But the hamster seemed a rounder personality so she was chosen in the end. The crow evolved in much the same way—from a crow to a dog, to a frog, to a duck, and back to a crow. He seemed right for someone omniscient about out of doors.

The function of the puppets evolved too. They were light relief at first—toy substitutes. Then they began to creep into draft scripts as scene-setters. They started to ask each other questions, display ignorance about each other's milieu, to insult each other, in a mild way, for being ignorant. Last of all, we realised they could tell the Mums what the programme was to be about. It took us even longer to realise that they are really the presenters—the regular point of reference. I hated them at first, but they're in residence now.

Filming Filming with a four-year-old may have its problems—but although we tell ourselves this before the event, we're not really quite sure what they will be, or quite how to solve them in film terms. We worry about a child's powers of concentration, access to lavatories, frightening him with a microphone that has to be strapped round his waist; strange people, noisy unknown surroundings. All these things are true, but even worse is the deadening effect of lining up camera shots, the slowness of lugging heavy equipment round, in this case, the supermarket. We have written lines—and a story. They hang like a lead albatross round the neck of the actress. She has to get the lines out some-how, to channel the child's interest into doing what the story says, not what he wants to do.

Learning from this we don't write elaborate 'plotty' stories any more. It is better to think up a situation—buying carrots, making a parcel, visiting a wood, that will illustrate your concept; tell the adult who's appearing with the child the questions you want asked, so that he really understands the idea—and then see what happens. Sometimes, the children will supply better lines than you could ever dream up. But you need two cameras shooting together to catch the good bits. So much for the unspoken belief among those who dish the money out that because children are smaller the budgets can be smaller too.

Piloting   Three programmes have been made—samples of the intended output for each day of the week—Monday, Wednesday, Friday. They have to be tried out with groups of children, so that we can see where things have gone wrong—or indeed if anything has gone right. Different sorts of audiences are waiting for our visits—nursery class, children at home, play-groups, etc. We go to the first, a nursery class in an Educational Priority Area. Predictably the projector fuses, and children play a circle game while we mend it. When everyone sits down, it is obvious that the adults—lecturer, teachers, nursery assistants, and programme-makers—are all very apprehensive. What strange beast is about to be unleashed? Will the children be totally bored, confused, uncomprehending? We forget that of all viewers in the room the children are probably the most habituated. Television is a way of life, life-long, not a habit acquired late in life. The children respond to the presenter, they answer questions, they comment, they concentrate for twelve minutes. There are all sorts of things that need altering in the pilots—but the fact remains you can get the attention of a four-year-old with real-life material, you can get him talking to a television set.

Born in travail, like all new series; and the simpler it looks when you see it, the more the travail.

'You and Me' and 'Playtime' are primarily for children below the age of compulsory school. But they are no doubt being used in some Infant classes too. When one adds them to the store of broadcasts already available to five and six-year-olds: on BBC TV, 'Watch!' and 'Words and Pictures', and more on ITV; on BBC radio, two 'Movement and Music' series, 'The Music Box', 'A Corner for Music', 'Let's Join In', 'Poetry Corner', and 'Listening and Reading', it is remarkable to reflect that in the early years of broadcasting the new medium was thought to have nothing to offer educationally to children so young. Infants' Schools are as enthusiastic to listen and view, and as rewarding to broadcast to, as any in our clientèle; and if broadcasting can doubtfully give headstarts, it can certainly help ensure that the early years of school are rich in imaginative experience.

This section has a postscript which after our coolness towards 'Sesame Street' may seem ironical. In its wake, the American 'Children's Workshop' produced 'The Electric Company', designed to help with reading; as brilliant as 'Sesame Street' in its ideas and its execution and also, being intended for older children, more sophisticated. BBC School TV will be putting it on next year, for illiterates in the secondary schools. We have no prejudices, you see; just good judgment, we confidently hope.

4 A STORY OF PARTNERSHIP

4.1 Council and programme committees

If BBC School Broadcasting is able to respond with enthusiasm and sensitivity to the major challenges which confront it, this is due to the skills of its producers and the sense of purpose which animates them. Equally, it derives from the closeness of the relationship which the BBC has been able to establish and maintain with the world of education at large. The relationship is manifested, at the policy-making level, in the constitution and the proceedings of the School Broadcasting Council and its Programme Committees (outlined in Appendix A); at the day-to-day working level, primarily through the activities of the Council's Education Officers in the field. Both the major post-war Government Committees of Inquiry into Broadcasting (Beveridge, 1951; Pilkington, 1962) have commended the success of the partnership: if the compliment is deserved, the success will not have been achieved without imagination and forbearance on both sides, for both are jealous of their independence. It is time to look at the BBC's partners in action, beginning with the Council and its Committees, and with the earlier days of school broadcasting.

The earlier decades

We have seen how the 'listening-end' inquiry conducted in Kent in 1927 told a number of home truths about the early broadcasts and the response of teachers and children to them; and how new ways of using the Fourth R were developed in consequence. Additionally, the Kent Inquiry convinced the BBC of two things: first, that a sustained study of the response to school broadcasts was indispensable if they were to make their mark; second, that a permanent body representing the world of education was needed to guide the service and commend it to practising teachers. Moreover, the guidance was to have teeth to it: there would be a Council with mandatory, not merely advisory powers, and an adequate staff in support.

The creation of this Council,[1] involving the abrogation by the BBC of a small piece of its cherished independence, was judicious. It has helped to protect the BBC from public controversy in an area where this would doubtfully have had any constructive effects. It has put the Council in turn under an obligation to use with great discretion its power to impose guide-lines and, in the last resort, to withhold sponsorship. It was an action designed to last; and so it has, in all its essentials, to this day.

Councils of this sort have to embody the idea of a represent-ative democracy. They must also operate in a way which will command the respect of those whose work is affected by their decisions: in this case, BBC producers. The double obligation was neatly met by making the Council itself predominantly a body of representative members appointed by educational organ-isations; and creating Programme Committees, through which the Council chiefly worked, composed of men and women chosen for the contribution they could make as individuals working at the educational coalface. Thus the Council, while rarely exercis-ing its mandatory powers except in a formal sense, could stand as the symbol of education's concern with broadcasting, and broad-casting's with education; while its committees could bring their personal experience to bear on the job of determining priorities, and hoist the red flag if they saw a serious danger of programme plans being unrealistic.

Experience has shown that these are normally the limits of an external Committee's useful functions in the business of pro-gramme building. Good programmes cannot be made by com-mittees; and devising appropriate machinery for a Council with mandatory powers meant, among other things, removing from its committees the temptation to try to do this. This was one of the lessons learnt from the experience of the 1930s. The Kent Inquiry had rightly emphasised the need for a more intimate

[1] The Central Council for School Broadcasting; reorganised in 1947 as The School Broad-casting Council for the United Kingdom (with parallel Councils for Scotland and Wales).

association between educationists and programme makers: the Council's committees were therefore constituted on the basis of subject specialisms, so that experts in each subject field could be involved in programme planning. In the early days, these might include people subsequently taking part in the detailed work of programme creation, and the Committee members also vetted, and made frequent comments on, drafts of the pamphlets which accompanied many of the broadcast series. But the expansion of the service into new fields soon threatened a proliferation of subject committees; moreover, valuable and stimulating as they often were, the system tended to create frustration because their function was too closely interlocked with that of the BBC producers: there would be excessive discussion of detail, insufficient standing back to reflect on larger issues. Experts in any case are rarely unanimous, so that changes in committee membership could result in capricious shifts in programme policy. The BBC can call in specialist experts when it comes to programme making: what is required of the Council's committees is a more broadly based educational judgment, applied to a store of information culled by their officers from the receiving end of the broadcasts.

This was an important conclusion of a review of the Council's machinery made soon after the war; a revised constitution and an enrichment of the Council's field staff duly reflected it. The Programme Committees now embodied expertise not in particular subjects, but in the educational needs of children at particular stages of school life. This ensured a broader perspective on programme plans, and was very much in tune with the shift in educational thinking generally from subject-centred to child-centred education. Moreover, to protect producers from possibly arbitrary judgments on programme plans, programme series were commissioned by the committees only after they had discussed detailed reports from the Council's Senior Education Officer, and then in terms which laid down broad objectives only. At a later meeting, when producers' plans for implementing these commissions were examined, outright rejection was in order only if they could be shown not to conform to the relevant commission; though members were also empowered to make 'suggestions', which if widely endorsed naturally carried considerable weight.

This marked a step forward; and over the years there were many civilised discussions on the larger issues of programme policy, if rarely that special spark of animation which gives a creative edge to the business of decision making. But discussion of producers' plans was often jejune, since the 'plan' for any single programme would often consist at this stage of a title only, supplemented perhaps by a few words from the producer on how he thought the topic would probably be treated (in several months' time, and in collaboration with a scriptwriter not yet engaged). Sometimes the old specialist committees were missed, not least by those producers who enjoyed the possibility of really picking the brains of fellow-specialists, or tilting a lance with them. For under the new system, a committee member would have to be very tough and persuasive to convince his colleagues, in the face of the producer's demurral, that the programme under discussion could not possibly 'conform with the commission' (for instance, that it would certainly not be suitable for thirteen–fifteen-year-olds of varying intelligence in Secondary Modern Schools). Such a member might well feel that to earn his lunch he should be able, if not to find chinks in a producer's armour, at least to be contributing more actively to keeping him 'on the right lines'; and the 'right lines' being enshrined in commissions, these tended to become over-elaborate, until members themselves felt cramped by the straightjackets they had helped to create (one member who chaired a committee with great distinction for several years always referred to the commissions as if they came from God). The rules of the game had become too obtrusive; and in an operation so professionally engineered by Council and BBC staff in concert, the amateur in broadcasting, as committee members felt themselves to be, seemed to have little scope.

For the newly appointed member the scene was, after all, fairly daunting. A mass of paper would reach him a week or so before the meeting. With little time to digest it or consult colleagues at all, he would arrive at Broadcasting House and take his place in the semicircular Council Chamber. Behind him, the portrait of Lord Reith, patriarchal and steely-eyed, flanked by successor Directors-General of the BBC: facing him, on either side of the Chairman, BBC Departmental Heads and producers to the left,

Council officers to the right – a formidable array, expounding, cajoling him to utterance, sometimes mysteriously sparring velvet-gloved between themselves in the hope, could he but realise it, that he might contribute to resolving some passionate disagreement between them. No wonder one of the qualifications for committee membership, as the staff saw it, was a willingness to stick one's neck out. A member who can sense this climate and find his way to make a constructive contribution within it, as so many have, does more than a little to make the partnership a reality.

The Committees in action in recent years

The 1960s saw some loosening-up of committee procedure, now too formalised properly to reflect the marked degree of confidence which over the years had developed between the partners. With the addition of TV and radiovision, school broadcasting's much enlarged output imposed on the committees the need to be selective in the programme plans they reviewed each year; while the surge of curriculum development schemes opened up new broadcasting opportunities in which the creation and trial of experimental programmes or series often preceded the formulation of specific policies, and gave the committees plenty of interest to chew on. Simultaneously, the new freedom in the discussion of controversial, and of delicate social and moral, issues which was pervading society generally was being echoed in the schools also, but to very varying degrees; divergencies of view on acceptable levels of forthrightness, realism or sophistication in school programmes became much more frequent; and the programme committees, inevitably and very properly, became often involved in such questions.

This involvement sharpened a dilemma which had always been there, but hitherto mainly latent: in sponsoring the service of school broadcasts, just what was the Council taking responsibility for? It had always been accepted that the BBC was responsible for 'presentation' and the Council for programme 'policy'; but the Council's committees had also concerned themselves with its interpretation, and that in considerable detail. Where does the interpretation of policy end and presentation begin? No one can say, of course. What is obvious is that no Council could underwrite, in the sense of accepting responsibility for, every single one of the hundreds of programmes broadcast annually under its banner; and no doubt programmes go out, from time to time, which some committee members would have been unwilling to approve as broadcast had they had the opportunity to preview them. Should the committees therefore preview those programmes which they consider are bound to tread delicate ground? To deny them this right would be to destroy public confidence in the service; but by the same token, for them to invoke it more than very occasionally, and with the willing assent of the production department concerned, would be to declare confidence in the executants of that service already undermined. It would, indeed, be to impinge on the acknowledged responsibilities of the production staff; for who, after seeing or hearing a programme, can forbear to voice his opinion on 'presentation' as well as 'content'; and how can such opinions, if endorsed even tacitly by others, be simply flouted by reasonable people?

'Reasonable people', I believe, epitomises the climate which successive Chairmen of Programme Committees have successfully created as the background to their members' decision-making job. It will not always seem so, of course, at the time. To a producer, intensively engaged on a current series and simultaneously preparing plans for a fresh one, getting those plans agreed by a committee may seem like having to surmount an uncomfortable hurdle unreasonably early. Many will at some time, at least in television with its greater production hazards, have had to weave some impeccable phrases of intent together with some hopeful 'e.g.s' (not all for certain realisable) into a paper of programme plans which leaves as many options as possible still open. Yet the discipline of having to clear one's thoughts, if partially only and prematurely, is usually salutary; and at the other extreme, a producer who has an original idea clearly formulated in his mind, and can speak to it with an enthusiasm passionate or temperate according to his assessment of the atmosphere, will rarely fail to win the committee to it.

A committee decision may seem perverse at the time but prove wise in the event. When French in Primary Schools was catching on fast, there was naturally committee discussion about a contribution from TV, as well as radio. Opinions were mixed – not so much about TV's potential as about the validity of the new impulse itself. I thought the production staff might help resolve the impasse if I got a pilot made, on a modest budget, illustrating the kind of studio-based series we might do to run through the year, if asked. My producer (he went on later to co-produce Kenneth Clark's 'Civilisation') made a very imaginative programme with a space-travel story line engagingly presented by Shusha, the Persian folk singer, whose French is impeccable: it had the blemishes inevitable in a hastily done experimental job but, I thought, great potential. But the committee turned it down flat: it lacked the one element they considered so essential – the flavour of the 'real France'. In vain I argued that for young children a strong story was the prime necessity; and that to shoot an acted story on location in France was a very expensive undertaking. A single term would cost as much as a year's studio programmes – and a single term would be a *bonne bouche* only, not a key contribution to schools' work. In that case, they replied, let us have a single term's TV, shot in France. The series they got in the event *(La Chasse au Trésor,* produced by Ronald Smedley) was splendid on both counts – a rip-roaring story and a most evocative French ambiance. It enhanced our reputation among modern linguists. But the use made of it, in quantity and still more in quality, was disappointing. So – and here lay part of the wisdom of the committee's decision – it could be quietly dropped after serving its small band of enthusiasts, without our having induced schools to build TV into their courses as a major element, only suddenly to leave them in the lurch by dropping out. Thus the Committee's doubts about this educational development on anything like a universal scale, and therefore about the case for strong and continuing support from TV, were faithfully reflected in the outcome. The wave of often undiscriminating enthusiasm for Primary School French which swelled in the 60s was a case of educational fashion getting the upper hand of really sound curricular development, and a most important job of the School Broadcasting Council's committees is to distinguish between the two. Not so easy these days.

On that occasion costs came into the debate, at least in a general way. They rarely do this, as the committees have no control over budgets: they simply have to be warned off if what they are asking for is manifestly beyond what the production departments have or can expect to get—and that is a sum which is never spelled out to them. It is remarkable really that decision-making bodies placed in this position should have contrived so consistently to achieve most of what they wanted, if not at once, then within two or three years. This has meant forbearance on their part, and a real willingness on the BBC's not only to act on decisions made, but to take note of the context in which they are made. Early in the 60s the broadcast provision in secondary school Science was reviewed. The Senior Education Officer's report suggested that the TV series 'Science & Life', after a six-year run in which those enthusiastic pioneers, Professor W. S. Bullough and Arthur Garratt, had distinguished themselves as presenters, was now, with the honeymoon period of school TV over, attempting to cater for too wide an audience: fresh planning was recommended. The BBC's response was to offer, as alternatives, a series supplementing the work of the abler and more motivated pupils, and assuming a fully-qualified specialist teacher; or one which set itself to interest the duller pupils, with probably less well-qualified teachers, in the science of everyday life. The committee plumped for the second, but by a narrow margin only. A couple of years later the BBC was able to come up with a plan to meet the other need as well.

The committee system, then, usefully ensures that worthwhile ideas which cannot be implemented at once remain in the pipeline and do not automatically have to defer to fresh enthusiasms which are sure to crop up meanwhile. The corollary is also true: that committee members tend to be conservative, reluctant to drop a tried series (especially if cherished in some member's own school) for something new and unproven, even if attractive— unless it stems directly from the recommendations of a substantial review. Fair enough: it is the business of a committee to be sceptical also: to suggest that the schools—and the BBC—can survive without that particular novelty. It will depend on their sense of the climate in the schools themselves. Each time TV has moved down the age scale—from ten-year-olds to eight, from eight to six, from six to four and five—there has been palpable resistance among some members of the committees concerned; for Primary

Schools since the war have been confident of their values and of the methods they have developed to foster these, jealous of inroads on precious time, and wary therefore of possibly superficial distractions. Whereas for teachers of young school leavers, less confident that their utmost efforts were bearing fruit, the widest possible choice of new stimuli has always been welcome.

Do Programme Committees then never take the initiative in proposing new departures? Indeed they do, and for being fairly rare these initiatives can have a useful shock effect, especially if they disturb conventional wisdom about the limitations, or the proper educational role, of the media. I can well remember the moment when, in the middle of a discussion of various sophisticated contributions TV might make to maths studies, a member suddenly said: 'This is all very well, but I haven't properly qualified teachers to handle my bread and butter A level work. Why can't you do something for me?' And carried the committee with him. We reeled a bit: broadcasting as a teacher substitute offended ingrained instincts; and we had come to regard exams as things schools no doubt had to do something about , but on their own, thank you, leaving us free to concentrate on loftier objectives. Yet the proposition had the spice of a challenge, and one where we could assume, from relatively mature students, relatively high motivation. The outcome was ninety-six programmes, over five terms, of Pure Mathematics, expounded by a Sixth Form teacher whose studio equipment was half a dozen blackboards, a sprinkling of more sophisticated visuals, and countless pieces of chalk. It certainly enlarged our perspectives on what BBC television might attempt.

Committees and Council

To sum up, then, on the role of Programme Committees: they can be reasonably detached judges, and occasionally effective initiators, of policy; they can contribute to that element of continuity which makes school broadcasting a genuine *service* to schools; and they do, by their sponsorship of that service, bear witness to the educational world that the basis on which the programmes are devised and prepared is educationally valid. While committees cannot help producers' creative processes, they are a useful sounding board of a type which if it did not exist already the production departments would probably feel the need to invent. So to the producers and, I think, the members themselves the Programme Committees have proved at worst acceptable; at best stimulating and enjoyable. But since their members speak as individuals, and although each committee includes an LEA official and an HMI, they do not carry a collective weight in the world of education at large; and the Council itself, which might in theory do so, is in practice insufficiently involved in policy making and programme building to develop much missionary sense of school broadcasting's potential. The Council has, indeed, always been a rather large body for effective debate; and until the late sixties, when its very formal Executive Committee was replaced by a Steering Committee with broader terms of reference, there were few occasions on which it really came to grips with larger issues of policy transcending the individual responsibilities of the Programme Committees.

Still less would Council members ever take the initiative in calling for a major new broadcasting venture in association with some important new educational development, discuss it, and conclude by instructing the relevant Programme Committee to get on with it. To purists in the workings of representative democracy this will appear a weakness, and perhaps it is; but the Council's forbearance has certainly made the effective operation of the partnership easier. For good broadcasts cannot be made to order: the timing of any new departure will depend on the necessary resources being available for it and the right person at hand to plan and produce it, and these may take as much as a couple of years to work towards. So it is more practical, even if also more comfortable, that such decisions should remain primarily in the hands of the BBC's production departments, provided of course these are sensitive to reasonable degrees of pressure.

In terms of its function as a pressure group operating in two directions—on the BBC on behalf of the schools, and on the educational world on behalf of the BBC's contribution to schools —the Council has, I think, been more successful at the first task than at the second; perhaps because it cannot escape appearing to some, despite its considerable independence of the BBC, as the BBC's creature as well as its creation. No machinery could, of course, be devised which 'represented the educational world' in a way which spoke with force to each and every member of that world; yet the impression, at least from inside the BBC, has often been that among the big battalions of education – the Ministry and the LEAs especially – school broadcasting speaks with a more muted voice than its relevance to the practicalities of educational need, and its actual following at the grass roots of education, seem to justify.

This could be simply the cry of an insider chagrined that all do not cherish him as much as he would like. It could just reflect the fact that school broadcasts, even though many have been available as more permanent recordings also, seemed at least until recently ephemeral things, transmitted at times when people are busy, so that many only knew them at second or third hand: they did not experience them in a way which galvanises to action. But it could also suggest that the partnership of broadcasting and education, while indeed harmonious in that the couple indulge in quite a warm embrace under the eye of Lord Reith, has not yet acquired the thrust to assault the power-houses of the education business.

It may be they are beginning to do so: that the hunger for 'resource material' which new approaches to curriculum building evoke will spell the end of polite nods of recognition towards broadcasting and a determination, instead, to make possible its full exploitation. Present activities, indeed, point in that direction; and if there is real progress by the time the next government Committee of Inquiry on Broadcasting reports, then the partnership can indeed be pronounced successful. Until then, I would call the pair just 'happily married', reserving 'success' for the day when they really are bringing home the bacon.

4.2 In the field

Committees with the wide-ranging responsibilities I have described need to be well serviced, and they are. Papers outlining specific programme proposals are, as we have seen, presented by the producers concerned: those which underlie the Committee's policy decisions are the responsibility of the Council's Senior

Education Officer, who is appointed (as are his colleagues) to the BBC's staff and seconded thence to the service of the School Broadcasting Council. In compiling these papers he draws on a number of sources. His Research Officer supplies him with information based on questionnaires to samples of schools: sometimes statistical information giving details of listening and viewing over the whole range of broadcast series; sometimes reports on special enquiries in specific fields, which give scope for teachers' comments also. The Senior Education Officer will also have reports of any specialists' conferences which may have been convened centrally or locally; he will have correspondence from teachers direct; and he will draw of course on any pertinent educational publications. Above all, he will have reports from his Education Officer colleagues in the field; some presenting a regional picture of educational development generally in a particular subject-area, some describing in detail (we had examples in the last chapter) the impact of particular broadcasts, the circumstances in which they were received, and the use made of them.

The Council's Education Officers do, of course, a great deal more than service the Council's Committees through their chief. They are indeed the prime agents of the partnership which is the subject of this chapter; for as members of BBC staff their knowledge of broadcasting, and of the whole range of its output to schools, is comprehensive, while their day-to-day work in the field keeps them in continual contact with schoolchildren, teachers and educationists of every kind. The 'field' is of course the whole of the United Kingdom: the Council's Education Officers number a score, and have their bases in the major cities. A permanent service on this scale in support of school broadcasting is unique in the world: its work deserves therefore a closer look.

BBC Education Officers in schools

The first BBC Education Officers were appointed in the early 30s as a direct result of the recommendations stemming from the 'Kent Inquiry'. Their job was—and still in a measure is—to be the 'eyes and ears' of producers at the testing point: the receiving end of school broadcasts; and to provide an objective, and some-

times unwelcome, view of just what happened there. The detail
is as important to the producer as the summarised impression;
the incentive given to an individual child as significant as a
class's general response; so he will particularly welcome comment of this nature:

It was noticeable that not only the very swish model Hovercraft attracted their interest, but also the much simpler design made by children.
This latter had prompted a boy in another class, who had seen an earlier
transmission, to try to make one himself at home. True, he didn't cut
any vent in the top of his brown paper model, so the air could not be
drawn into the fan . . . But he had tried to produce something on his
own, and in the light of what it did not do his design would be modified
by his group in class. He had at least learned that he could reverse the
direction in which his fan rotated by switching the terminals on his pair
of batteries.

As he builds up experience of the impact and the use made of a
particular series, the Education Officer will broaden his perspectives on it to take in wider questions of policy. We have noted
how the highly structured TV series 'Discovering Science' gave
place to the more flexible 'Science all Around' and 'Exploring
Science'. Here is an Education Officer commenting on two
parallel radio series:

Once again, one is made aware that with a tightly structured series like
'Junior Science' the children are at least regularly confronted with a
pattern of logical scientific thinking and some form of cumulative
effect throughout the school year; whereas the broader techniques of
a series like 'Discovery', which places far greater stress on the scientific
ability of the class teacher, runs the very great danger of being completely at the mercy of inadequate practitioners.

Here the Education Officer feels constrained to throw his weight
on the side of conservatism, and indeed it is often his duty to do
so; for he visits all sorts and conditions of schools, and he knows
that it is only the exceptional school, not the average one, which
is able to provide ideal conditions for the exploitation of broadcasts inspired by the more forward-looking and sophisticated
educational ideas.

Equally, when he finds himself in a school which seems to point to the shape of things to come, he will speculate on its implications:

It seems that where a number of small TV sets have been put to use in an open plan school (as here), pupils themselves will decide when to dip in and out of programmes; and this could result in a demand for broadcasts in five-minute sections, each on a number of discrete, but loosely coordinated topics. Over the weeks when a child, or group of children, was engaged on a particular project, he would wish to seek out broadcast contributions bearing on this project; and we would need to provide a termly subject-index: for instance, under the heading 'boats' a list of the dates and times when pupils would have to tune in to find information about boats on TV or radio.

Open plan schools, integrated days, group project work and several small TV sets take us a long way from the more conventional – and more usual – picture of a Primary School at work with which I started this book: but times change, and every change brings new problems for school broadcasting to which Education Officers cannot but be sensitive.

'Advanced' teaching methods may bring an Education Officer into situations where he feels that broadcasts are getting less than their fair chance of exercising their full potential. In our next school, the visiting Education Officer had come across an interesting and sophisticated example of team teaching, applied to the study of the USA and involving the use of a variety of audio-visual materials. Each week one of the teachers would make a carefully composed 'presentation' of a key topic, drawing on a number of such materials including the BBC TV series 'USA '72'. Subsequently the topic would be pursued in greater detail by the pupils, working in smaller groups. After observing the 'presentation', the Education Officer tape-recorded a discussion which he had with two of the teachers (one a Canadian):

E.O. May I now take you on to the question of broadcasts? What is your justification for using them? What special contribution do you expect them to make to this work?

HER A Pupil interest of course. Various visual aids of course stimulate children in different ways, but broadcast material more so; it's relevant and it's immediate.

TEACHER B I think it creates a different atmosphere. It can be very dramatic, a broadcast, and you can take that point and carry it through.

E.O. You particularly like broadcasts which make a powerful impact, then, do you?

TEACHER B Particularly if they create a very strong and accurate visual image. I've certainly found the kids in my groups will relate back to this.

TEACHER A A very important point here is the back-up materials – the booklets which come with the programmes. They're extremely useful, up-to-date sources of information.

E.O. Why this rather elaborate use? You were using a bit of radio, a bit of television, odd filmstrips and at one point an extract from the pupil's pamphlet, as part of the work.

TEACHER A I don't think one would always want to use so many different types of visual stimulus, although we quite frequently use both filmstrips and either a film or a television broadcast or a radio broadcast. We've selected from all of them the materials appropriate to the aim of the lesson or unit of work.

E.O. Do you feel any sense of loss at all in taking just a part of a programme? Did you feel that for example about the Dakota programme that they saw just now?

TEACHER B I don't think they're going to learn an awful lot more. The main point has been that it's flat, it's wide open, they use big machines, there's a problem of people leaving the land. And those points were made in the segment shown. That's what we wanted to show.

TEACHER A It's a question of time: if the television broadcast or what have you doesn't necessarily exactly fit the aim *we're* aiming to achieve, then we must cut bits of it out in order to allow time for other things to be taught.

E.O. If we can just pursue this for a moment. I don't wish to be critical of this scheme, but I see a danger when you take bits of a broadcast that you might simply be draining it dry of its *informative* content. In other words just taking out raw geographical data that you want for some specific purpose. In doing that you surely lose the other sort of impact that a broadcast can have; that is, to give children some kind of empathetic experience of another locality. A feeling that they've been somewhere, even if vicariously. And we do see this as a function of a broadcast. Do you?

TEACHER A I would agree with what you say, but we're up against a fundamental problem. We've talked about aims and I think each of us, in dealing with our topic, has had very closely defined aims: we have always included an amount of exposition, and this has had to come in because

we are working to an exam syllabus. I know, Bruce, you felt very unhappy about some of the things that we left out. You felt that perhaps
we were being a little too factual.

HER B Right. When we were doing California, I was glad to see that you used
the whole programme because I thought it brought out beautifully the
atmosphere of the area. It's an up-and-coming area, it's where people
go to be 'in'; and for these kids California won't just be mountains, the
Salinas Valley and vegetable-growing.

HER A I would agree, but I thought we had perhaps a little too much of the
problems of the migrant Mexican worker. I take your point but with
reservation.

The Education Officer on this visit was fulfilling, as so often, a
dual function. He will have observed the care, the efficiency and
the enthusiasm with which these teachers are tackling the opportunities, and the problems, of team teaching. He will have admired
the rigour with which they have thought out their aims and the
breadth of resources they have drawn on in pursuit of them. He
will have noted (not for the first time!) how large exams still loom
in the eyes of teachers in charge of classes soon to face them. But
he also, on his own and the producer's behalf, has been saying in
effect: 'Look, this programme was made for classes just like yours,
by a skilled director who is also a geography specialist, to give a
carefully balanced picture of life, and the "feel" of life, in
Dakota today. Are you sure your handling of it has done justice,
I don't say to the programme – a programme has no sensitivities –
but to the needs of your pupils themselves?'

I have just shown Education Officers in two rather 'avant-
garde' situations. Here is a different one, recalled by the Education Officer whose responsibilities extend from Deeside to the
Western Isles:

I was visiting a delightful little school in the wilds of Sutherland,
situated about five miles up the glen from the village. There is beauty
in the far view and the near – the loch sparkles in front, there's a moor
alongside and at the back, and as far as the eye can see there are the
glorious mountains. And I was sitting there, having tea with the headmistress, while the five pupils of the school were playing outside, and
she said to me 'Mr Harper, there's a very good series, I understand,
called "Singing Together". Many of my friends take it and they say that

it is excellent. Now I, myself, would like to take it, but unfortunately you always put it out at eleven o'clock on a Monday morning. Now that's the time of my morning interval – I wonder if you could change the time of the broadcast?'

'Singing Together' had been carefully placed for over a decade at a time which seemed admirably suited to the convenience of the great majority of the 15,000 schools following it. Yet for this Head the rhythm of her children's lives took precedence over any BBC broadcast; and who shall say that she was wrong?

I do not suppose there exists in Britain a school that small today[1]. But there are a number not so much bigger – of less than, say, fifty children – and back in the 30s there were very many more. Most are likely to be unusually dependent on the BBC for contact with the outside world and for providing varied stimulus for their children. Scotland, Wales, and Northern Ireland, parts of which still enjoy the blessings of remoteness, have a high proportion of them: so Sutherland will be my cue for an all too brief excursion into our Celtic fringe.

A digression: the Celtic fringe

All these three countries of the United Kingdom have not only their own BBC Education Officers, but their own school programmes too: in addition, they draw on the complete range of programmes designed for schools over the whole Kingdom. We have noted more than once Scotland's pioneering contributions over the years to nation-wide school broadcasting: its domestic programmes are naturally focused mainly on the Scottish scene, Scottish history, and Scottish literature – none of which can be adequately represented for Scottish schools in the programmes produced in London. Scotland has, too, its own School Broadcasting Council, and its representatives on the United Kingdom Council.

So has Wales; and Wales is, in a sense, pioneering all the time, since the Welsh Council is particularly active in seeking new fields

[1] Or so I thought until, on 13 June 1974, 'Nationwide' showed us a school with two pupils, also in Sutherland.

for the enlargement of Welsh children's acquaintance with the Welsh language. It is an engaging experience to attend a meeting of the Welsh Council as a visitor from London. The more formal business will be conducted in English; but soon, when advocacy must summon up the conviction or the cunning that brooks no resistance, everyone will drop into Welsh; and there will emerge yet another passionate resolution, for yet another series in the Welsh language. A noble cause; and if a little extravagant in its consequences, where can extravagance better be justified than in fighting for the survival of one's native tongue? To expect a neutered objectivity from a group of Welshmen invited to tell the BBC what it should do would be the extreme of naïveté.

Special programmes for Scottish and Welsh schools (and lest I be misunderstood, not all the latter are in Welsh) have a history as long as school broadcasting's itself. Northern Ireland came much later into the field—if we except some transmissions from Belfast in the earliest days when every local station was temporarily seized by the desire to put some 'experts' on the daytime air. For Ulster teachers were under the thumb of their Inspectorate, whose job it was (or so they interpreted it) to supervise observance of a very conservative curriculum. Small wonder that for a quarter of a century school broadcasting was mainly regarded there as a newfangled irrelevancy.

Moreover, all the available school broadcasts were London-produced: there were none specially made for Ulster's schools. By the 50s, there were Northern Irish members in the Programme Committees of the United Kingdom Council; and a more liberal spirit in educational practice in Ulster was finding expression in demands for special Northern Irish programmes. But Ulster's educational leaders were mainly lukewarm (at best) in support of this: in their view Ulster's schools should make more use of the United Kingdom series before they aspired to have their own also.

In fact, the developing use of school broadcasts in Northern Ireland during the 50s and early 60s owed a lot to the efforts of BBC Education Officers, who successively added to their responsibilities in the North and North-West of England the job of demonstrating and fostering understanding of school broadcasts through the length and breadth of Ulster. In the course of the 60s Northern Ireland got in turn its first specialist Schools' producer;

its first series about Ulster for Ulster children; its own Programme Committee (reporting to the United Kingdom Council); and its own, Belfast-based, Education Officer. Today it has one special TV series for schools, and four radio. One of these last must be singled out, for it is remarkable.

Children in Northern Ireland had not, until recently, the chance to learn Irish history. They might learn Irish Protestant history as an incidental to English history, or Irish Catholic history as a saga of heroic resistance, or (more probably) neither; but to attempt teaching Irish history as a whole would be trying to bridge the assumedly unbridgeable. Yet within a few years of the first special series for Ulster schools, the BBC's School Radio producer in Belfast, with the full support of his Programme Committee, came up with 'Two Centuries of Irish History' (since revised, extended, and improved; and now renamed 'Modern Irish History: People and Events'). The programmes in no way ducked major issues of sectarian controversy: yet they were universally acclaimed not only by schools, but in the Press and by casual adult listeners also. A distinguished Irishman described the series, with no exaggeration, as 'the first fully objective and non-partisan approach to the events of the last 200 years in Ireland'. In the following year the 'book of the series' was published, the first of a new wave of Irish history textbooks: it ran into several editions. It is idle to regret that this initiative came a quarter of a century too late; in a larger perspective of events than today's immediacies permit us, it will be recognised as a step which once taken can never be gone back on. And it is permissible to ask whether any less powerful or less independent force than the BBC could have been the first to breach the walls.

Education Officers as agents for School Broadcasting

In an earlier section we saw Education Officers as observers in schools, reporting and commenting on particular situations. In our brief survey of development in Northern Ireland we have seen them in a more missionary capacity. In both roles they are especially important in the 'Celtic fringe' countries: as missionaries, because their territories are extensive and include many small and scattered communities; as observers and reporters, because even there the bulk of schools' listening and viewing is to programmes coming from London, and for London producers it is vital to know whether the assumptions they make, and the accents in which they speak, are valid also for Caithness, Fermanagh and Montgomery.

To propagate understanding of the educational aims underlying school broadcasts and knowledge of the programmes themselves has always been, however, a function of the whole body of Education Officers. In the early days, when they were a handful only, it was indeed their main preoccupation, sometimes to be exercised in the face of opposition or, at best, cynicism. But there was plenty of encouragement too. Cyril Jackson, BBC Education Officer in Leeds at the time, recalls a demonstration to a branch of the National Union of Teachers in a Yorkshire town, shortly after Ann Driver's 'Music and Movement' came upon the scene.

The teachers, some of them, thought the wireless lacked the personal touch. So I arranged for two parallel classes. Ann directed one from a side-room with a loudspeaker in the hall. She ran the second in person. Believe it or not, the children reacted better to her voice over the speaker. The teachers admitted it.

Personal contact with the Local Authorities' Chief Education Officers and their staffs was, however, the key to making real headway, for here money was involved; and money had to be spent if reception in schools was to improve. On this issue, BBC Education Officers worked hand-in-hand with their Education Engineer colleagues, to whose cardinal part in the development of school broadcasting I have already referred.

BBC Adult Education comes into this picture too. In the 30s it was a very lively affair: all over the country, discussion groups met to chew over programmes they had heard together; and Area Councils were set up to advise. These Councils often drew Chief Education Officers into their ranks; and the BBC Education Officer might well find that the way in to persuading these holders of the purse strings to invest in school radio was through their involvement with BBC Adult Education programmes.

From the early 30s the Teacher Training Colleges (as they

were then called) were seen as prime agents in spreading understanding of the nature of school radio, the opportunities it offered
students for enriching their own teaching, and their responsibilities as users of the service. Colleges welcomed the arrival of the
BBC man with his 'box of tricks', but for very many years he remained, for most of them, just that: a purveyor of fringe benefits.
Not till well after the war, through the constant pressures of
individual 'BBC men', through Summer Schools, through the
increasing interest of the Inspectorate, and through the growth of
a more liberal view of the educational process, did the conviction
really gain ground that here in school broadcasting was something that touched at the heart of the Colleges' primary concerns.
Today, just as Local Education Authorities have assumed the
prime responsibility for the provision of sets, so have the Colleges
of Education for the job of familiarising their students with the
school broadcasting service; and to help them the School Broadcasting Council has created a rich and fascinating loan library of
study materials – including not only recordings of programmes,
but also teachers' accounts of how they used them, examples of
children's work stemming from them, and so on.

In the Training Colleges, the Education Officer's identification with the BBC was often a drawback to him: it meant he was
not a 'real educationist' (however long he might have served at
the coal face of education before). He was always the 'BBC
Education Officer': I have repeatedly used the same term myself,
to distinguish him from other Education Officers; but his correct
title is 'Education Officer of the School Broadcasting Council'. In
a school, on the other hand, the Education Officer's identification
with the BBC is usually a source of strength. He is not a servant of
the teacher's employers (though he is in the school with their
consent and good will); his view of what he sees there is irrelevant
to the teacher's, or the school's, reputation. As for the children,
they may even assume he is on familiar terms with Jimmy Saville.
He is a different sort of visitor, in fact. And incidentally, one who
may also have to carry the can for sins adjudged to have been
committed by the BBC in quite different quarters.

The Changing Role of Education Officers

Today, the Education Officers still visit individual schools (so do producers when they can spare the time). They still take part in Teachers' Conferences. But gradually their work in many respects is changing. First, the whole educational scene is becoming more complex, more variegated. School broadcasting, from being twenty or thirty years ago one of very few agents contributing nationally to change in educational thinking and method, is now one of many; and it has to take account of all these other agents of change. Again, school broadcasting's output has vastly increased in size and scope: no single person can now keep tabs on all the series, any more than he can digest all the scores of highly significant publications from, for instance, the Schools' Council and the Nuffield Foundation. In these circumstances the pull towards a measure of specialism among Education Officers is irresistible.

First, then, Education Officers are being increasingly selective in the areas of school broadcasting on which they focus attention at any given time: today, for instance, these include the area of pre-school broadcasting, or to take an example from the Secondary range, European Studies. 'Focusing attention' implies much more than studying the impact in the schools of programmes already planned and produced; it involves also testing pilot programmes, and before that even, studying the broader picture of educational thought and practice in that particular area. In a measure, Education Officers have long done this (every major new venture since the war has been preceded by background study); but today the process is highly intensified.

Secondly, much more is now done to capitalise each Education Officer's particular expertise. Traditionally, Education Officers have been generalists, reasonably at home with both 'Music and Movement' and 'Science for Sixth Forms'; but all of course bring to their job on appointment a special knowledge of one or more fields of education. The more they can exercise this, the more they can keep themselves masters of that field; build up contacts; and be of direct help to producers (themselves of course specialists) in the formative stages of their programme planning.

The trend towards specialism among Education Officers is, therefore, also drawing them further into the creative work of programme-making. Undoubtedly, a gain in job satisfaction for them: taking in other people's linen can be frustrating. A job calling for diplomacy and forbearance, too: the producer's responsibility for his own programmes cannot be eroded. And a job where involvement must still not blur the eye of objectivity. The Education Officer's strength has always been his keen sense of classroom realities: through it he has played his part in the creation of what was usually (not invariably!) a kind of constructive tension between producer and field observer. It is much harder for him to be a 'field observer' today: schools take many fewer programmes off-air at the 'BBC's times', and who shall know when they do take them? (not the Head any more, nor even the school secretary). Meetings of teachers known to be using particular series will, no doubt, in part repair the deficiency: but whatever the means, the Education Officer's job will still be to talk with producers from the point of view of teachers and children, remembering that broadcasts are for all sorts and conditions of both, and not just ideally postulated ones. Seen in this light, team work between producers and Education Officers in surveying the fields for possible action, in discussing the pitfalls and the opportunities of each, and in testing provisional assumptions, can be fruitful indeed.

But enough now of generalities: we will move in the next section to a particular broadcasting venture, in which Programme Committee, Education Officers and producers all combined – each playing a distinctive role – to pluck success out of danger.

4.3   Three-letter partners

Only one topic among the thousands BBC School Broadcasting handles in the course of a decade could have spawned fifty pages of press cuttings. And just for lack of a phrase, in all our glorious English language, to describe what we were up to. 'Human Biology'? Too broad, and too academic for programmes addressed to children of eight and nine. 'The facts of life'? Exact; but old-fashioned, musty, hilarious. If one wanted a portmanteau phrase it had to be, for all its misleading overtones, 'Sex Education'.

Delicate territory, but not new to school broadcasting. Twenty years earlier, school radio had been transmitting, in its General Science series for children of eleven and twelve, programmes about birth and the physical development of boys and girls. Much more recently, the smallest of the ITV companies, Grampian Television, had mounted a successful and quite detailed series for ten–twelve-year-olds. And school radio, in 'Learning about Life', had for several years dealt with sexual development and activity in the context of the maturation of the adolescent as a person. The enterprise now described was novel only in so far as the programmes were designed for children as young as eight and nine.

Public attitudes to sexual behaviour and to sex instruction for young people were moving rapidly in the 60s towards a greater tolerance and a greater openness. We could forget that not so long back some headmasters, before issuing certain radio pamphlets to their classes, would stick together two of the pages to protect their pupils from a diagram of a pregnant cow. But current opinions about sex education were far from uniform; actual practice, whether by schools or parents, still less so. What was common knowledge, and irrefutable, was that most boys and girls were maturing physically much earlier than formerly; and in the view of many teachers and most specialists sex education, in the sense of elementary biological instruction, was no longer a task which could be deferred till secondary school.

Preparing for the programmes

It was in 1967 that the School Broadcasting Council's Primary School Committee first discussed the possible help that broadcasting might give to teachers wishing to develop work in this field at an earlier stage. Clearly the task, if undertaken, would require the most careful handling; so before any decision was taken, the Committee asked its officers to ascertain the facts about current practice in Primary Schools, and to seek expert advice on the educational and psychological implications of sex education at this age.

Research by the Council's staff revealed that few Primary Schools had a worked-out policy for introducing sex education into their curricula. Many teachers thought that it was a responsibility of parents and that it would be wrong or unwise for schools to intervene. Many more thought that the subject was unsuited to class instruction and that teachers should simply answer individual children's questions honestly when they arose. But there was also evidence of a growing feeling that this was not enough.

Children who needed information and were ready for it were also conscious that sex was a taboo subject, better perhaps not broached in adult company. Teachers were aware, too, that many parents lacked the equipment and the confidence to deal with the subject to their own satisfaction, and consequently let it go by default. And even in schools which were ready to assume the task, there was a shortage of suitable visual material to help teachers perform it efficiently.

The consultant's report pointed in the same direction, and suggested that age eight or nine was appropriate for introducing the subject, since children were then growing out of the age of fantasy but had not yet become emotionally involved with sex. The Committee therefore asked the BBC to prepare and test pilot broadcasts designed for this age. These were not to be lessons complete in themselves, but audio-visual material which teachers could incorporate into a wider syllabus and use to illustrate and clarify their own work on the subject. The Committee thought that both radiovision and television had distinctive contributions to make, which could be used independently or to complement each other. It was important not to isolate sex education and give it an artificial significance: the programmes were therefore to be planned as extensions of existing series, and to fit quite naturally into them.

Responsibility now passed to the BBC, whose producers drew up their plans with advice from a wide variety of appropriate experts. First detailed proposals, then pilot programmes were shown to the Committee, and emended here and there. Then the School Broadcasting Council's Education officers came into the picture: their job was now to find schools, in different parts of the country and with children of differing social backgrounds, where there were teachers prepared to try out the material. The usual pattern was for the teachers first to view the programmes and confirm that they would be happy to use them; then to arrange for the children's parents to see them; and only then, and with appropriate preparation, to show them to the children themselves.

This operation went very smoothly, and gave us much encouragement. The children showed great interest, and remarkably little embarrassment or shock; parents and teachers were enthusiastic. A few more minor amendments, and the programmes assumed their final form. Meanwhile the co-operation of BBC Further Education had been enlisted to mount, in the late evening and some months before the transmissions to schools, a series of five TV broadcasts on Sex Education in the Primary School. These would be for the benefit of teachers and parents, and would include previews of key sections of the programmes for schools.

Meanwhile also, the Council's Education Officers were arranging to show the pilot programmes and discuss their use at meetings of teachers, Local Education Authority officials and others around the country; and a press conference was held so that the public could be informed of what was afoot. The press chose to make a field day of it; and some journalists, forgetting (if they ever knew) what is within the understanding and range of interest of eight-year-olds and what is not, drew some exotic conclusions from the absence in the programmes of specific reference to love and marriage. The stage army of instant heresy-hunters duly responded with indignant protests about programmes they had not seen. For the School Broadcasting Council's officers the job of allaying anxieties and correcting misunderstandings was time-consuming and the climate of controversy was not an ideal overture to the enterprise itself. Yet on balance I think the airing did good: the exposure of prejudice, and the opportunity to respond to genuine concern, helped move public opinion a little in the direction of sanity. Some critics had very fair points: it is not discreditable to believe that sex education is the job of parents; it is not unreasonable to question whether a whole class can be ready for particular information at a particular moment; it is altogether humane to be concerned for possible distress to an individual child. One simply has to weigh against these considerations the searing anxieties and the personal disasters that are the daily and inevitable consequences of the ignorance and distorted ideas about sex which in fact prevail.

The programmes themselves

I have described at some length the run-up to the programmes: what were they? Two fifteen-minute radiovision programmes: the first answering the questions, Where do babies come from? and How do they get out?; the second aiming to prepare children for the main changes characterising the onset of puberty. And three twenty-minute TV programmes: the first dealing with the development of humans and animals before birth; the second with birth itself; and the third with development from infancy to adulthood, the main differences between the male and the female body, and how conception takes place.

The radiovision programmes had, of course, pictures in colour, sensitively drawn by an artist to create an atmosphere of warmth and affection; the sound track was straight talk with musical punctuation. Two consecutive frames from the first programme are shown facing page 103. The programmes presented relatively few problems for teachers preparing to use them, as they could buy the filmstrips, tape-record the sound broadcasts, synchronise and play them back to parents, and consider at leisure how to use them with actual classes or groups of children. Most teachers decided that while the first programme was suitable for younger juniors, the second was best deferred for a year or two.

Television presented more problems because the programmes had to be taken off-air. Teachers were of course encouraged to view the evening series some months before, and a great many did so. Furthermore, film copies of the school programmes were made available, about three months before transmission, for Local Education Authorities to purchase, and a number of schools were able to borrow these for previewing, often with parents. But we had to reckon that many teachers would come to the programmes with no more foreknowledge of them than what detailed Teachers' Notes could provide.

Much thought was given, therefore, to the planning and timing of the TV programmes. We decided that they would be an appropriate element in the wide-ranging miscellany series 'Merry-go-Round', planned for age seven–nine (the same series which we met telling of the Vikings, in Chapter I). This would help take sex education, for the children at least, out of the realm of the extraordinary into that of the normal. We would put them on the air in June, when first-year juniors would be rising or turned age eight and second years around nine; and when they and their teachers would be on familiar terms.

Familiar, too, would by then be the regular presenter for the series. We wanted a style which combined warmth with matter-of-factness: a known and liked personality, at home in a TV studio and interested in the subject without being an expert (others could provide the expertise in his script), would be a far better mediator than an unfamiliar specialist, new perhaps to the difficult job of TV presentation.

The producers in both media (Margaret Sheffield for radio-vision, Claire Chovil for TV) had of course to wrestle with difficult problems, both of planning and of execution: I will confine myself to some of those encountered in television, since I was more closely associated with these. First, life begins with conception; but its process is not easy for an eight-year-old to grasp: apart from the delicacy of the subject of intercourse, micro-photography of a sperm joining an egg is difficult to relate to the normal world of men, women and babies. Claire Chovil decided therefore to leave conception to the end, and to begin the story with the development of living creatures before birth.

The producer also wanted the programmes not only to lead to discussion in class but also, like others in the series, to encourage children to undertake studies on their own, under their teachers' guidance. In the course of the first two programmes, therefore, she showed children making a graph of animals' different gestation periods, studying the operation of the heart (after hearing about the foetal heart), and comparing their own rates of development since babyhood.

Other problems: should an actual birth be shown, or drawings only? Children's curiosity would not be satisfied by drawings alone; and clarity and humanity both pointed to live illustration. Fortunately, there was a sequence shot two years before for an adult series which met our needs very well. As it showed a hospital birth, some Committee members thought that the atmosphere conveyed by white-coated hospital staff, as for an operation, was too clinical and might cause distress. But there was no evidence of this in the event: children were more upset, if at all, by the panting of a mother-cat as she gave birth to her kittens.

Would showing naked adults produce titters, or so shock the children by their 'rudeness' that concentrated viewing was disturbed? The producer felt, rightly I am sure, that the story of the life cycle could not be properly told without them; and that they should be seen where it was natural for them not only to be seen but to be drawn or photographed. So she went to a life class in an art studio. Not indeed a very familiar place to an eight-year-old, and I have heard it criticised on this account. Preferable, however, to shots of mum and dad in the bathroom, where the camera seems an odd intruder.

The response

So much for the programmes: how did schools respond to them? Not by any means all who were using radio's 'Nature' series or TV's 'Merry-go-Round' opted to take these particular programmes. This was neither surprising nor disappointing: there is no pressure on schools to follow these or any other broadcasts, and a great many Heads decided, either on general grounds or because of staff or parental resistance, that the time was not yet ripe. Thus, by August 1970 – several months after the radio transmissions – whereas 4000 schools had bought the Radiovision filmstrips, only one-third of these had as yet used them. The three 'Merry-go-Round' programmes were seen in about 2500 schools; but that was about a quarter only of those which viewed the other programmes in the series. To reach 3000 or more schools, and on average two or more classes in each, with one or both sets of programmes was nevertheless an achievement: more have joined in for the repeats in subsequent years.

This statistical information derives from questionnaires drawn up and analysed by the School Broadcasting Council's Research Officer. Meanwhile its Education Officers were busy in the field, visiting schools and reporting on the quality of response. There is room here for summary observations only: the whole project and its impact is described very fully in a report prepared by the Council.[1]

[1] School Broadcasting and Sex Education in the Primary School', BBC, 1971.

There was a wide scatter of critical comment on matters of detail, as was to be expected, and some more general dissatisfactions: for instance, many teachers thought the third TV programme was overloaded and in parts rather difficult; while others found the radiovision pictures, or music, not to their taste. These were nevertheless exceptions to the general tenor of comment, which repeatedly reflected teachers' welcome for the programmes and children's interest and absorption in them. It was noticeable, and not surprising, that children tended to identify with the babies rather than the adults, and centred their interest on the processes of birth and development rather than on the mechanics of conception. Nevertheless, discussion afterwards was wide-ranging indeed, as these children's questions, culled from some of the hundreds the programmes provoked, will testify:

How does the baby breathe in the uterus?
How was the baby fed in the womb?
How would a dead baby be born?
Why don't old women have babies?
Why does the baby come out head first?
Why was I born bottom and feet first?
Why do some women have their baby through a cut in their tummy?
How are Siamese twins born?
What happens if the lady wants to wee? Will the baby drown?
How do puppies know where to find milk?
Do you have to be married before you can have a baby?
What happens to the sperms that fail to fertilise the egg?
Who told the first people how to transfer the sperm?
Where did the first Mum and Dad come from to make the first baby?

On discussion generally, the Council's report has this to say:

The fluency and quality of the discussion periods following the programmes seem to have depended to a large extent on the adequacy of the preparation and the relationship established between teacher and children. Where these conditions were favourable, and in the great majority of cases they were, the children responded freely, frankly, with good sense, and with obvious relief at being able to talk about their misconceptions and their experiences.

And on the enterprise as a whole, this Head's comment was typical of many:

The programmes have made possible an approach to sex education which would have been quite out of the question before. We have scratched the surface in the past, but this year we have been able to cover all the ground appropriate to children of this age.

Even more heartwarming was the observation of many other Heads that quite apart from the intrinsic value of both television and radiovision programmes, all that was involved in using them, and particularly the associated staff and parents' meetings, had done a great deal to foster those close relationships between teachers, parents and children which are central to the well-being of a primary school.

To sum up, then, this enterprise showed that the apparently hazardous medium of broadcasting can indeed be harnessed to serve what is rightly regarded as a peculiarly personal and intimate need. Despite the variations between individuals, there is a common core of knowledge which all seek and welcome if it is presented in the right way. It showed, too, that young children can approach learning in this field in the same matter-of-fact and curious spirit of enquiry that they bring to other subjects, provided adults can avoid thrusting on them the burden of any neuroses of their own.

The enterprise was also a conspicuous example of the Council's Programme Committee, its Education Officers, and the BBC's production departments working in partnership to a single end. The initiative came, on this occasion, from the Committee itself: while we on the production side welcomed the challenge, we would doubtfully ever have laid our heads on the block uninvited. The role of the Education Officers in the field was cardinal—in arranging for the pilots, in propagating the intention, in observing response; as was that of the Council's Research Officer in building up the detailed picture. The producers were hard-pressed, and had to put up with more breathing down their necks than they could often bear; but their essential creative freedoms were kept intact. Five programmes, one reflects with relief, rarely or never in school broadcasting's day-to-day life get such anxious attention (short relief actually: four years later they are already due for 'updating', if that is what one does with sex). Yet the combination of forces which made them both possible and effective, though it is not often deployed with all guns blazing quite so fiercely, was by no means unique. It characterises BBC School Broadcasting's approach to all its major ventures into new territory.

5 PROBLEMS IN THE AIR

We have surveyed, in Chapter 3, a number of school broadcast series in relation to a succession of problems or opportunities thrown up by educational developments; and in the last chapter we have examined the part played by the School Broadcasting Council's Committees and staff in helping the production departments to respond effectively to these challenges. I shall now discuss some of the wider issues which have in recent years tended to recur in programme making, and particularly at the stage when one is encouraging adolescents to reach up into adulthood. They are problems of programme content, style and tone.

5.1 'Relevance'

When I was at school I 'did' the Peloponnesian War three times between the ages of twelve and seventeen. It never occurred to me, of course, to ask whether it was 'relevant' to my needs: both I and my teachers assumed that this was so. And not without reason. At twelve, the Peloponnesian War was a good story; at fourteen, it said quite a lot about human character and motivation; at seventeen, it was interesting to read what a contemporary writer had to say about it. We were not all academic specialists, either: even from the third stage, many would be leaving to work in banks, businesses, the Civil Service. To adjust, no matter how gradually and with what experience in between, from a base of this sort to participating in sensible decisions on what is relevant to the education of ordinary fourteen- to eighteen-year-olds today is something I have never found easy.

Today, if you want to know the answer to what is relevant to young people, you ask them. The Schools Council did it with young school leavers, in relation to school subjects, and got some disconcerting answers. Maths and English are relevant, because useful; also practical things like domestic science and workshop activities. The rest is mainly eyewash, and often boring too.

Broaden the inquiry a little, forget traditional school subjects, and ask them what they want to know about and discuss which relates to the adult world they are joining, and the answers are predictable: jobs, handling money, the family, getting on with parents, boy/girl relationships, love and marriage, authority, the police, crime, poverty. The older ones will add divorce, abortion, class, race relationships, women's rights, the mass media perhaps. Television can handle all these topics vividly, and well. Adolescents and young adults can discuss them well too, and often with a surprising perspicacity. Their teachers are keen on them. So we provide television programmes about them. And other agencies provide for them in their fashion too: kits galore. They have become the new orthodoxies.

I do not decry this mass movement towards what might be called selective elementary sociology. The topics are close to life as young people today know it or anticipate soon meeting it. I do not advocate substituting the Peloponnesian War for them. Ruthlessly contemporary though they are, they can and sometimes do serve also as starting-points for an element of historical study, which gives them a certain depth of focus. They can involve practical experience too–helping in the care of the old, the handicapped, the very young: they both reflect and foster a more open approach to and concern for the welfare of the weaker or the wayward in the community. Twenty, even ten years ago the notion that adolescent boys could be interested in caring for very young children would have been ridiculed: we have seen them on the job, coping with efficiency and pride, in the programme 'How Good a Parent', from 'Scene'.

Only, I wonder, has nothing but dead wood been jettisoned to make room for all this? From the late 50s through most of the 60s the School TV series 'Drama', in its search for plays relevant to ordinary boys and girls of fourteen–sixteen, ranged from Sophocles through Shakespeare and Marlowe to Shaw, Gogol, Ugo Betti, and Brecht. Living playwrights were represented too, in due proportion. For all, the producer's basic intention was the same. 'As the class watch each play,' wrote Ronald Eyre, 'their attention should be wholly on the people, the predicament they find themselves in and the conflicts that develop between and within them. And as they explore the fictional situations within each play, they should find that their own experience either validates or challenges what they see.'

In the 70s we still have the 'Drama' series, but without any conscious decision to exclude the timeless plays of the past, we have let it become a series of contemporary drama. We have moved with the times; and a dimension has been lost from the range of our audience's experience. Not all the plays we used to do spoke with force and clarity to each of our viewers, but the evidence is that mostly they did; if so, we may have narrowed our concept of relevance to their detriment, and this troubles me. Particular quotes are special pleading, but for the Secondary Modern girl who thus described the end of Marlowe's *Doctor Faustus* months after experiencing it in School TV, it was surely not irrelevant:

I like the bit at the end of Dr Faustus, when he was in his study and he was going to the devil. It had a balcony on the front and a big window. It was quite dark in there, and he had his study table. He was kneeling on the floor asking God for forgiveness because he'd sold his soul to the devil, and he asked the mountains to come and fall on him so the devil couldn't find him, and he asked the stars to turn him into dewdrops so that the devil couldn't find him, and he told his friends about it so they went outside and started to pray for him, on their knees to God, to ask for forgiveness, and he was still praying for forgiveness and then you saw on the television screen a picture of the Crucifix with Jesus's head on it. Then you saw the head of Jesus turn to the head of the King of the Devils, Lucifer, and then you saw all different devils all round the room. Very ugly devils, and you went outside then and you heard Faustus screaming and shouting and you didn't hear any more and then his friends did know that he went to the devil.

I do not suppose that girl believes in hell; perhaps not in the divinity of Christ either. But like the rest of us she had experienced panic, and hallucination too. So she rode the knobbly terrain of Renaissance language without a fall; and she sensed surely, through its nobility and despite its distancing effect, that the predicament of Faustus is part of the human condition in which we all share.

To choose a play with a contemporary or near-contemporary setting is not necessarily to extend the range of young people whose feelings can be engaged and whose sympathies enlarged. We chose, not long ago, for the 'Drama' series Shelagh Delaney's *A Taste of Honey*: it appealed to both the producer and me for its lyrical quality and its insight into young people's situations – the author was not a lot older than our audience when she wrote it. I watched part of it with a mixed class of fourteen- and fifteen-year-olds in the North of England. The girls lapped it up, and discussed the characters and their interaction with a maturity and a perspicaciousness which delighted me; the wiry, shock-headed boys, who seemed half the size of the girls, were completely at sea. It was not that one of the leading characters was a middle-aged woman, affectionate in her own fashion but fundamentally a selfish tart; and another a sensitive young man – kind, tender, and homosexual: the whole tenor and tone of the play escaped them. They were simply not ready for it.

Judgement in these matters is difficult. The teacher's judgement is involved too, of course: he has detailed Notes to guide him in deciding who is likely to view with profit; but then he also has the problems inherent in splitting a class. I have found it as easy to underestimate young people's range as to go beyond it. 'Scene' was presenting, a couple of years back, two contrasts in living. One, a documentary, was to depict the joys, and the limitations, of life for young people living in Benbecula, a small island in the Hebrides. The other, a play, would be about the pressures of life in high-rise flats.

The play, when it arrived, was indeed about this – and a great deal more. It told the story of a young mother so distraught by the loneliness and the boredom of her imprisonment on the twentieth floor up that she dumped her baby and rang the police, declaring it had been stolen from the courtyard below. We saw the police at work, interviews with the young mother and her husband, suspicions growing, the confession finally extracted. It was a fine play – moving, informative, thought-provoking. I wondered. There was indeed the resolution at the end of the play, pointing with tentative optimism to the future: the baby restored, the dawn of a new understanding of what was involved in a partnership. But were we really right to burden young people still at school with quite such searing adult problems?

The producer, it seemed, was surprised at my reservations. Well, I thought, he has almost daily contact with youngsters; I no longer have. We went ahead; and to judge from the schools' reports, he was amply vindicated. A great success: a play follow-ed with intense involvement and discussed with verve.

I am still not totally sure, of course–one rarely is. I wonder what the next lot of Geordie boys made of it.

5.2 'Impartiality' and 'Open-endedness'

The BBC has a recognised duty to be impartial: in News and Current Affairs, for example, to report the facts and to offer a wide and balanced range of comment upon them. From a cramp-ingly stringent observance of this injunction in the early days, it now permits itself a more relaxed interpretation: to achieve bal-ance over a series or cluster of programmes, for instance, rather than necessarily within each individual one.

There is also a general understanding that the BBC has a duty to cherish and not undermine the widely accepted and hard-won values of our society, broadly based on the Christian ethic: the brotherhood of man, the maintenance of government by consent, the tolerance of minorities, the rule of law–yet still to recognise that today's rebel may be tomorrow's prophet.

School broadcasting naturally takes its tone in these matters from general BBC policy; and broadcasting to the immature carries of course special responsibilities, as offended MPs and others can be quick to point out. There is a sense, however, in which pupils listening to or viewing school broadcasts are better protected than are the general public from the direct influence of partiality on the air: they are in the charge of an adult teacher, normally better than averagely well-informed on the matter, and the experience of the programme will be set in a special context provided by the teacher with the aid of the BBC's published notes. In this situation, what many teachers are looking for is a stimulus to discussion rather than a neat balance of argument which may appear to leave little or nothing to be said afterwards. The assumption is often made that the impact of TV is so powerful that no discussion afterwards can effectively redress imbalance; but in my experience this is not necessarily the case at all.

There can occasionally, then, be a conflict, not easily resolved, between the BBC's general responsibilities and one's conception of the special needs of schools. When controversial issues are under discussion in general programmes, the BBC's primary function is to cultivate a cool detachment in the adult viewer, so that he weighs opinions and reaches a reasoned judgement. But with young people in school one may be more concerned, in the first place, to get them to feel involved in the issue: for many, if the heart is not touched, there is little for reason to get working on.

This is often especially true when the issues are about events remote from familiar surroundings; but there are hazards. 1970 was a bumper year for the hi-jackers: we decided to do a programme about them, based on a single major incident—the hijacking of three international jets by Palestinian commandos in September 1970 and their destruction, anxious days later, on an airstrip near Amman. We wanted not only to state the facts of the case, but to set our young viewers thinking about why such acts of piracy took place. The programme stated the facts, over documentary film; then, borrowing perhaps unconsciously from the techniques used in 'Last Bus' (described in Chapter 3), the producer had elected to put two young actors representing two commandos 'in the dock', under cross-examination by another actor, the 'prosecuting counsel'. This looked promising: 'counsel' would be able to make a strong and irrefragable case for the maintenance of international law and order, dwelling on the horror of this use of human hostages and the wanton senselessness of the planes' destruction; the 'commandos', conducting their own defence, would display the hot-headed, intemperate sense of grievance which motivated their actions; the viewers would then be invited to sort out the rights and wrongs. In theory, a balance and an open-ended conclusion; in practice, for our audience, not. 'Counsel' spoke forcefully indeed, but he was the symbol of pontificating adult authority: the 'commandos', playing their parts brilliantly, and no doubt more attractive than their counterparts in reality, became the standard-bearers for passionate, rebellious youth, and stole the stage. A gripping programme; but one where strength of feeling hardly gave reason a look-in. That learning must involve feeling may be true: to range feeling against reason can, with the best of motives, be playing with fire.

Some teachers – there are fewer now – used to bristle at any programme (even a play) which appeared to invite criticism, or questioning, of traditional manifestations of authority: of Officers, by Other Ranks; of police, by long-haired youth. Production departments are in no position to be contemptuous of such reactions: they do not have the task of keeping from disintegration a piece of the fabric of our society; and for some teachers, in some circumstances, the daily round may mean at times just this. School Broadcasting exists to serve teachers, not to put thorns in their path. But broadcasting is part of the open society; and the open society, whether from deliberate choice or swept by the irresistible *Zeitgeist,* has elected to bring fractious youth too within the ambit of government by consent. Consent implies, or should imply, understanding; and the path to understanding lies through questioning. A Socratic ideal: brittle at the surface, easily trampled on by the undisciplined; but hard at the bed-rock, and the schools have plumped for it – here tentatively, there boldly; here with glittering successes, there with the outcome in the balance, or dipping adversely. Broadcasting must support them in their hazardous course, and in a tiny measure share in the rough time; for there is no universal consensus – nothing near it, either on educational methods, or even on objectives.

This is, perhaps, a little high-flown: I seem to hear the teachers themselves, earthy idealists mostly, pricking the bubbles. Let us be concrete again: here is a programme in the area we are discussing which resolved its problem rather happily.

The producer was planning a pair of programmes – play and documentary – about young people and the police. For the play, Colin Welland wrote a lively story called 'Bank Holiday', about two boys on a holiday trip to the seaside. The elder, Towzer, has left Secondary Modern and is at work; he has a fine bike; he's a steady type, rides it well. The younger, Tod, is at Grammar School still; bright and fiery, he puts on for the outing, over his leather jacket, a sleeveless denim coat festooned with medals and swastikas. On the way, they are stopped by a police car – not for wrongdoing, just checked as a precaution: these youngsters could be looking for trouble. They are not, actually; when a rowdy gang of 'greasers', who clearly are, enter the seaside café where Towzer and Tod are lunching, Towzer takes evasive action and pulls Tod out. But everyone assumes they're out to stir it up: they look dressed for the part. At night, they tog up and make for the dance hall: the bouncer throws them out – their hair is too long. They camp in an open space near the edge of the town, recommended by Tod's father: in the small hours the police arrive, make them get up and leave: camping was stopped there years ago. The boys ride off, come to a municipal garden, run their bike back and forth over it till the flowers are shattered. They have done what was expected of them.

I asked the producer what the play was about: he said, 'It's a cautionary tale about putting labels on people'. 'Yes, but it will be taken for an anti-police play.' Meanwhile, his co-producer was preparing the accompanying documentary. This was to be about real policemen, so he enlisted the co-operation of the Metropolitan Commissioner. Then he showed 'Bank Holiday' (not yet transmitted) to a group of London policemen, so that they would know what viewers had seen the week before the documentary. The reaction was immediate: they did not like 'Bank Holiday' at all – policemen would never behave like that. Fair comment on some of the acting, perhaps (actors find it difficult to play policemen quite 'straight'); hardly on the author, whose writing is always carefully researched. The producer, apparently in an impasse, saw his opportunity. 'Right, we'll show again in the next programme the police actions you've criticised, and you'll say what's wrong with them. Then we'll stage some other episodes, with real policemen operating as they really would.' Mollification all round; excellent co-operation from the police; and a good programme, 'The Police and You'. One little weakness: the last episode ended with a longish homily by the Chief Inspector to an erring youth. In the interests of truth – not to mention public relations – it had to stay, though we felt it would be counter-productive. It stayed; and it was.

We have seen examples of young people in rebellion, or provoking adults to believe them so. But few of them are, basically, rebels; despite occasional, or even frequent, acts of defiance they are mainly conformists – however outlandish, to an adult, their styles of conformity may sometimes appear. They are mostly insecure, and insecurity tends to breed a guarded conservatism. The adult world they are entering seems, for many, a harsh one, and it is; but they are not immune from lethargy, and it is safer to leave things as they are. Their outlook is limited, and they need to be stimulated, provoked even, into seeing that change is possible and that changes are brought about by people. Good teachers, I believe, and broadcasters too if their work is bound up with teaching, feel this as a duty: both, in consequence, are more apt to incur charges of being leftish than the reverse. One answer to this is that not all change is 'progressist' in even the faintest political sense: stimulate young people to see the importance of conservation, for instance, and they will respond with enthusiasm. I could multiply such examples, if my purpose was to make debating points, but the value of the exercise would be doubtful. School broadcasting's central task, for this audience, is surely clear: to make programmes as thought-provoking as it possibly can. There will be errors of judgement, here and there; but if ever it were to fall back from this objective, it would indeed be jibbing at a responsibility as welcome as it is sometimes onerous.

5.3 School Broadcasting for a multi-racial society

By the time School TV started race relationships were already a familiar problem in certain parts of Britain. In 1958 there were the Notting Hill riots; small affairs perhaps in the perspective of history, but they made a deep impression at the time. During the next few years the immigrant population increased rapidly: the face of parts of England was changing.

We treated this as a social problem; put on 'Current Affairs' programmes about it from time to time which were cool, presented the facts, avoided preaching of course, worked for understanding of and sympathy with the immigrants' situation. Teachers approved of these programmes; I wondered if they had much effect on those minds in which the seeds of prejudice were already sown. We tried short dramatised scenes: inevitably perhaps, with little room for development of character, they presented unconvincing stereotypes. The stock quasi-documentary situation, too, lost impact with repetition: the coloured man knocking at the apartment house, the brief exchange, the door closed in his face.

There was a more basic problem, however. Our audience consisted for the most part of all-white (or all-pink) classes of youngsters, many of them never seeing a coloured person from one year's end to another; but a substantial minority would consist of white and coloured together, and in some classes the coloured would outnumber the white. Yet we always seemed to be talking about coloured people in the third person. Who were 'they' and who were 'we'–all, surely, should be 'we'? I would pore over scripts, imagining both kinds of audience and how the programme would sound to each. I do not think there was a solution. If one were talking directly to these classes, one would use a different style of address for each; but broadcasts cannot differentiate. To stand right outside, to exteriorise the issues worked if the programme was speaking, say, to Sixth Formers about a specific measure–the 1971 Immigration Act, for instance; but with younger pupils this was too aloof. We tried West Indian presenters, including distinguished ones such as the author George Lamming: this was better; it gave a more personal slant to the story. But it did not quite circumvent the basic difficulty.

In the later 60s we changed our policy, partly because of doubts about the value of the head-on approach to a social 'problem' (a few teachers–not many–thought it could be counter-productive), partly because the climate was changing anyway. There were still–are still–deplorable incidents, and a feeling of alienation among many coloured adolescents; but there is also a wider recognition and acceptance of Britain as a multi-racial country, and some awareness of the indispensable part the new immigrants are playing in our society. More and more coloured children in school are second generation immigrants only. The proper course for school broadcasting, surely, is to reflect this change simply by ensuring that coloured people are properly represented on the screen, in both actual and fictional situations, as ordinary members of our community.

Actuality, in this context, presents few problems: in its plainest form, it simply shows children of mixed races working or playing at school together. Most production being London-based and London being a particularly cosmopolitan city, if children are brought to the studio or cameras taken to classrooms, shots naturally and without any prearrangement often include coloured children. Or to take another situation: in coming to decisions about jobs coloured youngsters, while they have special problems of their own, share many of their perplexities with their white counterparts. Personal relationships again, with parents for instance, present problems to all young people alike; though they differ between different national cultures – Indian and Pakistani parents, notably, are much stricter than ours, particularly towards girls – a common bond of sympathy which crosses cultural boundaries can be tapped.

A rather moving programme one of our producers made featured an Indian family living in West London. We saw the family at home, sensed the atmosphere of natural self-discipline, saw the mother preparing a meal (very Indian, and to adult eyes at least, succulent), the family at table, the girl at her Indian dancing class. We also observed a dawning love-relationship between young Indian boy and girl – the girl highly restricted in Western eyes by the traditions of her culture, the boy already largely anglicised, claiming for himself and yearning to claim for her also the freedoms taken for granted in his adopted country. For English youngsters to recognise, in a situation which would naturally evoke sympathetic response, that other youngsters from different backgrounds have personal problems which may be akin to their own, but are more deep-seated, more complex and more intractable, was an experience which both provoked thought among them and, one may hope, enlarged their capacity for fellow-feeling.

Fictional treatments require, of course, care and sensitivity on the part of writer and producer: it is the height of unreality, for instance, if not insufferable condescension, consistently to depict coloured people as more virtuous than the rest of us. Producer and writer together devised for a term of 'Television Club' a serial story in which the lead character was a West Indian 'innocent abroad' – a merchant seaman who took his discharge in London and at once got involved, all unsuspecting, in a robbery. In the subsequent adventure of getting on the track of the criminals he teams up with an English boy and girl who are often a jump ahead of him, but need his steadiness to see them through. Writer (Leonard Kingston) and actor (Kenneth Gardnier) between them achieved quite an effective mix of weaknesses and strengths in this West Indian character; and over seven weeks there was time, too, to develop his personality in some depth.

The driver in 'Last Bus', as we have seen, was West Indian too; and the writer made him at the crisis as guilty of cowardice as the others—more so, since a colleague was being attacked. But the mitigating circumstances in his case, if not exonerating, were certainly substantial: as the ensuing cross-questioning revealed, the consequences for him of disablement should he be seriously injured while helping his colleague were different in kind from those the white passengers would suffer.

In documentary programmes we naturally also looked beyond contemporary Britain: to how racism bred violence in Nazi Germany, in South Africa, in the United States. We told Primary School children, in a series of programmes introduced by Learie Constantine,[1] the story of the slave trade and of the pioneers who fought to rid our country of its shame: we paid honour to the name of Martin Luther King and his struggle in the cause of humanity. More simply, we tried to interest children in the background of our own coloured people by pictures of life in India and in the West Indies today. But perhaps educational broadcasting's most useful contribution to good race relationships in this country has been in two quite different fields.

The first was a series not for schoolchildren, but for teachers, produced by Felicity Kinross of the School TV Department for BBC Further Education, under the title 'In our Midst'. Its purpose was to illustrate and discuss some of the problems which schools encounter in providing for immigrant children and associating their parents with the school's aims and methods. One particularly successful programme showed five newly arrived children from a Punjabi village on their first day in the reception class of a London Primary School: it threw into sharp relief the bewildering strangeness of their surroundings by intercutting the

[1] The famous West Indian cricketer; afterwards, as Lord Constantine, a member of the Race Relations Board and a Governor of the BBC.

'Hello, Hello'—new audience: new series

routine of an English school with scenes from the life in India they knew. The contrasts came as a real shock to teachers involved with immigrant children.

The second significant contribution to immigrants' educational needs has been made by School Radio with the series 'Hello! Hello!' and 'Hello again'. Designed to help immigrant children learning English as a second language, the programmes consist of short plays, each containing a song: some have a contemporary English setting, some are based on folk stories from our immigrants' countries of origin. The series were produced in consultation with the Schools' Council team responsible for devising a new English course for immigrant children, and the language of the programmes was carefully graded to match a defined stage of this course. 'Hello! Hello!' was much appreciated in the schools; and though no longer broadcast it is still available for purchase as a set of tapes.

A few weeks ago I happened to switch on the TV towards the end of an evening programme: an Englishman was speaking, a potter, who had spent much of his life in Africa encouraging the development of pottery as an indigenous craft. His closing words struck me and I noted them; they ran something like this: ' . . . nothing so phoney as fostering good relationships between the races, but perhaps establishing some personal friendships between individuals.' Harsh words, but one saw what he meant: only human contact at the grass-roots of society can heal scars here, can effectively build for the future. The mass media with all their resources are strangely impotent. School broadcasting shares in their limitations, but it can help in practical ways, as we have seen; and if it cannot still unworthy passions, it can nevertheless inform, give pause for thought, and work for the day when racial differences among men will be neither blown up nor flattened out, but respected and cherished.

6 FRIENDS AND RELATIONS

BBC School Broadcasting is not an island: when we have considered its consumers together with its products, and the School Broadcasting Council's role in linking them, we have still, to avoid overcrowding the canvas, left out of account much else that is related to the service and may interact with it. For instance, the BBC speaks to children in school through its local as well as its national services; its school programmes are open to the eyes and ears of parents as well as of children; and BBC School Broadcasting is part of a national institution whose influence is worldwide. School TV in Britain, moreover, is also provided under IBA auspices, and by certain Local Education Authorities on closed circuits. Seen in this light, BBC School Broadcasting has a number of friends and relations, some close, some less so. In this chapter we pan across this extended family group.

6.1 BBC Further Education Broadcasting

The story of BBC Further Education (a term embracing the whole field of post-school education) would require a book in itself; and most of it has no place in this one. Yet we have already seen examples of how the Further Education Departments' work can support and nourish the work of School Broadcasting; and (as one would expect) the liaison between the production staffs of the two operations is such that of all School Broadcasting's 'friends and relations', BBC Further Education is the closest.

At the formal level, this is reflected most markedly in the persons of Sir Lincoln Ralphs, who is both Vice-Chairman of the School Broadcasting Council and Chairman of the Further Education Advisory Council (a body constituted in 1965 on broadly similar lines to the SBC, though with advisory powers only), and of John Robson, who as the BBC's Education Secretary serves both bodies equally. Among producers there have been over the years, particularly in television, substantial interchanges of staff, some on a temporary, others a permanent basis; in the field, the School Broadcasting Council's Education Officers frequently supplement the work of their much smaller team of colleagues specialising in Further Education. Close physical contiguity of the two radio output departments and the two Councils' HQ staffs next to Broadcasting House, and of the TV departments at Ealing, is also an important factor in promoting co-operation. Parts of the Further Education Departments' wide-ranging work are specially relevant to the story of school broadcasting, and deserve some consideration here: more detail is readily available in other BBC publications.[1]

Further Education broadcasting in the BBC, in the sense of broadcasts with a specifically educational purpose, and following an organised pattern, is as old as school broadcasting: it too dates from 1924. Many older listeners will still remember the satisfaction they got from following at home M. Stéphan's courses in French; others will cherish the stimulus of participation in one of the hundreds of discussion groups which were organised round broadcasts in the 1930s under the impulse of the Hadow Committee's report.[2] And although Further Education by radio was strangely slow (if one excepts the useful work of the Forces' Educational Broadcasts) in getting under way again after the war, by 1960 there had been experiments over a wide range of subjects and affecting many different categories of audience and of interest groups; while in some areas (notably language courses) the output was both substantial and sustained. In 1961 television, too, entered the field. Evidence to the Pilkington Committee was rich in requests from outside bodies for TV broadcasting time for adult education in specific areas and for specific audiences; and it was no surprise when the White Paper which followed close on the Committee's report foreshadowed a substantial increase in the air-time available, on ITV as well as BBC, for adult education.

---

[1] See 'BBC Further Education: an Introduction' (A BBC Further Education Bulletin); and BBC Handbook 1974.
[2] *New Ventures in Broadcasting: A Study in Adult Education*, BBC, 1928.

Neither the BBC's evidence to the Pilkington Committee, nor the Committee's report itself in 1962, made any reference to the uses of broadcasting in the in-service training of teachers. But this was soon to come: it derived from the surge of interest in curriculum development which was a feature of the early 60s (reflected in the creation in 1965 of the Schools Council), and the shift of emphasis from the quantitative to the qualitative aspects of teacher training once the major expansions of the Colleges of Education had been set in train. The first TV series specifically for teachers ('Mathematics '64') came with the opening of BBC 2; it was followed the same year by 'How and Why?', an exploration of new approaches to physics teaching. Both these series contained much which, ten years later, has become common coinage in mathematics and physics teaching. Who would have thought ten years ago, asks John Cain, producer of 'How and Why?' that most young children would today be bandying words like 'sets' around and even, occasionally, understanding them; and how many physics teachers would have foreseen it to be fairly common practice for teenage children to be measuring the size of a molecule?

By 1965, when by setting up the Advisory Council with its three Programme Committees dealing with both media, the BBC brought the structure of its Further Education service into line with that of its school broadcasting, this service's programme output also was on a scale comparable with that of the School Broadcasting Departments; and Donald Grattan, Head of Further Education's newly established TV Department, from the outset saw as one of its prime roles, and indeed its most distinctive one, the provision of short 'refresher' courses for a wide variety of professional or occupational groups: farmers, doctors, social workers, shop stewards, managers, nurses – and, inevitably, teachers.

Over the next few years, almost every major professional concern or interest among teachers was catered for somewhere or other on TV or radio: there were series for music teachers and for chemistry teachers; for teachers of young immigrant children and for teachers of general studies in technical colleges. A few series, such as 'Developing Maths Today' on radio and 'Sex Education in the Primary School' on TV had specific links with

Updating physics teachers—Sister St Joan of Arc with liquid nitrogen ('How and Why?')

series broadcast to schools. Some others ('Aids in Teaching' and 'Using School TV') dealt with applications of educational technology. Many more turned over, with conspicuously fruitful results, the soil in which the seeds of parent–teacher co-operation can best be sown because the concerns of each so manifestly overlap: the psychological development and upbringing of pre-school and primary age children.

In all such series the ideal situation at the receiving end – the picture every producer likes to conjure in his mind – is that of a group of dedicated practitioners (better still two or three dedicated who have roped in two or three more not quite so dedicated) gathered round the set and then discussing its challenging or provocative message into the dark hours. It does happen – sometimes with discussion separated from transmission by hours or days, because transmission times are rarely ideal – but of course exceptionally rather than normally. Where it does, the spirit of the 30s in adult education broadcasting has indeed been revived, and with the added edge that comes from professionals' succumbing to, or resisting, the urge to tear strips off fellow practitioners.

Fifty-odd short series in a few years were at least evidence of a stream of innovatory thinking and techniques in education, making the job of teaching more challenging than ever before. Much that was shown was valuable and appreciated; some was inspiring. Presenting teachers to teachers is a delicate job, for personality is dominant, even when it is quietly at work, guiding or probing, rather than conspicuous in virtuosity. It is good now and then to see a real genius in action (Dorothy Heathcote, featured in the series 'Improvised Drama' springs to mind); but even the teacher of outstanding talent must be shown with discretion, for what can the ordinary mortal do in response except goggle with admiration or, more defensively, seek to convince himself that this *trouvaille* of the BBC enjoyed advantages unknown to him in the liveliness of his pupils or the plushness of his working conditions? Conversely, to present teachers of no more than average capacity risks underpinning complacency rather than stimulating thought at the receiving end.

The programmes mainly steered successfully between these extremes; but as a service to teachers the enterprise suffered from three handicaps which school broadcasting escapes. First, the Further Education Departments lacked fully adequate resources for publicity and promotion. Secondly, because most viewing and listening took place at home, feed-back on the scale that the School Broadcasting Council achieves for school programmes was not possible. And thirdly, whereas the aim was to appeal to a broad cross-section of those teachers professionally concerned with the topic under discussion, in practice (such is human nature) it was mainly the initiated, the experienced and the knowledgeable – those least in need – who actually viewed and listened.

So there was a change of policy; and for 1972, the two Further Education Departments planned together a project on quite a new scale: a series of twenty TV and twenty radio programmes, 'ROSLA and After', with strong support literature, covering the whole range of problems and opportunities set for schools by the raising of the school leaving age to sixteen. As Roger Owen, the producer, put it:

We were going to put most of our eggs into one basket; we were going to choose an important basket; and we were going to make sure that as many people as possible knew what was inside it.[1]

The aim of the series reflected the fundamental nature of the challenge imposed by ROSLA: it was 'to explore the assumptions which informed the whole of "non-academic" Secondary education, and the practices they led to': its most significant point of departure was the Schools Council Inquiry of 1968 on Young School Leavers with its inescapable message (echoing many of the findings of the Newsom Report five years earlier) that much of what was offered to pupils of average or below-average ability was thought by them to be either 'useless', or 'boring', or both.

Some months before the series started, there was a big drive to enlist the interest of Authorities and schools: at twenty meetings, attended by 3500 people, excerpts from pilot programmes and samples of support literature were shown. To encourage group viewing and discussion in the schools themselves, each TV programme was given one of its transmissions at 3.45 pm. And to supplement the BBC's sources of feed-back, an independent assessment was undertaken by Ronald Seymour of the University of Keele Institute of Education. The course material each week consisted of a challenging essay on a defined topic ('Aims', 'Curriculum Building', 'Discipline' and so on) written by an expert practitioner; a TV programme illustrating the topic through one or more case studies of schools in action; and a radio programme following up this experience with comments from other teachers and, frequently, cross-questioning of the essay writer or TV presenter (often the same person).

The project was remarkable for the willing co-operation of Heads in allowing their schools' activities to be exposed to TV film cameras, with all this implies in disturbance and apprehension, and for the evidence of groups of teachers sustaining passionate discussion in schoolrooms from the programme's close at 4.15 till ejection by the janitor at 6.30. This is not the place for a detailed description of the programmes or assessment of their

[1] Report on 'ROSLA and After', BBC, 1974.

impact; but an observation in the Russell Report on Adult Education (published in 1973) is significant:

The BBC's massive 'ROSLA and After' operation demonstrated the power of educational broadcasting to bring about a change of climate within which individuals are helped to develop by taking part in learning groups using discussion, case-study material and the like.

The National Union of Teachers estimated that one in three Local Education Authorities used the series as a major element in their work of preparing teachers to meet the new situation.

From sales of support literature it seems likely that at least 50,000 teachers followed the first half of 'ROSLA and After' (apart from casual home viewers); but there was a fall-off in the second half, suggesting that so sustained an effort risked, for some participants, draining the subject dry. The successor to 'ROSLA and After' therefore, 'Early Years at School' (to be followed by 'The Middle Years'), has a modular structure of programmes and support material in which each module has an autonomous validity. To quote Roger Owen again, 'the big basket will be there, but no one will be expected to buy all the materials',

The same modular principle has informed the planning of Further Education's most substantial foreign language series for 1974-5: 'Kontakte', designed for beginners in German, and it too involving both television and radio. It is the latest in a long line of series – several annually in one or other medium – which have vastly enlarged opportunities for language-learning at home and reinforced the studies of those attending classes – besides being pleasurable viewing or listening in their own right. These TV language programmes are among those which now have daytime transmissions during the week also; so they are available to schools and colleges in session as well.

Looking further forward, Further Education's plans envisage an increasing attention to the needs of the disadvantaged in society. In particular, research is now in progress on a broadcasting project designed to help wholly or partially illiterate adults to achieve literacy. As we have seen, school broadcasting has for some years now been involved in preventive work in this field, helping to obviate initial difficulties some children experience in acquiring reading skills. Further Education will soon be joining in with its own distinctive contribution.

Remedial reading, therefore, and in-service teacher training are two fields in which the concerns of school and further education broadcasting overlap: there are many others. The very first educational TV series for a defined post-school audience was 'Engineering Science', produced in School TV Department in 1962, and designed to supplement the national 'G' course in Technical Colleges. This remains, to my mind, something of a classic in its adroit combination of efficient audio-visual teaching of principles with illustration of their practical applications in industry; and there has been regular provision in engineering for a similar audience ever since. Two years later a general studies series was started, mainly for day release students, which won a substantial – and critical – following in school Sixth and Fifth Forms also.

Meanwhile more pupils, by no means all academically minded, were staying on at school till seventeen or eighteen, while others were electing to continue their studies in what seemed to them the more free and grown-up atmosphere of the Colleges. This progressive blurring of the edges of the two types of institution is reflected today both in the breadth of educational TV programmes offered for institutional use in daytime hours, and in the 'adoption' by Colleges also of series designed primarily for schools. To the latter category belong, pre-eminently, 'Humanities' series such as 'Scene'; within the former are, currently, a language and an economics series, and (from the School TV stable) 'A Job Worth Doing?', a careers series designed for students with O level qualifications whether in schools or colleges. All these last, and their successors in 1974-5, can be seen at week-ends by the general public also.

Thus a strong element of cross-breeding has, happily, survived the growth of School and Further Education broadcasting to maturity. It has to be positively striven for, if the departmental rigidities endemic in as large an organisation as the BBC are to be avoided, for a close association has much to give to producers and users of both. There is every sign that the collaboration will continue, and grow.

6.2 ITV School Broadcasting

When one of the ITV companies, Associated Rediffusion Ltd, announced in December 1956 that they would be starting a service of school television in a little more than four months' time, they ruffled quite a few feathers. The National Union of Teachers asked what consultation there had been, and would be, with teachers: there had not been any. That was soon put right, however (there was some pained surprise in the other camp at the number of luminaries of the educational world who were happy to lend their names to sponsor the upstart). The School Broadcasting Council, which more than a year before had extracted from the BBC and made public a starting date of September 1957 for their service – still called 'experimental' – understandably turned up its nose at the rival and looked the other way. The BBC, in the person of Enid Love who was in charge of its School TV production team,[1] set about ensuring that when it went on the air it would do so with four series instead of the advertised two, making its output comparable in scale with Associated Rediffusion's.

Associated Rediffusion's initial programmes were transmitted in the London and Midland areas only, and were received mainly on sets loaned or given for the purpose. Over the next few years other ITV companies joined in – the larger ones as programme contributors, the smaller mainly as recipients of the service on the network. A liaison service with the consumers was developed, more complex than that of the School Broadcasting Council because of the independence of the companies in programming initiative, and never as strong. There was a somewhat edgy rivalry between BBC and ITV, manifest beneath the velvet gloves on occasions when, often in response to the wishes of the consumers, they shared a platform to expose their objectives and their products to audiences of teachers intrigued both by the potential of the new medium and by the breach of the BBC's monopoly. The rivalry was by no means altogether unhealthy: the BBC was a substantial and venerable enough institution to be fair game for a little tail-twisting (it was only later that it set itself

[1] She was later, in one of those moves which gave piquancy to BBC-ITV relationships, to leave and take charge of Associated Rediffusion's School TV.

on a firm course of shattering the 'auntie' soubriquet); and rivalry was anyhow tempered from the outset by a genuine effort, prompted by self-interest as well as by the consumers', not to tread in programme planning violently on each other's toes. Thus, in their first major statistical survey of what schools were following which series, the School Broadcasting Council gladly undertook to elicit information about ITV viewing also and to communicate the results to the ITA.

The BBC undoubtedly had, in these early stages, some built-in advantages. Some schools had sets which could only receive BBC; some teachers deplored the political decision to set up ITV in the first place, and judged from the quality of its general programming that it was unlikely to make a valuable contribution to serious broadcasting in any context; and the BBC's plans were rooted in much more intensive exploration by the School Broadcasting Council of schools' needs. Moreover after the first experimental two years the BBC agreed the Council's proposals for expanding its service on a scale which also established it, by something more than a short head, as the major provider of school TV programmes. Simultaneously the actual operators – the producers – in both camps were exploiting a common interest in the techniques of their trade and establishing mutual sympathies which ignored, and in a measure undermined, the more guarded stances of the policy makers. Thus attitudes developed, and fortunately persist, between friendly rivals in which the friendships are much more apparent than the rivalries.

It was probably wise on the School Broadcasting Council's part to carry on the business of developing its TV service without looking over its shoulder at what the other party was doing (ITV plans remained unknown to the Council's committees at the time of decision making, and its programmes were never discussed at their meetings). The Council's experience had made it very aware that to attract and maintain an audience of committed and purposeful users, continuity of plan was as important as innovation; and a pattern naturally developed in which the two services complemented each other. Both were often exploring new ground, but the BBC provided the major share of solid and sustained (though never rigid) programming in areas shown by the Council's field research to meet continuing needs, whereas

ITV took advantage of its multiple programme sources among the individual companies to probe in a more opportunistic way. Occasionally such probes might be undertaken by one of the smaller companies, at first within a local area only: it was Grampian TV, one of the smallest, which made the first venture into the sex education field.

During the 60s a kind of unexplicit gentlemen's agreement grew up between BBC and ITV production departments: a territory in which either had established itself over some time as an effective provider for a defined age of child would not be deliberately 'invaded' by the other. This was commonsense, for as ITV became recognised as a permanent part of the broadcasting scenery teachers increasingly surveyed the offerings of BBC and ITV with impartiality and without station loyalty; and they were also critical if they sensed that plans had been drawn up without any consultation between the parties. Liaison between departmental Heads became formalised, therefore, to the extent of two regular meetings annually – one at which embryonic outlines of plans for eighteen months hence were exchanged before they were submitted to the respective bodies' external Programme Committees; and a later one at which, as far as possible, undesirable clashes in times of programme transmissions were ironed out. This is a useful procedure: ideally, perhaps, it should be followed up by exchanges of more detailed information, and if necessary avoiding action, between BBC and ITV producers who might be cultivating similar ground (for instance, miscellany series for infants or juniors), where overlap or duplication may occur in details not decided till a later stage. Such exchanges do take place from time to time, but they are more difficult to ensure than might seem, and in the event dubiously valuable. The chance of a class's seeing the same topic handled in, say, consecutive weeks by both organisations is anyhow remote; and since the treatments will certainly differ, the experience is as likely to be educationally productive as the reverse.

Nevertheless there were voices – including that of the Pilkington Committee itself – which in the early years of school television declared with some force that guidelines for policy and the sponsorship of the services provided by BBC and ITA should be the responsibility of a single body: otherwise there would be wastefulness, even if rivalry meant no more than a healthy competition to achieve the higher quality of performance, with the ground rules and times of kick-off agreed and observed on both sides. In other words, if the School Broadcasting Council was really an independent body speaking for the world of education and not just a front organisation for the BBC, why should it not speak to, and for, both parties?

Compelling in theory, this change would have been, as the School Broadcasting Council observed to the Pilkington Committee, cumbersome and prejudicial to good relationships between Council and producers; we have heard less of it latterly, and for good reasons. First, with TV developing and radio expanding during the 60s, the School Broadcasting Council had more than enough on its plate already. A further score of series to cope with would either have required an increase in the number of its Programme Committees, reducing the field of each to a narrower spectrum of school life; or imposed on each so many responsibilities that little or nothing could have been discussed in depth or in detail. It would have burdened the Committees with an additional weight of officialdom (ITV programmes stem not from one source, but several), and the officials themselves with a time-consuming job of co-ordinating material from multiple sources for presentation to the committees. More important, it would have meant that departmental heads and producers in both organisations, instead of being anxious to share with committee members the full measure of their forward thinking and their problems, would have been inhibited from frankness by the presence of others whom, no matter how friendly, they knew to be combing the same beach. Petty? No, just human; and not only human, but professional. The Central Religious Advisory Committee, which does advise both BBC and ITV (but advises only) is rich in experience of the problems.

So we have been, surely, better off as we are. 'As we are' leaves room for major joint enterprises in field research, such as the newly published study,[1] in association with Local Education Authorities, of schools' use of broadcasts; it also results in a larger

[1] 'Using Broadcasts in Schools: A Study and Evaluation', by C. G. Hayter, BBC/ITV, 1974.

(though still small) number of representatives of the vast 'world of education' playing a practical part in broadcast policy making – which must be all to the good. That is not to say, of course, that the present arrangement (or agreement to have no arrangement) is valid for all time. Under the fiercest heat of economic or other pressures (to which ITV has recently shown itself the more vulnerable), combined rather than piecemeal resistance might serve both parties best. And any major change in, for instance, the funding arrangements for school broadcasts, or the networks on which they operate, would no doubt entail a review of their sponsoring mechanisms also.

Meanwhile, ITV's programmes enrich the choices open to schools, and both parties benefit from this. ITV series such as 'Picture Box', 'The Way we Used to Live', and 'Seeing and Doing' have a reputation in schools as high as the best of the BBC's, and nobody any longer supposes that ITV school programmes are any the worse for being financed by advertising. If I have a regret still, it is that producers in the two camps see too few of each other's programmes and have too few opportunities for sharing experience. A pity, but how much more fortunate our lot than that of Company Programme Heads and Controller BBC 1, watching each other hawklike to make, or forestall, the next audience-grabbing schedule change.

6.3 Closed-circuit television

Closed-circuit television developed, for a number of practical purposes, along with television broadcasting in the fifties. In the educational sphere, among others; for instance, in hospital training the uses of the electronic camera in giving groups of students an unencumbered view of complex operations quickly became apparent. And school television broadcasting had hardly begun before the possibilities of closed-circuit TV were being explored in a number of schools also. In the early sixties the College of Technology at Plymouth, as an offshoot of its job of providing basic training to students of electronic technology, co-operated with neighbouring Local Education Authorities in setting up a small network offering programmes to schools in the area. In

1965 Glasgow opened a TV service for all its city schools: three years later London followed suit. Meanwhile the enthusiasm had spread to Colleges of Education: many had equipped studios and were also using the new facility to extend students' experience of seeing classroom teaching in action.

The motives underlying this flurry of activity were various. Among the Local Education Authorities there was, first, the conviction that here was an enrichment of teachers' resources of enormous potential. Secondly, closed-circuit TV could not only cater for local needs in fields such as history, geography and careers guidance, using local illustrations which would be out of place on a national network; it could also help make good local deficiencies in specialist teaching expertise. Third, a cctv system could through its multiple channels carry a large load of traffic, mitigating timetable difficulties by offering several repeats of each programme; and there could be previews for teachers into the bargain. Fourth, because of the limited area of coverage, continuous contact and interchange of views between producers and users would be easy to ensure. Last, and most important, this would be a service in which many teachers, together with inspectors and advisers, would be involved not simply as consumers, but in programme planning and production as well.

Glasgow started its service with a Maths series for Secondary schools, and French for the Primaries. Interesting choices: nothing could have been less local in content. The aim was to support teachers wrestling with the 'new maths', or embarking on a subject which was new to many Primary Schools. The maths project, in particular, was well prepared: a completely new textbook had been written and issued to all schools concerned, and the precise contribution that each broadcast was to make was carefully dovetailed into the course plan. When I saw it in use, I was struck by the ease with which the teacher's work led in to the programme and the programme's material was taken up by the teacher at the end. In the studio, the visual devices used were simple and efficient; and the intimate atmosphere – so different from the forbidding vastness of the BBC Television Centre – made for easy communication between presenter and director, both experienced teachers who every few weeks changed roles.

London's service gave more attention to local material, but

was soon ranging widely. Training was thoroughly organised, with an effective screening process to ensure that the best available talent was taken on for production. The original idea was that teachers seconded as TV producers should revert to their normal jobs after two years. In fact the best proved too valuable to lose; and indeed the best of the Inner London Education Authority's TV productions have been of high quality, with relatively limited but not skimpy budgets often acting as a spur to imaginative and ingenious use of resources.

Yet over the country as a whole, while closed-circuit television in higher education has continued to make steady progress, the hopes of the school enthusiasts of ten years ago have not been fulfilled. Only a handful of Authorities are operating services for their schools on any scale, and even they have big question marks over their long-term future. Universities and Polytechnics can afford to cater for small minorities: L.E.A.-funded systems must, to be reasonably cost-productive, attract a substantial proportion of potential users as regular clients. In the event, and particularly at the secondary level, local enterprise has not escaped the problems familiar to the national networks also. Off-air viewing, even with multiple transmissions, is difficult to arrange: to maintain a comprehensive service of feed-back, despite the relative physical proximity of the clients, is still time-consuming, and quite a costly element in the budget. With high staff-turnover in big city schools, and amid the other stresses to which they have been exposed, the notion for the average teacher that this service has some special relevance or cachet by virtue of being 'our' service, provided by 'our teachers', proved chimerical. The reality is surely that however remote the school, if the broadcasts offered effectively meet a teacher's needs, he will feel in contact with the provider; and if not, not. It is precisely the remoteness of so many of their clients from the large urban centres which gives the national school broadcasting services the assurance of continued vitality for some time to come; for on a national scale the convenience, and the economics, of simultaneous distribution to so many receiving points is crucial. But in large cities, the increasing use of programmes as resource material, mainly not taken off air, is being matched by a parallel provision of documentation in print, picture and sound through their own

Resource Centres, supplemented by what is generated in the smaller Teachers' Centres and in the schools themselves; and in these circumstances the maintenance of an expensive distribution system of programmes by cable is bound to come into question.

Ten years ago it seemed that closed-circuit television might well develop to an extent which would impinge upon, and discernibly modify, what it was appropriate for the national networks to offer. It has not done so in the event; yet it is helping substantially to enlarge the arena in which television's potential for education can be discussed with knowledge and understanding. More directly, it is providing new insights into teaching method for all those who have actually been involved in programme production, and making them more informed critics of the productions of others. It has also served to take some of the mystique out of television, demonstrating that while TV needs resources on a national scale, and nationwide recruitment of talent, to achieve the highest sophistication of technique and to give scope to producers of outstanding flair, local studios can at the very least be manufactories of varied and good-quality audiovisual material for their Authorities' schools, and perhaps for a wider market. It seems likely that this is where their future lies.

6.4 BBC Local Radio

Observers of the educational scene in the USA are often struck by how deeply schools there are involved in the local community, and the local community in them. The same is true of educational broadcasting there (the term is used to describe the work of the hundreds of small non-commercial stations whose output is 'educative' in the broadest sense, but often includes programmes for schools). Standards in these local stations are often patchy: extreme decentralisation of effort, together with the absence of any licensing system for the funding of production, create recurrent financial problems which stand in the way of consistent development. Yet a visitor from Britain to one of the more flourishing of these stations is repeatedly conscious of the intimate, informal ways in which their output reflects the interests and talents of the local community.

In our much smaller country, once the national networks were established, the potential of local radio was for long not apparent: indeed in the educational field, as we have seen, it was not until the 1950s that the generality of schools were really coming to terms with what national broadcasting had to offer, and with what was involved for them in exploiting this. But by the end of the decade three factors were combining to turn the BBC's thoughts in the direction of local radio. First, TV was supplanting radio as the main source of entertainment and information for the mass audience, and thereby nudging radio into seeking new avenues for development. Secondly, this same growth of TV was throwing into relief how inexpensive a provider radio was. Third, and most important, these emerging pressures coincided with a surge of interest in community development, to offset a pervasive feeling among the public at large that the big battalions were increasingly taking over the control of human affairs. So the case for the BBC's developing local radio became embodied in its evidence to the Pilkington Committee, and that Committee's report in 1962 effectively brought the matter into the realm of public debate.

What the BBC had in mind for local radio was not simply a local application of traditional programme styles and content—either in the educational field or in any other. Education in particular offered opportunities for a new approach. Here is how Hal Bethell, BBC Local Radio Education Organiser, has put it:

We offered, as the basis for a practical working relationship with the local community, the concept of a productive partnership to which each party would bring its own special attributes. The BBC would put in its accumulated skills in broadcasting, its willingness to share these skills with others, an allocation of the station's general and supportive facilities and the salaried services of its Education Producer. To match this, we hoped that the educational world would provide specialised guidance, direct professional co-operation in the preparation of educational broadcasts and associated materials, and in the promotion, distribution and evaluation of these products. This was a scheme which, recognising the separate worth of distinct funds of experience, advocated that they should be pooled in the making of broadcasting an effective local educational resource.

Not so very different, then, from the partnership on a national scale we examined in Chapter 4, save in one important particular: 'direct professional co-operation in the preparation of educational broadcasts and associated materials' meant that the talents of the community would be drawn in to participate in the actual making of programmes, and take the prime responsibility for the production of their necessary accompaniments. The stations themselves, though part and parcel of the BBC, would have complete independence in their day-to-day running; the advisory panels set up for each station to guide the work of its single specialist educational producer would similarly be independent of the School Broadcasting Council, which limited its involvement to approving the constitution of the panels.

In relation to school broadcasts, enlisting the talents of the community meant of course, first and foremost, involving local teachers in the station's work – and not just occasionally, but also on a longer-term basis, as full working partners with the BBC's specialist. This is turn meant convincing the Local Education Authorities that here was an enterprise which deserved their co-operation because it would bring them benefits in return. How successful the local stations have been in this may be judged by the fact that since the first one opened in 1967 some four hundred teachers have acquired, in the stations, experience of radio production, while thousands more have made creative contributions to programmes. The key lies in the Authorities' willingness to second teachers from their school work to the service of the stations; the basis of secondment varies from a half-day weekly by several teachers to the attachment of one or two for a continuous period of up to two years.

With this kind of support the BBC's single specialist can achieve much. In the autumn of 1973, for instance, over eighty programme series for local schools were transmitted from the twenty local stations. Most of these programmes are related in some way to the locality: its history, geography, artistic achievements, social problems, job opportunities. But not all: particular talents cater also for particular local needs – in support of the teaching of French, for instance; or more general ones (though still often with a local flavour), such as stories and music for young children. And most important of all perhaps, teachers belonging to, or familiar with the problems of, the immigrant members of the community are drawn in to provide for their special needs, in school and outside it. The number of schools using the services of each local station varies between about one and seven hundred: in total, therefore, a very sizeable clientèle.

The job of the BBC educational producer and his seconded teacher colleagues is to get good programmes on the air—for adults as well as for schools. In pursuit of this, he is everywhere out and about—wherever potential programme material exists or can be stimulated: in Teachers' Centres especially, for these are both germinating points for new ideas and equipped with resources to produce new broadcast material. They can undertake the manufacture of supplementary materials too: Notes for the Teacher, illustrations, supplementary slides and so on. The larger Local Education Authorities' Resource Centres, particularly, are building up 'banks' of tapes and other audio-visual materials for schools to borrow: a two-way traffic is developing between them and the local stations. But on a smaller scale, the schools themselves are becoming potential contributors to local radio: several in Merseyside alone are planning to set up their own simple studios, on the inspiration of teachers who have acquired their experience through local broadcasting. Already, in Nottinghamshire, with help from the BBC producer, all the local programmes made for schools are being produced at the Authority's own School Broadcasting Centre: the local station transmits them over the air, but how long will this be necessary, if the tapes can be borrowed at discretion directly from the Centre itself?

Hal Bethell asks what local radio is to make of a situation where Local Education Authorities and others are becoming increasingly aware of the possibilities of thus 'going it alone'; and gives his answer:

Personally, I hold that we should welcome and encourage this and feel proud of any part which we may have been able to play in this development. Teachers, unlike lawyers, authors and journalists, achieve their greatest professional reward when they observe that their clients require fewer of their services. This should be equally true of teacher-broadcasters. To the extent that we are able to encourage teachers to pool their abilities with ours in coping with the endless chain of educational challenges which the future holds and yet, by a transference of skills, equally to encourage them to replace our services by theirs whenever educationally profitable – this is a consummation worth working for. History would speak well of us.

Meanwhile, there is much educational ground yet for local radio to till, and both BBC producers and the teachers who have worked with them will be active in tilling it. These teachers have a missionary feeling for what the future can hold : they even have their own journal, *The Studio*, started by and for teachers who had worked with Radio Merseyside, and now enlarged to serve as a national forum for all who have shared in such experiences. I will conclude this review of local radio by quoting from an article one of these teachers wrote for the first extended edition of *The Studio* :

Besides taking part in the work of the station I found a growing interest in making programmes with and for my own pupils . . . I wrote some playlets for radio presenting controversial situations in which listeners could sympathise with one or more of the offered points of view ; a girl caught shop lifting ; another who could afford fashion shoes for school, but not school fund ; pupils who defy school rules but expect the teachers to go by the book, and so on. They were fun to make and proved quite stimulating in provoking discussion, writing, and devising similar dialogues on other topics.

I like to think that the real value and effect of the secondment of teachers to Local Radio will snowball. There will be a growing system of links between schools and radio stations, with a two-way traffic in ideas, and an increasing number of pupils and teachers with experience and contacts in both fields. All this will be to everyone's benefit, since both schools and radio stations live by their positions in the communities which they exist to serve.

6.5 Friends abroad

The BBC started overseas broadcasting in 1932. Already, by then, its constitution as a public service organisation was being reflected by others around the world, and not in English-speaking countries only. Post-war Germany's debt to the BBC for re-establishing its broadcasting services on a sound footing is great, and fully recognised: Japan's NHK, reborn too out of the ashes of defeat and now one of the world's largest and most flourishing broadcasting organisations, also took the BBC as a model. Simultaneously, the expertise of BBC engineers and producers was being widely sought, and readily made available through secondments; so that patterns and styles of programming over much of the world often bear a family likeness to each other.

In educational broadcasting these links have been especially strong. Rex Lambert, a pioneer of BBC Adult Education, later went to set up school radio in Canada and ran it for seventeen years. Richmond Postgate, between being Head of BBC School Radio and its Controller of Educational Broadcasting, was Director-General of the Nigerian Broadcasting Corporation at a time of significant development in its educational work. Both the last and the present Heads of School Radio served abroad for several years in their earlier careers. Such examples could be multiplied; and the flow of producers (often two-way in the case of the Dominions), and to a lesser degree of School Broadcasting Council Education Officers, has been continuous.

Those of us lucky enough to get a taste of school broadcasting abroad have always found the experience stimulating. Full of surprises, too. I was once asked to conduct, single-handed, a week's course on School TV in Lagos for some fifty Nigerian teachers who were expected soon to have the opportunity to use it (the expectation proved, alas, premature). One day I showed them an elementary Science programme on 'Boiling Water'. I had warned them that afterwards I would want some to try their hand at conducting a few minutes' follow-up with the 'class' (the rest of them). They'd have to compensate for shortage of props (we'd no heating apparatus, for instance) by miming – at which they excelled. In the course of the programme we saw a kettle on the boil, and the presenter explained the phenomenon of the gap between the spout and the steam. One keen young teacher was very taken by this, and he'd discovered a gas ring fifty yards away from the studio. 'Look,' he asked me, 'if I boiled a kettle there and ran fast with it into the studio, do you think I'd still have the steam?' Of such enthusiasts are good users of broadcasts made.

Later in the course, I decided to show a teaching programme

on something they would know nothing about, so that they could judge of its effectiveness by reference not to hypothetical children, but to themselves. I chose an early programme from a series for beginners in Italian. It consisted of some simple acted dialogue, an instructional passage with pauses for viewers' responses, and a song. 'Response' was hardly the word for what the Nigerian teachers gave back. They bubbled over with their delight in echoing each speaker's new phrase–pause or no pause. The programme done, the studio erupted with cascades of Italian, punctuated by roars of laughter; then broke into a dance, improvised to accompany their rendering of the Italian song. Language for them was magic, caught as it flies. I thought of our tongue-tied group of English 'guinea-pigs', brought in to the Television Centre to be tested for audience response.

Japan, same year, 1964: more surprises. A primary school in Tokyo: 'Yes,' said the Headmaster, 'we have thirty TV sets, one in each class. And a small studio.' When I reached the studio, a ten-year-old was making an announcement to the whole school. I had expected much formality in Japanese schools: in the first classroom I went into, the class – also aged ten – had several floor-boards up. 'Practical activities', my guide murmured.

We went to a small country school in Hokkaido – all age, single teacher. He was giving a lesson to half his class. The other half were watching the TV, and listening – on individual earphones. A showpiece? Perhaps. But evidence that educational technology was well beyond the stage of pundits' talk. In some aspects of educational TV Japan was certainly ahead of us, and I suspect still is; but not in all. I have seen brilliant programmes there, especially in science; but also several designed to teach foreign languages, and none of them in the same class as our Italian one.

What more concrete than stimulus for individuals do BBC School Broadcasting's international connections give it–or others? In radio, there is the long tradition of drawing on French talent and French facilities to make recordings in France–indispensably, and for over a quarter of a century, in the case of Sixth Form programmes; equally usefully, and increasingly in recent years, to provide programme material for less advanced classes–right down to Primary School level. And the same goes for other languages, of course.

Reciprocally, BBC School Radio has for many years recorded each year in its studios a number of English programmes for broadcasts to Scandinavian schools. Originally produced with special regard for children's linguistic shortcomings, these programmes now offer English literature produced as for a domestic audience – even 'Juno and the Paycock' with Irish accents: a challenging reflection on the remarkable standards of English teaching in Scandinavia.

During the 60s the BBC was particularly active in giving help to both broadcasting organisations and educational institutions in the developing countries. In 1962 the Centre for Educational Television Overseas was inaugurated, and one of BBC School TV's producers left to take charge of production there. Simultaneously, in radio, an Educational Recordings scheme was set up, it too for the benefit of developing countries, by the BBC in partnership with the British Council, who financed it. Both organisations had similar objectives: to give advice on establishing school broadcasting in either medium, to assist with the training of indigenous staff, and to provide programme material (normally in the form of inserts rather than complete programmes) for developing countries' use, particularly in the fields of English teaching, science, and teacher training. 'Joseph and Sarah' was a particularly successful English teaching radio series: like others, it was sold for a nominal sum to educational institutions abroad as well as broadcasting organisations. Later in the decade both the Centre for Educational Television and the Educational Recordings Scheme became incorporated in the Centre for Educational Development Overseas, which is now a responsibility of the British Council.

In television, the expense of production, as well as the universal coinage of pictorial communication, has been a spur to programme sales and co-operative activities internationally. 'People of Many Lands' is a BBC series ranging over the five continents: its sales have a distribution equally wide. The Australian Broadcasting Commission, in particular, offers Australia's schools many other BBC programmes too: the BBC, for its part, has co-operated with the Commission in making filmed programmes on Australia, with BBC producers, at both primary and secondary levels, and for the benefit of schools in both countries.

During the 50s and 60s most European countries started School TV services, opening up the prospect of collaborative work beyond the field of language programmes. The European Broadcasting Union – an association of all the major broadcasting organisations of Western Europe – had been fostering international radio for general audiences since well before the war, music and sport being naturally the chief beneficiaries: with television, these activities received a new impulse and the promise of wider horizons. In 1961 the EBU set up a group now called the 'Working Party for School and Educational TV', to act as a forum for the exchange of ideas and programmes: its present chairman is a Swede, Rolf Lundgren. In the same year, the first World Congress on Educational Television and Radio took place at Rome.

International contacts do not automatically lead to international co-operation, and this is particularly true of school broadcasting. Educational systems differ from country to country; the nature of their relationship to broadcasting still more so. Objectives may be fundamentally different: Italy, where school TV was early in the field, set up 'Telescuola' to make good an absolute deficiency in secondary school places. Youngsters who had no school to go to assembled in front of TV sets at convenient centres to follow a replica of the normal secondary course, under the guidance of a monitor (not a trained teacher): their written work was sent to Telescuola headquarters in Rome for correction. It was not always easy to believe that Italian youth was watching the programmes, once the novelty had worn off, with quite the degree of enthusiasm credited to them: still, it was a remarkable initiative in using the medium for quite basic purposes. Back in the 50s, too, Italian TV devised an impressive series, with a presenter of genius, designed to impart reading and writing skills to illiterate adults ('Non è mai troppo tardi' – It is never too late). We have just got around, in this country, to realising the extent of our own deprivation in this respect, and to considering the uses of TV in alleviating it.

Telefis Eire, when it started School TV in the mid-60s, was actuated by the need to remedy teaching deficiencies in maths and science, and made no bones about 'direct teaching' either. Naturalness in front of the camera seemed to come easily to the

Irish temperament, and an early series on the 'New Maths' quickly attracted international admiration. But 'direct teaching', whether Irish or Italian style, was not what most European countries' schools were—or are—looking for from TV (in the USA, by contrast, there is a great deal of it, as we have noted). The Scandinavian broadcasting organisations' approach to programmes for schools has much in common with our own, and their achievement (in terms of the percentage of the potential audience actually viewing) is more impressive; for they have the advantage of working within a framework of nationally planned curricula. France has similar advantages from broadcasting's point of view; but French teachers were for long more suspicious than most of the intruder in the classroom: school radio had not blazed the trail there as it had in Britain and Scandinavia. In Germany, despite the conspicuous success of radio, TV for schools was relatively slow in coming, partly because German teachers had, in the Institut für Film und Bild at Munich, a rich source of educational film unrivalled anywhere in Europe.

Programme initiatives and programme styles reflect, of course, national characteristics. School TV in Germany is sometimes hampered in its development, it seems to me, by an almost excessively conscientious teaching profession, reluctant to allow TV to range outside the context of curricular studies in the way it does here. Yet I have seen, as a contribution to the political education of adolescents that has been so marked a feature of post-war German education, a documentary programme about Goebbels which brilliantly reflected not only the malignity of his philosophy but, equally, the charm which gave him his insidious hold over his contemporaries.

French educational TV, brilliantly led for many years by Henri Dieuzeide, is (as one would expect) often inventive and highly imaginative. What would happen here if you took cameras to Trafalgar Square, set them up by the Underground exit and started, with a blackboard, to give a lesson on some of the finer points of the English language? You'd get a crowd, no doubt—of speechless gogglers: hardly a participatory programme. A French producer did it in Paris, and got passionate argument about French vocabulary and syntax from all and sundry. The heart of French education was being probed.

Sometimes, I have felt, French cleverness can border on the perverse. School broadcasting in France is a function of the Ministry of Education. A few years ago it produced a skilful programme designed to make Fénelon's *Télémaque* more accessible to today's schoolchildren. It would surely have been kinder, and more economical, simply to have banished this hoary classic from their curriculum.

Different countries: different structures, also. School broadcasting in France not only serves a nationally planned curriculum; it is also part and parcel of the machinery for producing audio-visual materials of every kind for every stage of education. In consequence, there is a logic in the planning of such production which is non-existent in Britain (where even within the BBC, broadcast programmes and their accompanying materials are quite separately accounted for, and transfer of money from the one to the other is impossible). Thus, a few years ago the French decided, after wide-ranging experimentation in maths programmes for secondary schools, to forgo further broadcasts for pupils, and to use the resources thus saved for making TV programmes for teachers of maths, and short mathematical films for schools. Not necessarily the right solution elsewhere; but for them it seemed to be what the situation demanded, and nothing stood in the way of their doing it.

In Sweden school programmes are produced, as with us, by the national broadcasting organisation, Sveriges Radio. But radio, television, and the associated materials for both are jointly planned, in a much closer sense than applies in the BBC. Thus a group of radio and television programmes, with printed matter, slides and so on in support, will quite frequently be offered to schools as a single unit, with each medium playing its appropriate role. This is a procedure which, as we have noted, has been introduced into the planning of some Further Education programmes in Britain, but not as yet into school broadcasting. The spread of the recording habit in schools makes it much more practicable than it used to be; and opinion in Sweden is that the response of schools to it, and the stimulus given to producers by the teamwork involved, justifies the extra expenditure of time, and the possible human frictions, which are endemic in it. That is not to say that we should at once follow Sweden's example: it is possible to over-complicate teachers' lives; and in Britain, where variety of curriculum and teaching method is so cherished, the widest possible range of less elaborate offerings, giving maximum choice to the user, may be preferable.

European co-operation on the school front is not limited to the West: I have shown the BBC's sex education programmes, described in an earlier chapter, to an enthusiastic Teachers' Summer School in Southern Hungary – surprisingly enthusiastic to me, in a country one might suppose to labour under a mainly Catholic tradition overlaid with Communist puritanism. But not on this occasion; and certainly not in Magyar TV's School Broadcasting Department where, for instance, drama documentaries on teenage problems – not excepting unwanted pregnancy – feature quite naturally in programmes for schools.

Yugoslav radio, in its programmes for young people, established a tradition of teenagers interviewing grown-ups. Miro Jevtović, Director of Educational Programmes, describes it thus:

At school, paradoxically as it may seem, those who know usually ask questions of those who don't. In my radio programmes, I have done the opposite. Once, before Sputniks and satellites were ever sent up, I invited teenagers to join me on a flight to the Moon. This is when the idea was born to make youngsters interview grown-ups and learn how they should prepare themselves for a flight to the Moon. The result was a long-running and imaginative radio series on Selenites – young people who have established the international city of Selenopolis on the surface of the Moon.

In the series 'Sexual Education', it was again teenagers who sought answers from their elders. Boys and girls in the studio would say what they wanted to know about sex and would suggest that young radio listeners should interview their parents, relatives and older friends. They sent the answers to our department. So, in the programmes, the questions were theirs and the answers were provided by the grown-ups.

I became aware that the young had great problems with their parents and older relatives, and here too I used the same technique. I was surprised by both the teenagers' questions and the parents' answers. They covered a lot of ground. It was clear that teenagers exerted a strong influence on the grown-ups, in fact educated them, as it took a lot to get a father to allow his daughter to wear a mini-skirt, let his son sport long hair, or stop enjoying his favourite folk music to make room for his children listening to pop hits.

International contacts are stimulating, and nowhere more so than in the seminar for practitioners in educational broadcasting which Frank Tappolet, of the Société Suisse de Radiodiffusion, organises annually at Basle under EBU auspices, and where producers meet to exchange ideas, see each others' programmes, and work together on practical projects. Screening sessions, here and elsewhere, can bring to one's attention material made by others which, with editing, is adaptable to the needs of one's own country. Personal contacts open up, too, the possibility of international co-production; but in limited areas, mainly confined to film: differences of educational outlook and structure as well as of language are an impediment. Our first essays in European co-production for school TV were much too ambitious: they envisaged series on Western European geography involving separate contributions from eight or ten different organisations: the result, an uncoordinated hotch-potch. We have learnt wisdom from our Scandinavian colleagues, who by close co-operation on detailed planning, and clear agreement on executive control, produce programmes which all four countries can use and none could afford to make with their own resources alone. The BBC's 'USA 1972' followed this example: it could not have been achieved without Bavarian Television's co-operation, but the responsibility for making the film remained ours, with our partners free to adapt it if desired for their own purposes.

Intercommunication with our European neighbours is as yet defective: even to keep cognisance of each other's plans demands substantial time and effort, and the machinery for keeping track of exchangeable products hardly exists. But collaboration will grow; and we have much to learn from each other. It will grow on the wider, world scene too: the Commonwealth Broadcasting Conference, a biennial event, always includes discussion of educational broadcasting, and in 1975 is holding an extraordinary meeting devoted exclusively to this topic. The longer-term possibilities for BBC School Broadcasting of working co-operatively with friends abroad have hardly yet been broached.

6.6 Parents generally

BBC School programmes are part of BBC1 and Radio 4: in homes where there's a set, they can all be seen and heard like any others. Quite a lot of parents take advantage of this on their own account: especially of radio, which can be combined with some of the household chores – though you need a VHF set to receive school broadcasts nowadays. I have met graduate housewives who keep up their French with the radio programmes for Sixth Forms; I used to delight in the occasional letters from adult viewers of the current affairs series 'Spotlight', saying how much more clearly a knotty political issue had been explained to them than on any other programme; I knew an octogenarian whose annual greeting to me was a whiff of grapeshot peppering the doctrinal imperfections of religious programmes for schools.

Some parents with children at Primary School – but too few – are aware that school programmes may be something they at home can share with their children in school. A six-year-old in an Infants' School is as likely as not to be a regular viewer of the series 'Watch': it could be an experience to be talked about with pleasure to both over tea. Teachers can help with encouragement here; and many do.

There are other school programmes of which parents should at least be aware. The sex education broadcasts are an obvious case; and as we have seen, programmes discussing the family as a social unit, or dealing more directly with teenagers' problems in living with parents (and vice versa) feature strongly in several of the series designed for older children. Of course, opportunities for daytime viewing or listening will be at best occasional for most parents; for some, impossible ever. But the programmes are listed in *Radio Times*, in however small a print and whatever bareness of bone: series titles and timings in some newspapers too. *Radio Times*, for all the pressures on it, ought now and then to find the means to do better – the occasional editorial to foster the use of this home-school bridge. Schools are closed institutions no more – nor should school broadcasting appear to be.

A word of caution, however, to parents who may read this. Children at home and at a loose end in school time are most often pre-school children, or on leave from Primary School with a minor ailment. Some parents, as I know from correspondence, imagine that any programme labelled 'for Schools' will at least be 'safe' viewing for children on their own, however young. Thirty years ago this may have been true; but by no means always today: we would be failing in our duty to maturing youngsters if it were so. An intelligent interpretation of series titles will help: 'Drama' is much too grand a word to signal a play suitable for young children. But there are still pitfalls. For instance, a story for children of eight may be one designed, among other things, to help them come to terms with fear—a necessary part of their education, and usually a pleasurable one in the secure circumstances of group viewing with an adult at school. A five-year-old seeing—or hearing—the same story alone at home might be left with a gnawing, destructive feeling of insecurity and alarm.

The series specially made for pre-school children are well known: 'Listen with Mother', 'Watch with Mother', 'Playschool'. This year there are two additions, already referred to: on radio 'Playtime', on TV 'You and Me'. These last are primarily designed for children in nursery classes, but seek deliberately to bring in parents with small children at home, so letters from parents about them, as well as from teachers, are both welcome to the producers and important.

Parents often deplore the fact that there are no educational programmes for children of school age during the holidays—not even repeats of those broadcast during termtime. Broadly this is true—though in the Christmas and Easter holidays BBC and ITV both show, for the benefit of teachers, some samples of forthcoming school programmes. The answer is primarily economic: repeat programmes cost much more than the public imagines, and their number is often limited by contract too; so any substantial number of holiday repeats would be at the cost of the schools' service itself.

So far I have only touched on what the BBC makes available, to schools and homes alike. But our traffic with parents has not been one-way: we have much cause to be grateful for their help in school broadcasting's development. Many smaller schools especially owed what value they originally drew from school broadcasting to the generosity of parents, whether through parent-teacher associations, or more informally; for time was when a wireless set in a school was considered such a luxury that for many it owed its existence to the profits of a school bazaar. Today the picture has changed fundamentally; but for some schools – such are the economic pressures bearing on the provision of school equipment – a TV set was till recently ranked as something desirable rather than essential, and for most a colour set is still a luxury. Yet programmes for young children especially gain enormously from colour, and every year there are more colour transmissions for schools. Before long, on present trends, colour sets in homes will outnumber black and white. Parent-teacher Associations have still a part to play in helping ensure that schools do not lag too far behind.

On some bodies concerned with school broadcasting abroad I believe that parents have formal representation. That is not our way in this country: it must be even harder for one person, or even several, to represent 'parents' than to speak for 'consumers'. But in a host of informal ways they are becoming increasingly involved with the life and work of their children's schools. It is a healthy, and an overdue, development; and now that broadcasts and activities stemming from them are such an integral part of that work, the more parents can know about them and contribute to their vitality, the better. And this goes, of course, for local radio's community stations just as much as for the national services.

Education, from being a neglected topic twenty years ago, is today a journalist's pet; and the sources of information and advice for parents about education are legion. Few are more stimulating than the BBC Further Education programmes to which I have already referred; but for direct impressions of the sometimes bewildering changes in what schoolchildren today are learning about, and how, school broadcasts themselves can be an illuminating source for parents.

6.7 The parent BBC

The BBC spends about £2½ million a year, nearly 2½ per cent of its income, on School Broadcasting, including School Broadcasting Council staff. Quite a lot, but not substantially more, proportionately to its total domestic service expenditure, than it was, say, twenty-five years ago. More is spent by the schools in using the broadcasts and their associated materials (only a small proportion of this, of course, reverts to the BBC as licence fees).

As we have seen, the BBC started school broadcasting on its own initiative, and developed it in its early years in the face of much indifference and some hostility. Its obligation, in terms of its charter and licence, to provide the service has always been self-imposed. The BBC has found it a useful exhibit to put in the shop window as a symbol of virtue in the face of Committees of Inquiry and on other public occasions. Between times, its generosity has naturally fluctuated in relation to other pressures on its resources. Until recently, the BBC has enjoyed a steadily expanding revenue, first from radio, then from TV licences. In the mid-50s, however, it was slow in getting School TV under way, partly because of a chilly economic climate generally, partly because the arrival of ITV inevitably spelt rising costs for general programmes. But by 1959, when licence income was booming, the BBC volunteered a major expansion of School TV a year earlier than the School Broadcasting Council had asked for it. By the mid-60s, licence revenue from monochrome TV was drying up, and there was the new Further Education service to be financed; so School TV's expansion was halted. Now colour licences are boosting revenue again, but barely enough to offset inflationary costs; and since no other major source of new income is in prospect, the future of school broadcasting's funding is for the first time in its history finding itself in the melting pot. Other factors than money are involved in this, however: I shall take up the question in the next chapter.

The BBC, to its credit, has always recognised that school broadcasting is not a service to be run on the cheap. Of course it has never had all the money it would like: school broadcast producers often think they are hardly done by, but the same is true of producers in all departments. School programmes do not use expensive star performers, but hour for hour of original transmissions they are by no means the least expensive—largely because short programmes cost more per hour than longer ones of similar type. The balance is more than redressed, however, by school broadcasting's liberal use of repeats.

School broadcasting can sometimes be in competition with other claims on the BBC for airtime as well as for money. It is vital to the schools' service that its airtime, agreed and published long in advance, shall be protected; and apart from occasional impingements, when the national interest has been adjudged paramount in admitting a special event within 'school time' and at the expense of a school programme, this need has been honoured. Today, with daytime radio listening in the ascendant and the de-restriction of TV broadcasting hours, the picture is different. School radio has been confined to the VHF band: School TV's continued occupation of substantial time on BBC1 has been helped by the BBC's lack of money for extension of general daytime television.

The pressures to which the BBC is subject in determining the allocation of its resources are of course enormous. Some are mainly unformulated except in terms of the glow of individual gratitude or the howls of individual protest; others are highly articulate—and these include pressures from educational interests. 'One of the most intemperate of the lot', an exasperated Managing Director of Television has been heard to observe, 'and what's worse, they always have morality on their side.' So it is not surprising to find in the BBC a certain ambivalence of attitude towards its educational services. It respects their good name, yet it sometimes treats them as if they were hardly a part of itself, but rather the embodiment of a problem imposed on it by this powerful and appallingly respectable pressure-group. Further Education, rather than school broadcasting, has to bear the brunt of this ambivalence, since it competes much more directly with the general service for airtime, and its subject-matter frequently overlaps that of general programming. However, the channel Controllers feel perfectly free to comment on, and even on occasion to intervene, in Further Education programme plans (the Further Education Council's role is an advisory one only); consequently, they may feel some personal commitment to what is eventually broadcast. Not so with school broadcasting, unless— a most rare occurence—some demonstrable conflict with general BBC policy can be detected. A channel Controller whose powers of effective intervention are, in practice, so tenuous is likely to feel that school programmes are not in any real sense his responsibility, or even his concern. A pity, nevertheless; since it may close his mind to the notion that a programme made for schools could be successful in the context of general programming also (as some could); and it results, at the level where power is felt to count, in more isolation of school departments from the mainstream of broadcasting than is desirable or healthy.

Intervention or attempted intervention in plans, on the rare occasions when it happens, is more likely to be on matters of detail than on broader issues which could involve confrontation with the School Broadcasting Council. A production by any department which involves filming abroad, and therefore foreign currency, is subject to special scrutiny; and I once had to defend a producer's intention to set up a café discussion on current life-styles among Parisian lycéens to a Controller who insisted that the essence of life for a French lycéen could be quite adequately conveyed by having a cameraman shoot him with his satchel bulging with books. To be left to one's own devices and ignored, one sometimes felt, was the lesser of two evils. One could even take it as a backhand compliment–being trusted to get on with the job.

If school broadcasting sometimes seems a foreign body in the BBC's eye, it is easy to exaggerate this. The people on whom producers really depend for making good programmes–cameramen, sound recordists, editors, designers, studio staff–do not, with the rarest exceptions, so feel it; and BBC school broadcasting is what it is because of the quality of their services. The BBC's staff structure does not distinguish between schools' and other production staff; so that one of the strengths of its school broadcasting service lies in its ability to recruit both from the world of education outside and from within the other parts of the Corporation (and, equally important, to offer opportunities of moving on to positions of higher responsibility within the BBC as well as elsewhere). At the highest level, too–the level from which BBC school broadcasting derived its first impulse–the march of events has brought the BBC's educational services into the forefront of its thinking to an extent hardly paralleled since Reith's early days.

There is a negative reason for this. People with heavy responsibilities tend to exclude things from the forefront of their minds until they become problems; and as we have seen, problems of finance and of airtime, due in part to the development of its educational services, pursue the BBC into *impasses* from which an escape must nevertheless be found. But there are positive reasons too, and one of them is surely the conspicuous success of the Open University. The BBC entered into partnership with the Open University with some misgivings – shared by many others. It was a pioneering venture involving a form of partnership of which the BBC had no experience. It would obviously be – and has so proved – even more demanding of airtime than the BBC's existing educational services. But the BBC put its best talents and much skill and effort into ensuring that the partnership worked, and it cannot but take some share of the credit. The unique nature of the operation has attracted world-wide interest: the BBC's stake in education – and in a prestigious field of it – has been reinforced. Its other educational departments are indirect beneficiaries of this heightened involvement.

If the BBC's stance towards education is ambivalent, so, often, is education's to the BBC. For while educationists share the view, repeatedly propounded by the BBC itself and endorsed by the Pilkington Committee and others, that the BBC's major educative contribution lies in its general programmes, many of them quite often also find themselves at cross purposes with an organisation which when wearing its 'showbiz' face cannot possibly 'always have morality on its side', and which when addressing itself to a mass public cannot altogether forgo the more trivial forms of journalism. They recognise, sometimes with envy, that the educative programmes the BBC offers – in which they would certainly include 'Z Cars' and probably 'Monty Python's Flying Circus', though not, perhaps, 'The Pallisers' – are often more lively and vigorous than anything they can provide; yet they must sometimes feel that the social mores which the BBC helps to propagate, if only by reflecting them, make their job of slogging away at the coalface of education even more arduous than it is anyhow. Yet teachers (to drop the ugly, rebarbative portmanteau 'educationists') are human, too, and therefore not immune to the mesmeric effects of contact with the BBC's rather grand world: if one of them seems a little distrait when engaged in earnest discussion over lunch at the TV centre, it may be because he has just bumped into Stratford Johns in the lift. Even while he recognises that his job as a teacher must be motivated by moral purpose, his attitude to broadcasting is as likely to draw on the philosophy of Carleton Greene as on that of John Reith. For he shares the dilemma of the BBC itself: schools are no longer closed shops, they have opened their doors to a society which is pluralist, tolerant, exploratory; they too are engaged in the unending quest for a stance which will let them communicate with their society on its own level, and yet stand up for the values they see as the highest it can set itself.

David Attenborough, when he was Director of BBC TV Programmes, once told me he regarded its school broadcasting service as the conscience of the BBC: he meant, I think, that the extent of the BBC's commitment to schools was one of the touchstones of its determination to discharge its obligations to society generally. That was well said. He might even have meant that the values reflected in its school programmes symbolised those he felt should underlie BBC broadcasting as a whole. That, in the view of teachers who share with the BBC the responsibility for the schools' service, would be even better.

7 PROSPECT

The picture I have given of school broadcasts in the earlier chapters has no doubt been coloured by my own enthusiasms; and the programmes I have selected for description and comment have mainly been ones which, though not necessarily outstanding, were of above average interest. The total view is of course a little more mundane: there are school programmes of workaday quality only, and a few (a very few I think in relation to the total output) which have failed because they were found boring.

Alternatively, some readers may have formed the impression of a service which is innovatory to the point of trendiness – flitting as it were from flower to flower of educational fashion. Not so either: school broadcasting has conservative programmes, too, for conservative teachers. Some of these, perhaps, outstay their time: it is difficult to kill off a tried and still welcome favourite. There is, besides, a certain relish in playing it occasionally against the grain. In the sophisticated age of the anti-hero I judged there was a missing element in School TV's output, and took pleasure in devising a straightforward series which presented traditional portraits of heroism: climbers of Everest, pioneers of the American West, David Livingstone, Thor Heyerdahl. School radio for its part, alongside the avant-gardish Music Workshop and Music Club, this summer has Country Dancing.

Again, BBC School Broadcasting has a good repute; it has been called a success story. But it rides on the back of the BBC, and with a 'captive' audience too: given its problems here and there, has not the ride been by and large quite an easy one? I think not: indeed it is hard to point to a time when school broadcasting's future, across the whole range of its output, has seemed totally secure. There were the early struggles for recognition in the world of education at large, and for the achievement of

tolerable reception in classrooms; there were the growing problems, in the 50s, of reconciling BBC timetables with those of
Secondary Schools, and the certain prospect of a diminishing use
of school radio until tape-recording came to the rescue (and, with
tape-recording, the fertile mind also of Norman Lloyd Williams,
who was in charge of school radio through the 60s). In the 60s,
the multiplication of exams and exam syllabuses threatened to
cast into limbo whatever Secondary School offerings from radio
or TV were not pertinent to them; while in today's Primary
Schools the break-up of traditional class organisation, though it
provides new opportunities for broadcasting, is disturbing the
pattern of week-by-week listening or viewing which in the past
has ensured large audiences. In recent years, too, while there is
much to school broadcasting's credit, there have been disappoint-
ments also. TV has not, despite early hopes, and successes here
and there, made to education in the visual arts the massive and
sustained contribution which radio has to the appreciation of
music. And neither medium has been able to match the growth
of Sixth Forms with any corresponding increase in the number of
pupils it reaches there. The path, then, is not all strewn with roses.

Nor, for that matter, is it overgrown with nettles or bitingly
windswept. Again my picture may need refocusing; for when
Education seeks to explain her ways, her temptation is to adopt
a pose more heroic, to project a vision more high-minded than
truth can wholly underwrite or common humanity endure. Let
me declare therefore that school broadcasts are often relaxed,
sometimes even funny (I mean intentionally: the unintentionally
so are of course legendary); and let me salute in passing the
natural clowns – I think of Charles Mason in radio and Michael
Simpson in TV – who over the years have added circuses to the
daily bread of school broadcasting.

7.1   Recording, and its consequences

Today School broadcasting has both new opportunities and new
problems; and both are more fundamental and far-reaching than
the past ones I have mentioned. In Chapter II we noted the
growing practice of recording BBC programmes in schools, and

the parallel increase in audio-visual materials available to them from other sources; we observed how, in some fields, this could result in changes of programme structure, making the product barely suitable for off-air reception, and questionably therefore for broadcasting at all. As Leslie Ryder, a Chief Inspector for the Inner London Education Authority, has put it:

With the advent of the cheap video-tape recorder alongside the very cheap audio-tape recorder, what advantages are there in live broadcasting apart from ease of distribution? Most of the output is already pre-recorded. Does the encouragement now given to the secondary use of material mean that ultimately the broadcasting organisations will be producers of educational resource material rather than broadcasters?

We must examine this briefly, distinguishing radio from TV, Primary Schools from Secondary, the longer term view from the shorter. Virtually all schools have the means to record radio programmes if they so wish. By the end of the decade, given reasonable economic circumstances, the same may be true of TV in Secondary Schools, and perhaps in 'Middle Schools' for age nine–thirteen also; but in the case of Primary Schools the process will surely be much longer: many of them will continue to need TV off-air for the foreseeable future. Ease of distribution over the air remains a potent factor even for Secondary Schools: Local Education Authorities may achieve a relaxation of the present recording agreements (listed at Appendix C), which could enable them both to record and to copy tapes for schools to draw on at will; but other factors apart, this is not necessarily the cheapest and most convenient method of distributing programmes.

We have also noted how this development in recording programmes within schools, while it may contribute to the better use of programmes, tends to draw a dividing line between school broadcasting and ordinary broadcasting. The goal of promoting better use is admirable: there has been, throughout school broadcasting's history, too much wastage here, by no means all to be blamed on the shortcomings of teachers; for circumstances have often been against them. But the consequences of simply letting this division happen could be regrettable too. We have noted how schools have become more open places, increasingly interacting with the life and activities of the community at large; and both general and school broadcasting have significantly contributed to this welcome change. We have observed the involvement of parents in aspects of school and further education broadcasting, and have seen broadcasts as a potential link between school and home. These developments, too, are to be cherished and fostered, not simply cast aside if they do not fit the pattern emerging elsewhere.

Let us suppose, however, that the factors tending to separate a part at least of the output for schools from main-line broadcasting persist. Whether this material is distributed in other ways than over the air, or whether it continues to be broadcast—possibly no longer during the day, but in the small hours to free the daytime air, with schools recording by pre-set timing devices: in either case the material becomes not only a specialised product for specialised use, but one among many specialised products for schools, part of the 'software' whose proliferation we have already noted. And to quote Leslie Ryder again:

With BBC, ITV, local radio, and Local Authority closed-circuit TV we shall have a welter of broadcast material at our disposal. How much longer can we afford to have these various agencies, together with those of the diversified publishing companies, producing their own sets of material, seldom if ever coming together for discussion? Going their own separate ways, it is purely accidental whether they produce complementary, or competitive, materials. Is this not all rather too important and too expensive for us to ignore?

We may even ask, as we saw Hal Bethell asking in relation to local radio, whether the end result of all this should not be to unhitch the 'broadcast' element in this 'welter' from its moorings in the national broadcasting organisations and bring it within the scope of educational 'factories' equipped and staffed to make and put at schools' disposal the whole range of audio-visual products. The larger Local Authorities already have such factories, producing slides, filmstrips, sound tapes, reprographed documents— a whole plethora of material. Some have TV studios and film facilities too: might they not take on the whole job of audio-visual production and distribution, with a body such as the National

Council for Educational Technology acting as a co-ordinating agent? For the BBC is not without its weaknesses as a servant of the schools. Its school broadcasting staffs are not in day-to-day contact with other educationists producing other kinds of educational materials. The funding of what it produces has to follow the logic of an organisation whose primary imperatives are geared to broadcasting: the logic of providing for educational needs over a broader spectrum is different. We have seen, in France, this logic effectively applied: the planning and producing of school broadcasts and their associated materials has always been a function there of a branch of the centralised Ministry of Education. For long this branch looked to ORTF, the national broadcasting organisation, to provide studios and related facilities for radio and TV, together with technical staff; but this did not work happily, and educational specialists, under the acronym OFRATEME, now take charge of the whole process of production and distribution, for the whole range of audio-visual materials.

From one point of view this is a neat solution, though harder to realise in our country, where educational administration is decentralised. But from another, the losses surely far outweigh the gains. First, the BBC is no inflexible monolith, standing apart from developments at the grass-roots of education and reluctant to adapt to them. On the contrary, it has in many ways shown over the last decade a remarkable flexibility in serving education's needs. There is the record of its association with the Open University to bear witness to this; there is also the phenomenal expansion of BBC Publications Department's services to schools. The years since 1960 have seen not only a marked increase in its output of the traditional Pupils' Pamphlets, Teachers' Notes and Wallsheets; but also a new profusion of filmstrips, slides, film loops, sound tapes and discs, work cards, folders of study documents, storybooks, and even educational games, in response to the importunate demands of producers and committees. To commission all this and to distribute it to schools has not been achieved without some hitches and some financial headaches for BBC and schools alike; but it stands as a considerable achievement to all concerned, including of course the producers who edit and mainly write the copy. There may be disadvantages in the

BBC's isolation from producers of parallel products, but no one could fairly claim that its primary job has inhibited it from an appropriate diversification. The present question is rather whether some of this material (it is sold to the schools at cost price) could not achieve a wider distribution by more extensive forms of promotion.

Secondly, can one imagine that for programmes made in, say, a Local Education Authority's Resource Centre, or perhaps under the aegis of the National Council for Educational Technology, the same range of high talent which the BBC attracts to its service would be available? For production, possibly; for technical services, conceivably; but in respect of actors, writers, and other professional free-lancers, surely not—not, at least, if one looks at the whole range of school broadcasting. What if one looks at a part only? Some school broadcasts are akin to general programmes: these are usually the ones which draw most on the artistic talents of the community at large. Other broadcasts are much more specialised, and call above all for deep understanding of educational method and the sophisticated application of broadcasting techniques to specific educational ends. There is much overlap, of course, between these two types; and where both as at present are produced by colleagues working side by side, there is a cross-fertilisation of ideas between them. But it is just possible to envisage them as separable kinds of contribution, each of which might still flourish in a rather different ambiance. Whether such a separation would be desirable or practicable is another question.

7.2 Pressures on the BBC

We have been looking at a complex situation related to technical development, the needs of schools, and the place of school broadcasting within the large national broadcasting organisations. We must now shift our angle of vision and consider the future of school broadcasting from the viewpoint of the BBC as a whole.

I have remarked on a certain ambivalence in the BBC's attitude to its educational services: it is only fair to recall, therefore, that its commitment to these services was publicly underlined by its Director-General in a speech at the Inter NAVEX exhibition in July 1972. He said:

The BBC has made a steadily increasing commitment to education over the last 40 years, so that now BBC educational broadcasting costs £5 million each year, provides nearly 600 hours of radio and 700 hours of TV and employs 150 senior production staff. In addition we are partners in Open University operations financed by the Department of Education which could occupy up to 30 hours each week of radio and TV airtime by 1975. This is the extent of our commitment to education and it is a commitment which we shall do everything in our power to sustain.

But the BBC, as we noted in the last chapter, is subject also to the pressures of circumstance, and the financial pressures today are becoming more acute than ever before. The BBC is therefore entitled to ask whether its school broadcasting service, costing at least half of a sum now approaching £6 million, is properly a charge on its licence-payers rather than on the Department of Education. Indeed, they put this point to the Department some years ago, but received a fairly dusty answer. Of course, either way the money comes from the pockets of individual citizens, but it is generally regarded as healthy that a government Department should pay for services it receives; and the broadcast licence fee, being a flat-rate contribution from all sorts and conditions of men, is in effect a form of regressive taxation. So the BBC certainly has a case for off-loading this expenditure: it is not improper to feel committed to the next round and yet not to insist on paying for it–particularly when you realise that if you did, you wouldn't be able to afford to take your guests to that football match.

The BBC now has a precedent, too, in the Open University for outside financing of its educational activities. How would BBC School Broadcasting, then, and the School Broadcasting Council, who would of course have an interest, view the change? With some misgivings, no doubt. The Open University situation is not quite parallel, for the rest of its expenditure is also met by the Government; so that if, within the measure of what the BBC could undertake, the University wanted to spend more of its total resources on broadcasting, or less, there could hardly be any objection in principle. It is for the University, and not the Government who provides the cash, to decide whether it is getting value for money from the BBC's co-operation. But BBC school broadcasting, like its External Services which are financed by the Foreign Office, would be more vulnerable: the provider of cash and the judge of cost-effectiveness would be one. I would not myself, on school broadcasting's behalf, welcome the change: the External Services have had to struggle for over twenty years to prevent erosion of a service acknowledged to be of outstanding quality; and although two or three millions is peanuts to a government department but quite a lot to the BBC, I would have more confidence, in the crunch, in the BBC's determination to sustain and nourish what is its own child than I would have in a government Department. Others, I know, think differently; and it may be that in the longer run the BBC will have no choice but to press its case more strongly, if it is convinced that the standards of its general programmes and its ability to compete with ITV are seriously jeopardised for lack of money. If the School Broadcasting Council, on behalf of BBC School Broadcasting, were pressing for an expansion of its services, the BBC's case for financial relief from the added burden would soon be irresistible; but the Council is not pressing this. Naturally it wants to offer schools a wide variety of choice, but in school radio at least the choice is already lavish; and the result of the practice of recording in schools, and the better and more intensive use of the recorded material that should follow from it, could be that they would be satisfied with a smaller number of programmes on offer.

The second main pressure weighing on the BBC is the shortage of air-time, and the principal sources of this pressure at the moment are educational: firstly the needs of the Open University, and secondly the demands for broadcast support for the various kinds of *éducation permanente* discussed in the Russell Report. In both cases, however, the need is for broadcast time when working adults are free to view and listen – including some peak hours; so these needs can only be properly met by additional networks on both radio and television (as the BBC stressed in a memorandum last year to the Minister of Posts and Communications on the subject of a fourth TV channel). School broadcasting, therefore, will hardly be touched by these claims on air-time. The growth of daytime listening and viewing, however, which stems from a gradual increase in the leisure time of the population at large, is a different case. It does not as yet bear heavily on School TV, largely because the BBC lacks the money to fill daytime hours on two channels with general programmes: the threat is rather to school radio. It can indeed be argued that, since schools are now equipped with audio-tape recorders, the whole of this provision could be made, before long if not now, through tape cassettes distributed to individual schools along with accompanying materials. We are brought back to the questions put by Leslie Ryder earlier in this chapter – but also to the reservations I have already made about drawing a sharp dividing line between broadcasts for schools and broadcasts for the whole community.

7.3 A look into the crystal ball

It is proper for a book of this kind to expose this complex web of issues: it is doubtfully within my capacity even to try to resolve them. To have been engaged for years on the shorter-term problems of school broadcasting is no qualification for the task: it is rather an impediment. One is trammelled by the past one has enjoyed, and a little dismayed by a future which for all the promise it holds could deny these same satisfactions to others. The task of unravelling that future belongs to Lord Annan's Committee, in whose report BBC school broadcasting can only be a very minor, but nevertheless I hope an important chapter. I do not think that the problems inherent in the developments and the pressures I have described are so urgent that their resolution cannot wait a few years: indeed, the situation in which schools are recording programmes on a large scale and school broadcasting is beginning to take account of this in structuring them is a very new one, at least in TV; and it is wise, for a little while yet, to watch how this develops.

To speculate beyond a few years' hence, and from outside the arena, is an act compounded of foolhardiness and either self-indulgence or masochism (I am not sure which). But it is cowardly to deny readers the pleasure of picking holes in ill-substantiated arguments, so I will chance my arm.

I think there may in the longer term be a broad choice for BBC

School Broadcasting between two courses. It could accept whole-heartedly a situation which implies a continually diminishing off-air use of its products in return for a more intensive use by schools of these products as recorded resource material. It would then recognise school broadcasts as essentially a specialised product for a specialised market; accept – even welcome – the transfer of their funding to the Department of Education, trading as it were the possible hazards of some consequential loss of independence for the expectation of a more assured provision of all that schools need to exploit this specialised material to the full. It may be that BBC School Broadcasting could continue, and flourish, on this basis for a decade or more: the BBC has recently declared that it would wish to retain school TV programmes on one of its main channels. But a specialised service, financed from outside and scarcely used off-air by its intended beneficiaries, would surely be a very vulnerable part of a national broadcasting organisation. Would it not inevitably, as the pressures mounted, at least be hived off to a channel serving specialised interests exclusively, should one be available; and eventually, very likely, be shunted off the air altogether? And once this had happened, would not the question have to be faced whether the production of school programmes was any longer a proper function of the BBC?

The precedent of the Open University might suggest there are no grounds for thinking thus. The BBC takes pride in its association with the University and its key part in the University's broadcasts; and even if, as the University would wish, its broadcast production centre is transferred to the University's campus at Milton Keynes, BBC staff will go with it. Yet will not the logic of events take the University's programmes sooner or later out of the hands of the BBC – just as we have seen BBC local radio, for instance, beginning to relinquish its hold on educational programmes when others are ready to take over?

At present, the BBC's position as provider of school broadcasts is of such unique strength that a change of this order is hard to contemplate: but the BBC itself is of course not eternally secure, and it is by no means certain that the BBC, given its survival for say fifteen years at least, would by then seem the most favourable base to which to anchor a service to schools.

A possible alternative line for school broadcasting might be this. First, to consider the schools less as consumers of specialist products than as human institutions in a larger society with which they are increasingly interacting and ever more closely bound up; and the potential of school broadcasts in furthering this process. Then, to look at the broadcast provision for them and see it as indeed specialised in certain respects – notably where the acquisition of particular skills is concerned: reading, number, language, notation; but in others becoming if anything progressively less specialised, more akin to the products of general broadcasting. For this is the reality: more pure documentary, uncommented drama or literature is what schools tend to ask for, in series after series; less intervention by an intermediary or, should one be indispensable, the purging from his intervention of any element of 'schoolsiness'. There was once a 'Talks' Department in BBC TV: it disappeared, I think, because people wanted less of being talked at, or even talked to. The same has happened in the schools.

Next, school broadcasting might look at BBC departmental structures and question whether what now obtains will necessarily provide the best service for young people in the longer future. There are the School Departments covering the whole range from age four to eighteen for in-school programmes; there are the Children's Departments serving out-of-school needs up to age about twelve; for teenagers out of school there is little specifically provided, if one excepts the area of pop music. There have been sporadic incursions here into other territory, but no sustained effort; the conclusion has been that youngsters prefer normal 'adult' programmes anyhow. One may question this: is it perhaps simply that nobody with the qualities of a Mary Somerville has emerged to take on the task, and that it is easier therefore to ensure audiences by a facile ministering to the teenage sub-culture?

The School Departments look, above all else, compact and unified of purpose, and so they are. But they are discrete entities partly because they are necessarily geared to a structure of school years and terms, with all that this implies for publicity, production of associated materials, and so on. Once the overwhelming majority of schools are no longer taking a series off air, the need for it to be accommodated to this rigid pattern becomes less clear-cut; and as such series multiply, the pattern itself can begin to be broken up, for an intricate schedule of delivery dates for each product is then no longer a prime factor in planning; nor need one automatically assume that each series must be fathered by a specialised and unitary School Department.

At this stage it is worth reconsidering the point I have made before: whether the more highly specialised work of the School Departments is necessarily inseparable from the rest; whether there could not be gains, even if there were also losses, in such material being produced, under different auspices, by teams involved also in making other audio-visual materials. These could find themselves in a more genuinely 'workshop' setting than the BBC can readily provide – at least for TV – and with opportunities for practical research in depth into audio-visual communication which are lacking within the present organis-ational structure. The last thing I want to suggest is that such specialised programmes require less sophisticated techniques than the others; but their sophistication is of a different kind from that involved in the production of, say, 'Top of the Pops' or 'Dad's Army', to which the provision of BBC facilities is, in the main, quite properly geared.

A possible different pattern of school programme production is now beginning to emerge, with specialised school programmes produced, and funded, outside the BBC; and others, more closely related to general programmes, within it. Some of these would be the responsibility of a Department catering for young children both in and out of school; others of a second Department similarly providing for teenagers. The stimulus from colleagues for pro-ducers in all three areas could be not less than what the existing School Departments offer; and though new anomalies would be created (I am aware that I have, for instance, left the School Broadcasting Council out of account), some old ones would disappear.

The BBC would be relieved of some financial pressure, and some pressure on air-time (in the case of radio, where the greater pressure is on airtime, the most practical course might be to retain all production within the BBC, but distribute the more specialised parts of the product on cassettes). In return, the BBC should accept that those school programmes it retained would be part of its general output for the public at large – geared indeed to the needs of a particular section of society, but available to all, and of intrinsic interest whether for their own sake, or as a means for adults to share in the concerns of the young. One transmission of each programme should be within school hours; but repeats for some school programmes at other times (at week-ends during the day for instance), reaching a wider audience, should be the norm and not the exception. The BBC's guiding instinct would be to display its programmes for the young – all of them; and no longer to divide them in two and tuck the meatier half away. Only then would it be truly recognising the changing relationship between our schools and society, and between learning and living.

Here, then, are two contrasted lines of thought. Partisans of the first will assume that the needs of schools will always be distinctive, indeed unique; and should be met by whatever agencies are best fitted, at any given time, to devote themselves single-mindedly to these very specialised needs. They will see schools as institutions subject of course to change, but certainly more permanent in character and structure than broadcasting is likely to be. As they look back, therefore, over fifty years of BBC School broadcasting, they may well salute this happy conjunction of education and broadcasting, yet recognise it, in the larger perspective, simply as a transitional phase – a kind of apprenticeship, for education, in coming to terms with a new development which it should very soon be able to handle on its own.

Advocates of the second course will see schools as subject to no less rapid change than broadcasting; broadcasting as something which has shifted, for good, the focus of educational thinking and whose unique contribution to the schools has derived from, and is dependent on, its larger role as universal educator and universal entertainer. They will recognise that there are certain services of a very specialised kind which the BBC at present provides for schools but which lie sufficiently far from broadcasting's mainstream to be doubtfully its longer-term responsibility. But they will see the BBC as deserving by its record, and likely through the prestige and the popularity it still enjoys, to preserve into the foreseeable future its essential character as a unique national institution; and they will wish the schools to share in that future and the BBC to ensure that they do.

Between the two courses there is, no doubt, many a half-way house. I leave the issue open-ended, not seeking to convince, but hoping rather to provoke. As school broadcasts try to do.

APPENDICES

A The School Broadcasting Council for the United Kingdom and its committees

Since 1929, the BBC has observed the principle that the guidance and sponsorship of the school broadcasting service should be vested in a body representing the educational world. The BBC broadcasts to schools only series and programmes requested by the School Broadcasting Council for the United Kingdom, and for which that body stands sponsor vis-à-vis the educational world.

The School Broadcasting Council studies educational practice and trends in the schools in the United Kingdom and considers in what ways the education which they provide can be aided by school broadcasts. It formulates the general educational policy of school broadcasting and determines the scope and purpose of each series. It considers plans for the implementation of its policies submitted by the BBC and recommends their adoption, rejection or amendment. It obtains and assesses evidence on the suitability of school broadcasts and makes known to the schools the BBC's provision of broadcasts and accompanying publications. The Council has a full-time professional staff, and its work is financed by the BBC.

The Council consists of representatives proposed by the main educational organisations (including representation of educational interests in Scotland, Wales and Northern Ireland) and members appointed by the BBC because of their particular educational interests or experience. The majority of members are appointed by the educational organisations: The Department of Education and Science, the associations of local education authorities, the various teachers' associations, the association of teachers in colleges of education, the association of local education authority inspectors and organisers.

In respect of programme policy the Council works through three Programme Committees, which are responsible for broadcast series for children up to age eight/nine, age eight/nine to twelve/thirteen, and age twelve/thirteen to eighteen respectively. They consist mainly of teachers invited because of their known ability and interest in educational broadcasting, with other representatives from the Department of Education and Science, the local education authorities and the teacher-training world.

These Committees are concerned with the purposes, nature and suitability of series intended for their respective age groups, while the Council has regard to the overall balance of the output.

The Council itself meets twice a year. It has executive powers and appoints the members of the three Programme Committees. These meet three times a year. The Council's decisions are assisted by the work of a Steering Committee which includes the Chairmen of the Programme Committees. The Steering Committee makes recommendations to the Council but is not itself an executive body.

Scotland, Wales and Northern Ireland

There are separate School Broadcasting Councils for Scotland and Wales and a special Programme Committee for Northern Ireland. These have responsibilities for the series produced and transmitted only in those countries. All are represented on the School Broadcasting Council for the United Kingdom.

B **BBC School Broadcast series 1974-5**

Note: Series vary in length from 5 to 28 programmes. Those series printed in italics are not broadcast but are available on sale. After each series the target age is given.

For Infants and young children

Playtime, radio, 4 and 5
You and Me, TV, 4 and 5
Let's Join In, radio, Infants
Poetry Corner, radio, Infants
Watch!, TV, Older infants
Listening and Reading I, radio, Older infants
Words and Pictures, TV, 6-8

Movement and Music Stage I, radio, Younger infants
Movement and Music Stage II, radio, Older infants
A Corner for Music, radio, Older infants
The Music Box, radio, Older infants

Junior miscellanies

Merry-go-Round, TV, 7-9

Springboard, radio, 7-9

For the middle years ten—twelve

Learning about Food, radio, 10-12
Animals Real and Unreal, radio, 10-12
Into the Future, radio, 10-12

Young Europeans, radio, 10-12
Orchestra, radio, 10-12
Think, radio, 10-12
Exploration and Discovery, TV, 10-13

English and drama

Stories and Rhymes, radio, 7-9
Hello! Hello!, radio, 8-11
Living Language, radio, 9-11
Drama Workshop, radio, 11-14
Listening and Writing, radio, 11-14

Adventure, radio, 13-16
Speak, radio, 14-16
Books, Plays, Poems, radio, 14-17
English, TV, 14-17

English: Reading series

Listening and Reading II, radio, 8

Listening and Reading III, radio, 11-13

Look and Read, TV, 7-9+

Look and Read: radio resource material, 7-9+

The Electric Company, TV, 10-16

Geography and environmental studies

A Year's Journey, TV, 10-13

Exploration Earth, radio, 10-12

People of Many Lands, TV, 10-12

Geography: USA and Ghana, TV, 13-16

Our Changing World, radio, 13-16

History

History: Long Ago, radio, 8-11

Out of the Past, TV, 9-12

Man, radio, 10-12

History in Evidence, radio, 11-14

History in Focus: The 20th Century, radio, 14-17

British Social History, TV, 14-16

History 1917-73, TV, 14-16

Mathematics

Maths Workshop: Stage 1, TV, 9-10

Maths Workshop: Stage 2, TV, 10-11

Countdown: mathematical starting points, TV, 14-16

Modern languages: French

Nous y sommes!, radio, 11-14

Meet the French, radio, 12-15

Tout compris, TV, 12-14

Quatre coins de la France, TV, 12-14

French for Beginners, radiovision, 11-12

Allons-y!, radio, 12-14

Radio Jeunesse, radio, 12-14

La Parole aux Jeunes, radio, 13-15

La France aujourd'hui, radio, 14-16

Horizons de France, radio, 15-17

Voix de France, radio, 16-18

Modern languages: German, Russian, Spanish

Frisch begonnen . . ., radiovision,
   Secondary
Halb gewonnen!, radio,
   Secondary
In Germany, radio, 12-15
Da sind wir wieder, radio, 14-16

Deutsch für die Oberstufe, radio,
   16-18
Privyet!, radio, 2nd year Russian
España es diferente, radio,
   Secondary
Unos minutos nada más, radio,
   Secondary

Movement and dance

Movement, Mime and Music
   Stage I, radio, 7-9

Movement, Mime and Music
   Stage II, radio, 9-11
Country Dancing, radio, 8-11

Music

Time and Tune, radio, 7-8
Music Time, TV, 8-9
Music Workshop Stage I, radio,
   8-10
Music Workshop Stage II, radio,
   10-13

Singing Together, radio, 9-12
Music in Action, TV, 10-13
Music Club, radio, 13-16
Guitar School, radio, 13-18

Religion

A Service for Schools, radio, 8-12
Quest, radio, 9-11
The Bible: How and Why, radio,
   11-13

Material for Assembly, radio,
   11-16
Christian Focus, radio, 14-16
Religion and Life, radio, 16-18

Science

Sex education for children of
   8-10:
   Merry-go-Round, TV
   Nature, radiovision
Nature, radio, 8-10
Nature, radiovision, 8-10
Discovery, radio, 9-11

Junior Science, radio, 9-11
Science All Around, TV, 9-11
Exploring Science, TV, 11-13
Life Cycle, radio, 11-13
Science Extra: Biology, TV,
   13-16
Science Session, TV, 14-16

For the less able (Secondary)
Television Club, TV, 12-14

Humanities
Art and Humanities, radiovision, 13-16

Inquiry, radio, 14-16

Learning about Life, radio, 14-16

Scene, TV, 14-16

Outdoor Education, radio, 14-18

Careers
Going to Work, TV, 14-16

The World of Work, radio, 14-16

A Job Worth Doing?, TV, 15-17

General studies
Art and Experience, radio, 16-18

New Horizons, TV, 16-18

Prospect, radio, 16-18

Special programmes
Special Programmes, TV, 9-18

'Out of School' television previews

For Schools in Northern Ireland
Today and Yesterday in Northern Ireland, radio, 8-11

Ulster in Focus, TV, 10-13

Explorations, radio, 14-15

Modern Irish History: People and Events, radio, 14-15

For Schools in Scotland
From Seven to Nine, radio, 7-9

Let's See, TV, 7-9

A Religious Service for Primary Schools in Scotland, radio, 8-12

Exploring Scotland, radio, 9-11

Scottish History, radio, 11-13

Around Scotland, TV, 9-12

Scottish Magazine, radio, 11-14

Living in Scotland, TV, 14-16

Questions of Living, radio, 14-16

Geography Studies, radio, 14-16

O-Grade History, radio, 14-16

Scottish Writing, radio, 16-18

For Schools in Wales

Un, dau, tri!, radio, under 5
Ffenestri, TV, 5-7
Symud a Chân, radio, 5-7
Gair yn ei Le, radio, 7-9
Sain, Cerdd a Chân, radio, 7-9
Gwrando a Darllen I, radio, 6-8
Gwrando a Darllen II, radio,
    9-11
Hwnt ac Yma, TV, 8 and over
Byw a Bod, radio, 9-11
Hel Hanes, radio, 9-11
Stories from Welsh History,
    radio, 9-11
Y Byd o'n Cwmpas, radio, 9-11
Dwedwych Chi, radio, 9-12
News in Wales, radio, 9-12
Newyddion yr Wythnos, radio,
    9-12
Let's Look at Wales, TV, 10-12
Gwlad a Thref, TV, 10-13
Wales and the Welsh, radio, 15+

c Recording of BBC programmes in schools[1]

Schools and educational institutions of all kinds within the British Isles which provide further, higher and adult education courses under the guidance of qualified teachers or instructors may record respectively 'off the air' BBC School and further education broadcasts (other than Open University broadcasts) provided that *radio, radiovision and television* recordings are:

1 made by a teacher or student in the course of instruction;
2 used for instructional purposes only in the premises where they are made;
3 destroyed within 12 months of their being made, or, in the case of radiovision recordings, by the end of the third school year (i.e. recordings made during 1973-4 may be retained until July 1976). Responsibility for ensuring that these conditions are fulfilled rests with the head or principal of the institution concerned.

Radio and television broadcasts in the BBC general output

These may not be recorded without the prior consent of:

1 the BBC (except for private purposes at home);
2 the holders of the copyright in musical and literary material;
3 the performers (except for the private and domestic uses of the person making the recording); and
4 any gramophone companies whose records are included in the programme.

[1]Tape recording and video-tape recording of BBC educational broadcasts (other than Open University broadcasts) by schools and other educational institutions for classroom use.

D A select bibliography

Educational Broadcasting

The Listening Schools. K. V. BAILEY (BBC, 1957) The author pays particular attention, in chapters V-VIII, to children's responses to school programmes and teachers' uses of them. Chapter IV gives a detailed description of the making of a school radio broadcast for the Primary School series 'World History'.

School Broadcasting in Britain RICHARD PALMER (BBC, 1947) Describes in detail the nature and range of BBC School Radio at the time of its coming to maturity. Contains a chapter by Mary Somerville on how school broadcasting began.

Teaching and Television GUTHRIE MOIR (ed.) (Pergamon Press, 1967) A number of essays by various authors.

Broadcasting and the Community JOHN SCUPHAM (Watts, 1967) A broad survey of broadcasting's place in the national culture. Includes chapters on broadcasting as an educational force and on educational broadcasting; also a detailed bibliography.

Using Broadcasts in Schools: A Study and Evaluation C. G. HAYTER (Published jointly by BBC and ITV, 1974) Describes, with detailed case studies, the use made of BBC and ITV school broadcasts in some 100 schools spread over the UK and adequately equipped to exploit them fully as resource material.

The BBC

The History of Broadcasting in the United Kingdom (4 vols) ASA BRIGGS (Oxford University Press; vol. 1, 1961; vol. 2, 1965; vol. 3, 1970; vol. 4 in preparation) Vol. 2 has a chapter on BBC educational broadcasting up to the war.

The Biggest Aspidistra in the World PETER BLACK (BBC, 1972) A personal celebration of fifty years of the BBC.

BBC Handbook (published annually) A mine of hard-core information on all its services. Includes a bibliography.

School Broadcast Production

The Informing Image RODNEY BENNETT (Educational Explorers Ltd, 1968) The author describes his work as a BBC educational producer. He includes detailed accounts of the making of both radio and TV programmes.

Television for the Teacher FELICITY KINROSS (Hamish Hamilton, 1968) About the basic principles of studio production, and designed especially for teachers working in close-circuit systems.

Scene Scripts MICHAEL MARLAND (ed.) (Longman Group Ltd, 1972) Contains the scripts of seven of the earlier TV plays written for 'Scene', also a chapter by Ronald Smedley on the production of one of these.

Occasional Publications by the School Broadcasting Council

The School Broadcasting Council publishes periodic Bulletins for Colleges of Education on particular developments in BBC School Broadcasting. (These are available for study on application to The Educational Secretary, BBC.)

Also useful for reference are:

BBC School Broadcasts: An Introduction (includes a bibliography)

BBC School Broadcasts: Facts and Figures: A Statistical Digest

Annual Programme of BBC Radio and Television for Schools and Colleges (published each year in March)

INDEX

Adam, Duncan, 43
Adult Education, 125, 153, 155, 172
aerials, 20
'Alistair Cooke's America', 24
Albert Memorial, the, 9, 10
Alexandra Palace, 21
Alf Garnett, 1
Alfred, King, 10
Allan, Douglas, 43
anchorman, 23
Annan, Lord, 196
Annual Programme of BBC Radio and TV for Schools and Colleges, 211
Arabian Nights, The, 85
Aristotle, 47
Armstrong, Harry, 59
Associated-Rediffusion Ltd, 160
Attenborough, David, 187
Audio-visual software, 40, 191
Australian Broadcasting Commission, 174
autocue, 24

backward children, programmes for, 93-4
Bacon, Roger, 47
baffleboards, 20
Bailey, K. V., 84, 210
Bartók, Béla, 1
Basle, 179
battery sets, 20, 21
Bavarian TV, 179
BBC (general)
   Adult Education on, 125, 172
   (see also Further Education)
   airtime for school broadcasting, 183, 184, 195-6
   attitudes to school broadcasting, 182-7, 193-6
   BBC 1, 164, 180, 184
   BBC 2, 154
   Central Religious Advisory Committee, 163

Charter, 183
Children's Departments, 198
cost of school broadcasting, 182, 183, 194
Current Affairs programmes, 142
daytime listening to, 184
Education Secretary, 153
External Services, 195
Further Education, 131, 149, 152-9, 182, 184
References to series titles (radio):
   Developing Maths Today, 154
References to series titles (radio & TV):
   Early Years at School, 158
   Kontakte, 158
   Middle Years, The, 158
   ROSLA and After, 156-8
Reference to series titles (TV):
   Aids in Teaching, 155
   Engineering Science, 159
   How and Why?, 154
   Improvised Drama, 156
   In our Midst, 149
   Mathematics '64, 154
   Sex Education in the Primary School, 131, 154
   Teaching Maths Today, 62
   Using School TV, 155
Further Education Advisory Council, 152, 154, 184
Programme Committees of, 154
Handbook, 153n., 210
licence fees, 183, 194
Local Radio, 16, 167-71, 191, 197
   Advisory panels for, 169
   Radio Merseyside, 171

News programmes, 142
Overseas broadcasting, 171
partnership with Education, 106-116, 186
Publications, 153, 192
Radio Times, 180
Radio 4, 180
staff structure, 185
TV Centre, 165, 173, 186
TV Enterprises Department, 26
TV Talks Department, 198
BBC School Radio
List of current series, 204-8
Reference to series titles:
   Art and Design, 35
   Bible and Life, The, 67
   Boys and Girls of the Middle Ages, 45
   Citizenship, 66
   Corner for Music, A, 104
   Country Dancing, 188
   Current Affairs, 50-3, 66, 146
   Discovery, 118
   Drama Workshop, 84
   Exploration Earth, 6-7
   For the Fourteens, 66
   General Science, 54, 129
   Hello Again!, 151
   Hello, hello!, 150-1
   History in Evidence, 12
   How Things Began, 49-50, 84
   Inquiry, 70
   Jacksons, The, 94
   Joseph and Sarah, 174
   Junior Science, 59, 118
   Learning about Life, 69-70, 129
   Let's Join In, 104
   Living in the Country, 29
   Living Language, 85, 88-90
   Listening and Reading, 96, 104
   Listening and Writing, 85-8
   Looking at Things, 66

Man, 84
Modern Irish History, 124
Movement and Music, 3-5, 104
Music and Movement, 1, 4, 47, 125, 127
Music Box, The, 104
Music Club, 93, 188
Music Workshop, 84, 92, 188
Nature, 37, 134
News Commentary, 50
Playtime, 101, 104, 181
Poetry Corner, 104
Poets and Poetry, 84, 85
Prospect, 15-16
Religion and Life, 67
Religious Service for Schools, 49
Science and the Community, 54, 66
Singing Together, 5-6, 49, 121, 122
Speak, 85
Stories and Rhymes, 37
Talks for Sixth Forms, 47
Travel Talks, 46
Two Centuries of Irish History, 124
Unfinished Debates, 50
World History, 35
World of Work, The, 66, 68-9

References to individual programmes:
Elephants in East Africa, 6-7
Five Members, The, 45-6
Horses of the Sun, The, 87
Juno and the Paycock, 174
Mangrove Swamps of the Rufiji Delta, The, 46-7
Marshall Plan, The, 51
Means Test, The, 50
News, The, 15-16
Rain Horse, The, 86
Thatcher, The, 29   45
What the Potboy Saw,

References to Radiovision series:
French for Beginners, 13, 35
Frisch Begonnen, 35
References to individual RV programmes:
Courtship and Marriage in Painting, 33-4
Depression South of Iceland will move, A, 33
Everything New, 37-8
Joan of Arc, 35
Stanley Spencer, 36
Vincent van Gogh, 35-6
BBC School TV
List of current series, 204-8
References to series titles:
British Social History, 9-12
Chasse au Trésor, La, 112
Countdown, 64
Discovering Science, 55-8, 65, 118
Drama, 71, 139-41, 181
Exploring Science, 58, 118
Exploring your World, 59
Going to Work, 68
Job worth Doing?, A, 159
Living in the Commonwealth, 28
Look and Read, 96-8
Looking at TV, 67
Making a Musical, 92-3
Making Music, 90-2
Mathematics and Life, 61, 67
Maths Today, 62-3, 65
Maths Workshop, 2, 63-4
Merry-go-Round, 2-3, 96, 132, 134
Middle School Mathematics, 61
Middle School Physics, 66
People of Many Lands, 174
Pure Mathematics, 114

Scene, 70-83, 139, 141, 159
Science all Around, 59-61, 62, 118
Science and Life, 67, 113
Science Extra: Biology, 12, 59
Science Extra: Physics, 59
Science for Sixth Forms, 127
Science Session, 13-14, 59
Spotlight, 51-3, 70, 180
Television Club, 94-5, 96, 148
Tout Compris, 39-40
USA '72, 119, 179
Watch!, 99, 104, 180
Words and Pictures, 7-8, 96, 104
You and Me, 101-4, 181
References to individual programmes:
Alternative Society, The, 47
Ballad of Ben Bagot, The, 77-82
Bank Holiday, 144
British Columbia, 28
Calley Case, The, 47
Doctor Faustus, 140
How good a Parent?, 83, 139
Immigration Bill, The, 47
Joe and the Sheep Rustlers, 97-8
Last Bus, 71-7, 143, 149
Midnight Thief, The, 90-2
Palace of Glass, The, 9-12
Pattern and Shape, 63
Police and You, The, 145
Raven and the Cross, The, 2-3
Sam of Boff's Island, 7-8
Sentence of the Court, The, 76-7
Streamlining, 60-1

References to individual
programmes (cont.) :
Taste of Honey, A, 141
£60 Single, £100
Return, 71
Benbecula, 141
Bennett, Judy, 101
Bennett, Richard
Rodney, 90
Bennett, Rodney, 211
Bethell, Hal, 168, 170,
191
Betti, Ugo, 139
Beveridge, Sir William,
47
Beveridge Committee
of Enquiry, 106
Beveridge Report, 20
Bible, The, 85
Black, Peter, 210
'Blue Peter', 99
Bowery, 1
Boyd Orr, Sir John, 47
Braden, Bernard, 28
Brecht, Berthold, 139
Bridges, Robert, 43
Briggs, Asa, 210
Bristol, school
broadcasts from, 48
British Council, 174
Broadhead, Peggie, 28
Broadway, 1
Bullet Express, 60
Bullough, Prof. W. S.,
113
Burghclere Memorial
Chapel, 36
Butler Act, the, 51

Cain, John, 62, 154
Canada, school radio in,
172
capitation allowance, 2
careers broadcasts, 68-9, 159
Carnegie Trust, 44
Carruthers, Herbert, 43
Central Council for School
Broadcasting, 19, 107n.
Technical Sub-
Committee of, 19
Centre for Educational TV
Overseas, 174
Centre for Educational
Development Overseas,
174

Charles I, 45-6
Chataway, Christopher, 51
Chesterton, G. K., 47
Childers, Erskine, 51
Chovil, Claire, 95, 101, 133
Churchill, 50
'Civilisation', 112
Clark, Kenneth (Lord
Clark), 112
closed-circuit TV, 16, 164-7,
191
Colleges of Education, 126,
154, 165
Bulletins for, 211
Commonwealth
Broadcasting Conference,
179
conservation, 6, 146
Constantine, Learie (Lord
Constantine), 149
Cooke, Alistair, 24
co-production,
international, 174, 179
CSE, 9, 13, 64
curriculum development,
154
Czechoslovakia, 1

'Dad's Army', 199
Dakota, 120-1
Darwin, C., 59
Davies, Sir Walford, 18, 43
Day-release students, 159
Delaney, Shelagh, 141
Demonstrations to teachers,
18, 47, 125
Dewhurst, Keith, 71
Dieuzeide, Henri, 176
Dimbleby, Richard, 51
discussion groups, 125, 153,
155, 157
Dixon, George, 18, 45
Domestic Science, 139
Doolan, Moira, 85
Driver, Ann, 47, 125

Ealing, 153
earthing of sets, 20
economics, 159
Education, Department of,
25, 116, 194, 197
'Education: a Framework
for Expansion', 100
Education Engineers, 18,
19, 20, 125

Educational film, 24-6
Educational Priority Areas,
100, 104
Educational Recordings
Scheme, 174
Educational Technology,
40, 155, 173
National Council for, 192,
193
Eire, school broadcasting in,
175-6
Eliot, T. S., 47
English, 13, 85-90, 139-41,
174
as a second language,
151, 174
Epicurus, 47
Europe, school broadcasting
in, 175-9
European Broadcasting
Union, 175, 179
European Studies, 127
Evans, Edith, 47
Evesham, school broadcasts
from, 48
Eyre, Ronald, 72, 139

Fénelon, 177
Festival of Britain, the, 12
film, 16mm, 26
copies of school
broadcasts, 132
cassettes, 12
loops, 62, 192
projector, 8
educational film, 24-6
filmstrips
in association with
broadcasts, 31-2, 192
in radiovision
programmes, 31-8
in support of broadcasts,
40
Fisher, H. A. L., 42
Forces' Educational
Broadcasts, 153
Foreign Office, 195
Forster, E. M., 47
France
recording for School TV
in, 173
Educational broadcasting
in, 176, 177, 192
French see Modern
Languages

'G' Course, 159
Galbraith, Kenneth, 47
Galileo, 59
Gaping Ghyll, 29
Gardnier, Kenneth, 149
Garratt, Arthur, 113
Gauguin, 36
GCE, 59
  A level, 114
  O level, 12, 159
general studies, 15, 158, 159
geography, 6-7, 119-121
Germany
  her broadcasting's debt
    to BBC, 171
  Nazi, 149
  School broadcasting in,
    176
  'Sesame Strasse', 99
Gittings, Robert, 84, 85
Glasgow School TV Service,
  165
Goebbels, 176
Gogol, 139
Golding, William, 75
Goya, 33, 34
Gramophone Company, 28
Grampian TV, 129, 162
Granada TV, 67
Grattan, Donald, 61, 154
Great Exhibition, 12
Greene, Sir Hugh, 187
group working, 3, 14, 60,
  119, 157
Gwynne Jones, Eurfron, 59

Hadow Committee, 42
  Report (on The
    Education of the
    Adolescent), 48, 153
Haldane, J. B. S., 47
'Half our Future', 67
Hall, Geoffrey, 57
Hardcastle, William, 15
Harper, Jack, 121
Hayter, G. C., 31n., 163n.,
  210
Heathcote, Dorothy, 156
Herbert, A. P., 47
Herschel, 59
Heyerdahl, Thor, 188
Hinduism, 1
history
  for Primary Schools, 2-3,
    35, 49-50

for Secondary Schools,
  9-12, 45-6, 53
  Irish History, 124
HMI's, 56, 115
Hokkaido, 173
Holden, David, 51
holiday repeats of school
  broadcasts, 181
Homer, 85
Hosier, John, 90, 91, 92
Hoskin, Dr Michael, 59
Hughes, Ted, 86
humanities, 9, 12, 15, 159
Hungary, school
  broadcasting in, 178

IBA, 152
'idiot-boards', 24
immigrants, 146-52, 170
  Immigration Bill, 47
  Immigration Act, 147
Indians in school broadcasts,
  148-51
Inner London Education
  Authority, 165, 190
in-service teacher training,
  159
Institut für Film und Bild,
  176
Inter-NAVEX Exhibition,
  194
Iron Bridge, the, 32
ITA, 161
Italy, school broadcasting
  in, 175
ITV, 16, 183, 195
  School TV, 153, 160-4,
    191
  Titles of series:
    Messengers, The, 67
    Picture Box, 163
    Seeing and Doing, 163
    Way we Used to Live,
      The, 163

Jackson, Cyril, 125
Japan: NHK, 172
  School broadcasting in,
    173
Jevtović, Miro, 178
Johns, Stratford, 186

Keele, University of, 157
Kennedy, President J. F., 52
Kent Education Authority,
  44

'Kent Inquiry', 18, 44-5,
  106, 107, 117
King, Martin Luther, 149
Kingston, Leonard, 97, 149
Kinloch, Bruce, 6
Kinross, Felicity, 149, 211
'Kubla Khan', 78

Lambert, Rex, 172
Lamming, George, 147
Langstaff, Jack, 91
language laboratory, 8
LCC (London County
  Council), 19
LEAs (Local Education
  Authorities), in relation
  to educational
  broadcasting, 19, 25, 116,
  126, 132, 152, 158, 163,
  164, 165, 166, 169, 170,
  190, 191
  LEA Advisers, 56
  Chief Education Officers,
    125
  officials, 115, 131
  Resource Centres, 40,
    167, 170, 193
'Listen with Mother', 181
'Listening Schools, The', 84
literacy, 158
Liverpool FC, 1
Livingstone, David, 188
Lloyd Williams, Norman,
  189
'Lord of the Flies', 75
'Lord of the Rings', 84
Love, Enid, 160
Lundgren, Rolf, 175

Machiavelli, 47
Magyar TV, 178
maintenance of audio-visual
  equipment, 9
Marland, Michael, 211
Marlowe, 140
Martin, Prof. Charles, 43
Mason, Charles, 189
mathematics, 61-5, 114,
  139, 165, 177
  'New Maths', 61-3, 165,
    176
  teaching of, 154
McQueen, Edith, 42
Merseyside, local radio in,
  170, 171

Metropolitan Commissioner
of Police, 144
Middlesex Education
Authority, 21
Milton Keynes, 191
Mitchell, Denis, 29
modern languages, 13, 34-5,
39-40, 111-2, 158, 173,
180
Moir, Guthrie, 210
Molyneux, Andrée, 97
'Monty Python's Flying
Circus', 186
Morecambe & Wise, 1
Morris, Johnny, 33
Morris, Dr Joyce, 96
MPs, 142
multi-media production,
156-8, 177
multi-racial society, 146-51
music, 3-6, 90-3

National Union of
Teachers, 125, 158, 160
'Nationwide', 122n.
Nature Study, 59
Newsom Committee, 67
Report of the, 157
Newton, 59
'New Ventures in
Broadcasting', 153n.
Nicolson, the Hon. Harold,
47
Nigeria
Nigerian Broadcasting
Corporation, 172
teachers in TV Course,
172-3
'Non è mai troppo tardi',
175
Northern Ireland
School broadcasts for,
123-4, 207
Programme Committee
for, 124, 203
Notting Hill riots, 146
Nottinghamshire School
Broadcasting Centre, 170
Nuffield Foundation, the,
58, 127

objectivity in broadcasts,
15, 142-6
Observer, The (in 'How
Things Began'), 50

Observer, 75
off-air viewing, 166, 190
OFRATEME, 192
'Onward Christian
Soldiers', 1
Open Society, 144, 187
Open University, 63, 186,
192, 194, 195, 197
Orff, Carl, 90
ORTF, 192
overhead projector, 8
Owen, Roger, 156, 158

Pakistan, 148
Palestinian commandos,
143
'Pallisers, The', 186
Palmer, Richard, 210
parents
and school broadcasting,
100, 152, 180-2, 191
and sex education,
129-32, 134, 136
involvement in schools,
182
parent-child relationships,
69-70, 178
parent-teacher
co-operation, 155
Parent-Teacher
Associations, 181, 182
Pasteur, 59
Paterson, Swinton, 43
Peloponnesian War, the,
138, 139
Phaethon, 89
photo-copying, 12
Photoplay, 14
physics teaching, 154
Pilkington Committee of
Enquiry, 106, 153, 154,
162, 163, 168, 186
pilot programmes, 21-3,
104, 130, 157
Plater, Alan, 71
'Play School', 99, 181
Plowden Report, 98
Plymouth College of
Technology, 164
Pompeii, 35
Postgate, Richmond, 172
Posts and Communications,
Minister of, 195
Power, Rhoda, 42, 45, 84

previewing of programmes,
9, 165
Punjab, the, 149
Puppets, 8, 102-3

Race Relations Board, 149n.
radiovision
definition of, 31
examples of, 31-8
strengths of, 32
(for series and programme
titles see BBC School
Radio)
'Railway Children', 64
Ralphs, Sir Lincoln, 152
reading, programmes to
help with, 7-8, 94-8
receiving apparatus, list of
suitable, 19
reception in schools, 18-20,
26
recording
by BBC:
on disc, 18, 28
on film, 38
on tape (audio), 29, 68
on tape (video), 38-9
on transmission, 18
in Schools:
agreed conditions for,
30, 190, 209
demands made on
teachers by, 30, 31
effect on programme
structure, 39-41
new flexibility in use,
63
on tape (audio), 2, 13,
30, 189
on tape (video), 9,
39-41
refresher courses, 154
Reggae, 1, 93
Reith, John (Lord Reith),
42, 109, 116, 185, 187
Robson, John, 153
Russell Report, 158, 195
Ryder, Leslie, 190, 191, 196

Saville, Jimmy, 126
Scandinavia
School programmes made
by BBC for, 174
School broadcasting in,
176, 179

Schools, in relation to
broadcasts,
Grammar, 144
Infants', 104, 180
Middle, 190
Nursery classes, 100, 101,
181
Open-plan schools, 119
Pre-school broadcasting,
127
Primary, 1-8, 180, 189
School Leaving Age, 51,
67, 156
School Managers, 19
'School Radio and the
Tape Recorder', 30n.
Schools' Council, 52, 58,
127, 138, 154, 157
Secondary Modern, 51,
56, 94, 109, 140, 144
Secondary
Comprehensive, 8-16,
92
Technical Colleges, 154,
159
School Broadcasting
Council, the, 25, 106-116,
117, 122, 134, 152, 156,
160, 161, 163, 169, 182,
183, 185, 194, 195, 199,
202-3, 211
Commissions from, 108,
109
Constitution of, 108, 201
Education Officers of the,
21, 55, 56, 60, 73, 83,
106, 117-28, 130, 131,
134, 136, 153, 172
Executive Committee of
the, 115
for Scotland, 122, 202
for Wales, 122, 123, 202
Loan Library, 126
N. Ireland Programme
Committee, 124, 202
Programme Committees,
106-116, 128, 129, 136,
138, 161, 162, 163, 202
Report on the first 18
months of School TV,
52
Report on School
Broadcasting and Sex
Education in the
Primary School, 134-6

Research Officer, 117,
134, 136
Senior Education Officer,
108, 116, 117
Steering Committee, 115,
203
Summer Schools, 126
Television Sub-
Committee, 25
School Broadcasts (general)
(for particular titles see
BBC School Radio,
BBC School TV)
as basis for scheme of
work, 9, 54-5
as bridges between
subjects, 64
as 'direct teaching',
54-6, 65-6, 114, 176
as 'enrichment', 54, 66
as 'resource material',
13, 40, 66, 166, 197
as school-home links,
96, 180-2, 191
as teacher refresher
courses, 88
as stimulus to creative
work, 3, 5, 8, 37,
84-93, 118
authority in, 144-6
children's absorption
in, 2, 5, 57, 60, 74,
75, 135
children's participation
during, 4-6, 8
children's recall of,
10, 140
children's response to,
7, 25, 60, 74, 75,
80-2, 86, 92, 101,
134-6, 140, 141,
143-4
class follow-up of, 3, 7,
8, 10-12, 13-14,
15-16, 61
controversial issues in,
124, 143
discipline during, 5, 10
film cassettes to
accompany, 12
folders to accompany,
12, 192
fortnightly broadcasts,
9, 60, 62
future of, 41, 196-201

impartiality in, 124,
142-6
origins of, 42-3
pamphlets for, 2, 5, 6,
8, 10-14, 45, 48,
55, 192
relevance of, 139-42
selective use of, 6, 68,
120
Teachers' Notes for,
4, 9, 27, 55, 56, 62,
132, 141, 142, 170,
192
teacher's preparation
for, 2, 6, 9-10
to provoke thought,
146
used without teacher,
15-16, 49
science, related to school
broadcasts, 12, 13-14, 32,
49-50, 53-61, 118, 128-36,
159
Scotland
first school broadcast
from, 43
first series for backward
children, 94
pioneer of school
broadcasting, 42
School Broadcasting
Council for, 122, 203
'Singing Together'
emanates from, 49
small schools in, 122
special programmes for,
122, 123, 207
use of filmstrips with
broadcasts, 31
Scupham, John, 67, 210
Serraillier, Ian, 90
Sex Education
in Primary Schools,
129-30
programmes on, 128-37,
162, 178, 180
Seymour, Ronald, 157
Shakespeare, 1, 12, 139
Shaw, Bernard, 47, 139
Sheffield, Margaret, 133
Shusha, 112
Simpson, Michael, 187
Sister St Joan of Arc, 155
Sixth-Form Programmes,
15-16, 47, 59, 61, 114,

127, 147, 159, 173, 180, 189
Smedley, Ronald, 71, 112
Société Suisse de Radiodiffusion, 179
sociology, 139
Socrates, 48
Solzhenitsyn, Alexander, 15
Somerville, Mary, 42-8, 85, 198
Sommerhof, Gerd, 55
Sophocles, 139
South Africa, 149
Squiers, Granville, 46
statistical surveys, 161
Steele, Dickon, 44, 48
Stéphan, E. M., 153
Stobart, J. C., 42
Stoics, 171
Sutcliffe, Jean, 42
Sutherland, 121, 122n.
Sveriges Radio, 177

tape recording *see* recording
Tappolet, Frank, 179
Taverne, Dick, 51
Taylor, Duncan. 35
team teaching, 119
Technical Assistant, in school, 9
teenagers, 178, 180
'Télémaque', 177
Telescuola, 175
television
    Colour TV, 17, 182
    compared with film in education, 24-6
    directors in, 26-7
    impact of, 142
    'Main Experiment' in, for schools, 22
    on-camera performance in, 23
    personality in, 23-4
    'Pilot Experiment' in, 21-4
    Producers in, 26-8
    start of, 21
    studio rehearsal for, 26
Television Enterprises, 26
Terson, Peter, 71, 77
Thatcher, Mrs M., 100
Thomsett, Sally, 64
Tizard, Sir Henry, 47
Todmorden, 97

Tokyo, 173
Tolkien, J. R. P., 84
'Top of the Pops', 199
Trafalgar Square, 176
transistorised sets, 21

Udall, Rita, 68, 69
Ulster, 123-4
USA
    'Children's Workshop', 98, 100, 104
    educational stations in, 167
    'Electric Company', 104
    racism in, 149
    School broadcasts in, 55, 176
    'Sesame Street', 98-100, 104
    study of, 119
'Using Broadcasts in Schools', 31n., 163n., 210

Van Gogh, Vincent, 36
Vermeer, Jan, 33, 34
VHF, 180, 184
Victoria, Queen, 10
Vikings, 2-3, 132
violence in school TV, 71-6
visual arts, broadcasts on, 33-6, 189

Wales
    School Broadcasting Council for, 122, 123, 203
    small schools in, 122
    special programmes for, 123, 208
    Welsh language, 123
wartime, school broadcasts in, 49
'Watch with Mother', 181
Weathercote Cave, 28
Welland, Colin, 71, 144
West Indians in school broadcasts, 147-9
West Riding, 29
Wimbledon, 50
Wiseman, John, 20
Work Cards, 62, 64, 192
Working Party for School and Educational TV, 175
workshop activities in schools, 139

World Conference on Educational Broadcasting, 32, 175

Yugoslavia, radio programmes for teenagers in, 178

'Z Cars', 186